CW00470355

ISBN 978-1-331-98442-9
PIBN 10089546

This book is a reproduction of an important historical work. Forgotten Books uses
state-of-the-art technology to digitally reconstruct the work, preserving the original format
whilst repairing imperfections present in the aged copy. In rare cases, an imperfection in
the original, such as a blemish or missing page, may be replicated in our edition. We do,
however, repair the vast majority of imperfections successfully; any imperfections that
remain are intentionally left to preserve the state of such historical works.

A

BOOK OF BURLESQUE

𝔖𝔨𝔢𝔱𝔠𝔥𝔢𝔰

OF

ENGLISH STAGE TRAVESTIE

AND PARODY

BY

WILLIAM DAVENPORT ADAMS

Author of " A Dictionary of English Literature," " Rambles in Book-Land"
etc., etc.

WITH PORTRAITS OF F. C. BURNAND, W. S. GILBERT,
AND G. R. SIMS

LONDON

HENRY AND CO., BOUVERIE STREET, E.C.

1891

PREFACE.

IN the pages that follow, I make no attempt to supply a consecutive and comprehensive history of English stage travestie. This would have been impossible within the limits assigned to me. My object has been simply to furnish an introduction to such a history, supplemented by sketches of the various groups into which English stage burlesques naturally fall, with such extracts as might serve to exhibit the respective methods of individual travestie-writers. My business has been with the literary rather than the histrionic side of burlesque—with the witty and humorous, rather than the purely theatrical, features of the subject with which I had to deal. At the same time, I hope that the details I have been able to give concerning dates, and "casts," and so on, may be useful to at least a large section of my readers.

I ought to say that, while I have endeavoured to mention all the most representative burlesques of which our stage history keeps record, I have intentionally left outside of my scheme all "extravaganzas," "bouffoneries musicales," and other such miscellaneous varieties of comic literature,—confining myself to definite and deliberate travesties of subjects previously existent.

I have to thank more than one kind friend for information and material supplied, and more than one living writer of burlesque for the opportunity of consulting his " prompt books " and thus quoting from unpublished work.

DAVENPORT ADAMS, JUN.

NOTE.—Those who desire to extend their acquaintance with the literature of English stage burlesque may be recommended to turn first to the travesties published by Mr. French, which include those by Planché, and many by the Broughs, H. J. Byron, Talfourd, F. C. Burnand, etc. Mr. Gilbert's "Rosencrantz and Guildenstern " is to be found in his volume entitled " Foggerty's Fairy, and Other Stories." A large proportion of the burlesques discussed, quoted, or mentioned in the following chapters are out of print, and to be seen only at the British Museum, on the second-hand bookstalls, or on the shelves of private collectors.

[*We beg to acknowledge the courtesy of MM. Walèry, Limited, in permitting us to avail ourselves of their photographs of Messrs. Burnand and Gilbert ; and of Mr. Bassano for the same permission in regard to that of Mr. G. R. Sims.*—ED. *W. L.*]

CONTENTS.

WHO shall say when the spirit of burlesque first made its appearance on our stage? There were traces of it, we may be sure, in the Mysteries and Moralities of pre-Elizabethan days; the monkish dramatists were not devoid of humour, and the first lay playwrights had a rough sense of ridicule. The "Vice" which figured in so many of our rude old dramas had in him an element of satire, and the pictures drawn of his Satanic Majesty were conscious or unconscious caricatures of the popular conception of the Evil One.

In all these cases, however, the burlesque was general. It was of the nature of travestie, and of the vaguest sort. Of particular parody one finds but few signs in the Elizabethan drama. There is a little of it in Shakespeare, where he pokes fun at the turgidity of contemporary tragedy or at the obscurity of contemporary Euphuism. The Pyramus and Thisbe episode is less burlesque than satire. It is an *exposé* of the absurdities of the amateur performer,

W. L.—V.

I

for whom Shakespeare, as a professional actor, could have only an amused contempt.

"The Bard" parodied, but he did not burlesque. That was left to the initiative of the gifted literary Dioscuri, Beaumont and Fletcher. "The Knight of the Burning Pestle," which saw the light in 1611, is not wholly a travestie, but it contains a travestie within itself. In the main it is a dramatic exposition of a love story, the scene of which is laid in the middle-class life of the time. Ralph, the Knight of the Burning Pestle, is by no means the hero of the tale; rather is he an excrescence upon it. A grocer and his wife sit on the stage, and suggest to the actors that Ralph, their apprentice, shall take part in the performance. They want a play in which a grocer shall do "admirable things," and Ralph is bound to do them. The apprentice, it would seem, is an amateur actor—he "hath played before," and so finds no difficulty in adapting himself to the situation. When he enters, it is "like a grocer in his shop, with two prentices, reading 'Palmerin of England.'" This gives us the key to the satire. Ralph is to burlesque the romances of chivalry, which were then so common in England, as elsewhere. "Palmerin of England" had been "translated out of French" by Anthony Munday and assistants, and published between 1580 and 1602. Ralph starts with a quotation from it, and then goes on to say :—

Certainly those knights are much to be commended who, neglecting their possessions, wander with a squire and a dwarf through the deserts to relieve poor ladies. . . . There are no such courteous and fair well-spoken knights in this age.

He whom Palmerin would have called "Fair Sir," and she whom Rosiclear would have called "Right beauteous

Damsel," are now spoken of opprobriously. But why should not Ralph be the means of wiping out this reproach ?—

Why should I not pursue this course, both for the credit of myself and our company? For amongst all the worthy books of achievements, I do not call to mind that I yet read of a grocer-errant: I will be the said knight. Have you heard of any that hath wandered unfurnished of his squire and dwarf? Thy elder prentice Tim shall be my trusty squire, and little George my dwarf. Hence, my blue apron! Yet, in remembrance of my former trade, upon my shield shall be portrayed a burning pestle, and I will be called the Knight of the Burning Pestle. My beloved squire, and George my dwarf, I charge you that henceforth you never call me by any other name but "the right courteous and valiant Knight of the Burning Pestle"; and that you never call any female by the name of a woman or wench, but "fair lady," if she have her desires; if not, "distressed damsel"; that you call all forests and heaths "deserts," and all horses "palfreys."

After this, Ralph reappears at various points in the action. He interposes, Quixote-like, in the aforesaid love-affair, and gets belaboured by the favoured lover for his pains. Later, he puts up at an inn, and, about to leave, is surprised when the tapster draws his attention to the fact that the reckoning is not paid :—

> *Ralph.* Right courteous Knight, who for the order's sake
> Which thou hast ta'en, hang'st out the holy Bell,
> As I this flaming pestle bear about,
> We render thanks to your puissant self,
> Your beauteous lady, and your gentle squires,
> For thus refreshing of our wearied limbs,
> Stiffen'd with hard achievements in wild desert.
>   *Tapster.* Sir, there is twelve shillings to pay.
>   *Ralph.* Thou merry squire Tapstero, thanks to thee
> For comforting our souls with double jug :
> And if adventurous fortune prick thee forth,
> Thou jovial squire, to follow feats of arms,
> Take heed thou tender ev'ry lady's cause,

Ev'ry true knight, and ev'ry damsel fair,
But spill the blood of treacherous Saracens,
And false enchanters that with magic spells
Have done to death full many a noble knight.

Host. Thou valiant Knight of the Burning Pestle, give ear to me: there is twelve shillings to pay, and as I am a true knight, I will not bate a penny. . . .

Ralph. Sir knight, this mirth of yours becomes you well;
But, to requite this liberal courtesy,
If any of your squires will follow arms,
He shall receive from my heroic hand
A knighthood, by the virtue of this pestle.

The host, however, insists upon receiving his twelve shillings, and the grocer's wife, in great fear lest harm shall befall her Ralph, requests her husband to pay the money. In a subsequent scene, Ralph conquers the giant Barbaroso, and releases his captives. By-and-by he goes into Moldavia, where he touches the heart of the king's daughter, but tells her that he has already pledged his troth to Susan, "a cobbler's maid in Malte Street," whom he vowed never to forsake. At the end of the play he comes on to explain, at length, that he is dead, taking the opportunity to recount his various performances.

The fun is never very brilliant; and the "Knight of the Pestle," albeit by writers so distinguished, is not, for the present-day Englishman, particularly exhilarating reading. One can imagine, however, how droll it seemed to our ancestors, with whom it remained popular for over half a century, surviving till the time of Mistress Eleanor Gwynne, who once spoke the prologue to it.

Our first burlesque, then, was a satire upon exaggerated fiction. Our second was a satire upon extravagant plays. It is possible that "The Rehearsal" was represented before

Your Details

Michael Mills
56 Waveney Drive
LOWESTOFT
Suffolk
NR33 0TW

Order date:	26/02/2018
Order reference:	AUK-33167463
Dispatch note:	20180231431001

Your Order

ISBN	Title	Quantity
9781331984429	A Book of Burlesque, Sketches of Engl...	1

For returns information visit wordery.com/returns. Please keep this receipt for your records.

**Thank you for your Wordery
order. We hope you enjoy your
book #HappyReading**

20180231431001

"The Knight of the Burning Pestle " left the boards. Begun in 1663, and ready for production before 1665, it was first performed in 1671. It is ascribed to George Villiers, Duke of Buckingham; but probably there were several hands engaged in it. It was the outcome of the boredom and the laughter caused by the wildness and bombast of the Restoration plays. There were some things in the stage of that day which the wits could not abide :—

> Here brisk insipid rogues, for wit, let fall
> Sometimes dull sense ; but oft'ner none at all.
> There, strutting heroes, with a grim-fac'd train,
> Shall brave the gods, in King Cambyses' vein.
> For (changing rules, of late, as if man writ
> In spite of reason, nature, art, and wit)
> Our poets make us laugh at tragedy,
> And with their comedies they make us cry.

So runs the prologue to "The Rehearsal," which was destined to strike the first blow at the mechanical dramas that had succeeded the masterpieces of the Shakespearian period. Bayes, the playwright whose tragedy is supposed to be "rehearsed," is usually accepted as a skit upon Dryden, whose dress, speech, and manner were openly mimicked by Lacy, the interpreter of the part. But there is reason to believe that Davenant first sat for the portrait, and in the end Bayes became a sort of incarnated parody of all the Restoration playwrights. This preposterous play travesties a whole school of dramatic writing. Dramas by Dryden, Davenant, James and Henry Howard, Mrs. Behn, and Sir William Killigrew and others, are directly satirised in certain passages; but in the main the satire is general. For instance, in one place fun is made of the prevalence of similes in the dramas aimed at. Prince Prettyman, in the rehearsed play, falls asleep, and Chloris, coming in, finds him in that situation :—

Bayes. Now, here she must make a simile.

Smith (one of the spectators). Where's the necessity of that, Mr. Bayes?

Bayes. Because she's surpris'd. That's a general rule: you must ever make a simile when you are surpris'd ; 't is the new way of writing.

Elsewhere it is confusion of metaphor, very common among the second-rate " tragedians," that is derided. Says the physician in the play :—

All these threat'ning storms, which, like impregnant clouds, do hover o'er our heads (when once they are grasped but by the eye of reason), melt into fruitful showers of blessings on the people.

Bayes. Pray mark that allegory. Is not that good?

Johnson (another spectator). Yes, that grasping of a storm with the eye is admirable.

In one place, Smith, the aforesaid onlooker, complains that, amid all the talk, the plot stands still ; to which Bayes replies, "Why, what the devil is the plot good for but to bring in fine things?" At another juncture we have the first hint of a bit of persiflage which Sheridan afterwards imitated in " The Critic." It has reference to the portentous reticence of some of the dialogue in Restoration plays. An usher and a physician are on the stage :—

Phys. If Lorenzo should prove false (which none but the great gods can tell) you then perhaps would find that—— (*whispers*).

Usher. Alone, do you say?

Phys. No, attended with the noble—— (*whispers*).

Usher. Who, he in grey?

Phys. Yes, and at the head of—— (*whispers*).

Usher. Then, sir, most certain 'twill in time appear,
These are the reasons that have induc'd 'em to't ;
First, he—— (*whispers*).
Secondly, they—— (*whispers*).
Thirdly, and lastly, both he and they—— (*whispers*).
[*Exeunt whispering.*

"Well, sir," says Smith to Bayes, "but pray, why all this whispering?" "Why, sir," replies the dramatist, "because they are supposed to be politicians, and matters of state ought not to be divulg'd."

In its direct travestie "The Rehearsal" is often very happy. Dryden had claimed for his tragedies that they were written by "th' exactest rules"; so Bayes exhibits to his friends Smith and Johnson what he calls his "Book of Drama Commonplaces, the mother of many plays," containing "certain helps that we men of art have found it convenient to make use of." "I do here aver," he says, "that no man yet the sun e'er shone upon has parts sufficient to furnish out a stage, except it were by the help of these my rules." Davenant, in his "Love and Honour," had portrayed a mental and spiritual struggle between those potent forces. Bayes, accordingly, is made to introduce a scene in which Prince Volscius, sitting down to pull on his boots, wonders whether he ought or ought not to perform that operation :—

My legs, the emblem of my various thought,
Show to what sad distraction I am brought.
Sometimes, with stubborn Honour, like this boot,
My mind is guarded, and resolv'd to do't :
Sometimes, again, that very mind, by Love
Disarmèd, like this other leg does prove.
Shall I to Honour or to Love give way?
Go on, cries Honour; tender Love says, Nay;
Honour aloud commands, Pluck both boots on ;
But softer Love does whisper, Put on none.

In the end, he "goes out hopping, with one boot on, and t'other off." Again, there was a passage in the drama called " The Villain," in which the host supplied his guests with a collation out of his clothes—a capon from his helmet, cream out of his scabbard, and so on. In like manner, Pallas, in Mr. Bayes's tragedy, furnishes forth the two usurping kings :—

> Lo, from this·conquering lance
> Does flow the purest wine of France :
> And to appease your hunger, I
> Have in my helmet brought a pie ;
> Lastly, to bear a part with these,
> Behold a buckler made of cheese.

Of the direct parody in the burlesque a few instances will suffice. Almanzor, in "The Conquest of Granada," becomes the Drawcansir of Mr. Bayes's work ; and while the former ejaculates—

> He who dares love, and for that love must die,
> And, knowing this, dares yet love on, am I,—

the latter caps it with—

> He that dares drink, and for that drink dares die,
> And knowing this, dares yet drink on, am I.

Again, while Almanzor says to his rival in love—

> Thou dar'st not marry her, while I'm in sight ;
> With a bent brow, thy priest and thee I'll fright,—

Drawcansir, snatching the bowls of wine from the usurpers, cries—

> Whoe'er to gulp one drop of this dare think,
> I'll stare away his very power to drink.

The simile of the boar and the sow has often been quoted ;

it seems to have been always a favourite with our playgoing ancestors. In "The Conquest of Granada" we read :—

> So two kind turtles, when a storm is nigh,
> Look up, and see it gathering in the sky. . . .
> Perch'd on some dropping branch, they sit alone,
> And coo and hearken to each other's moan.

Mr. Bayes imitated this in what he called "one of the most delicate, dainty similes in the world, egad" :—

> So boar and sow, when any storm is nigh,
> Snuff up, and smell it gath'ring in the sky. . . .
> Pensive in mud they wallow all alone,
> And snort and gruntle to each other's moan.

The example set by Buckingham in "The Rehearsal" was followed, more than half a century later, by Henry Fielding, in "The Tragedy of Tragedies, or the Life and Death of Tom Thumb the Great." This was brought out in 1730, in two acts, and was so immediately and largely successful that the author was induced to expand its two acts into three. It was afterwards published, with elaborate notes, setting forth a number of "parallel passages" from Dryden downwards, and with a preface, in which the supposed editor, H. Scriblerus Secundus, gravely assigned the origin of the "tragedy" to the age of Elizabeth. Apropos of parallel passages, the editor says :—

Whether this sameness of thought and expression [on the part of the authors quoted] . . . proceeded from an agreement in their way of thinking, or whether they have borrowed from or author, I leave the reader to determine. I shall adventure to affirm this of the Sentiments of our author, that they are generally the most familiar which I have ever met with, and at the same time delivered with the highest dignity of phrase ; which brings me to speak of his diction. Here I shall only beg one postulatum—viz., that the greatest perfection of the language of a tragedy is, that it is not to be understood; which granted (as I think it must be), it will necessarily follow that the only ways to avoid this is by being too high or too low for the understanding, which will comprehend everything within its reach.

The editor goes on to say that " our author excelleth " in both these styles. " He is very rarely within sight through the whole play, either rising higher than the eye of your understanding can soar, or sinking lower than it careth to stoop."

Fielding does not adopt in " Tom Thumb " the machinery of " The Rehearsal." [" Tom Thumb " is a burlesque tragedy, standing by itself, and intended for representation in the serious spirit which should animate all true burlesque.] Tom Thumb is " a little hero, with a great soul," who, as a reward for his victories over the race of giants, demands in marriage the hand of Huncamunca, the daughter of King Arthur. As he observes :—

> I ask not kingdoms, I can conquer those ;
> I ask not money, money I've enough ;
> For what I've done, and what I mean to do,
> For giants slain, and giants yet unborn
> Which I will slay—if this be call'd a debt,
> Take my receipt in full : I ask but this—
> To sun myself in Huncamunca's eyes.

" Prodigious bold request," remarks the King ; but he decides, nevertheless, to give Huncamunca to Tom Thumb. Unhappily, Lord Grizzle is enamoured of the princess, and, in revenge, leads an insurrection against the Court. He is, however, conquered by the little hero, who is about to be wedded to his charmer, when, alas ! as he is marching in·triumph through the streets, he is swallowed by " a cow, of larger than the usual size." Queen Dollallolla, who is in love with Tom, slays with her own hand the messenger who brought the news. Thereupon, Cleora, who is in love with the messenger, kills the Queen. Huncamunca, by way of reprisal, kills Cleora. A certain Doodle kills Huncamunca; one Mustacha kills Doodle; the King kills Mustacha, and then kills himself, exclaiming—

> So when the child, whom nurse from danger guards,
> Sends Jack for mustard with a pack of cards,
> Kings, queens and knaves throw one another down,
> Till the whole pack lies scatter'd and o'erthrown;
> So all our pack upon the floor is cast,
> And all I boast is—that I fall the last.

We have here a happy satire upon the sanguinary conclusions given to the tragedies of the seventeenth century. Great pains, too, are taken, throughout the "tragedy," to travestie that *bête noire* of the humourists, the dragged-in simile, to which not even "The Rehearsal" had given the *coup de grâce*. The ghost of Tom Thumb's father is made to say—

> So have I seen the bees in clusters swarm,
> So have I seen the stars in frosty nights,
> So have I seen the sand in windy days,
> So have I seen the ghost on Pluto's shore,
> So have I seen the flowers in spring arise,
> So have I seen the leaves in autumn fall,
> So have I seen the fruits in summer smile,
> So have I seen the snow in winter frown.

Whereupon the king says, "D—n all thou hast seen!" Grizzle, when on the point of expiring, cries—

> Some kinder sprite knocks softly at my soul,
> And gently whispers it to haste away.
> I come, I come, most willingly I come.
> So, when some city wife, for country air,
> To Hampstead or to Highgate does repair,

Her to make haste her husband does implore,
And cries, " My dear, the coach is at the door ' :
With equal wish, desirous to be gone,
She gets into the coach, and then she cries, " Drive on ! "

Some of the mock similes in " Tom Thumb " are among the most familiar things in literature. We all remember the lines—

So, when two dogs are fighting in the streets,
When a third dog one of the two dogs meets,
With angry teeth he bites him to the bone,
And this dog smarts for what that dog has done.

And these—

So, when the Cheshire cheese a maggot breeds,
Another and another still succeeds ;
By thousands and ten thousands they increase,
Till one continued maggot fills the rotten cheese.

The burlesque contained within the pages of " Tom Thumb " covers a considerable field. Dryden is once more very freely satirised, some nine or ten of his plays being held up to ridicule. But much attention is at the same time paid to dramas which saw the light after the production of " The Rehearsal." Thus, there are allusions to the " Mithridates," " Nero," and " Brutus " of Nathaniel Lee, which belong to 1674—1679; to the " Marius " of Otway (1680); to the " Anna Bullen," " Earl of Essex," " Mary Queen of Scots," and " Cyrus the Great " of Banks (1680—1696); to the " Persian Princess " of Theobald (1711), to Addison's " Cato " (1713), to Young's " Busiris " and " The Revenge," and even to Thomson's " Sophonisba," which had come out only in the year preceding that in which " Tom Thumb " was performed. " O Sophonisba, Sophonisba O " (which had already been parodied in the

form of "O Jemmy Thomson, Jemmy Thomson O") is
here laughed at in "O Huncamunca, Huncamunca O!"
[In "Cyrus the Great" the virtuous Panthea remarks to one
lover—

> For two I must confess are gods to me,
> Which is my Abradatus first, and thee.

And, in a like spirit, Huncamunca, after wedding Tom
Thumb, is quite willing to wed Grizzle :—

> My ample heart for more than one has room :
> A maid like me Heaven form'd at least for two.
> I married him, and now I'll marry you,—

thereby reminding us of the obliging defendant in Mr. Gilbert's "Trial by Jury," who is ready to "marry this lady
to-day, and marry the other to-morrow."] In the third act
of "Cato" is a simile which Fielding parodies thus—putting
it into the mouth of Grizzle :—

> So have I seen, in some dark winter's day,
> A sudden storm rush down the sky's highway,
> Sweep through the streets with terrible ding-dong,
> Gush thro' the spouts, and wash whole crowds along,
> The crowded shops the thronging vermin screen,
> Together cram the dirty and the clean,
> And not one shoe-boy in the street is seen.

Finally, we have this equally well-known passage, suggested
by the remark of Lee's Mithridates that he "would be
drunk with death" :—

> *Doodle.* My liege, I a petition have here got.
> *King.* Petition me no petitions, sir, to-day ;
> Let other hours be set apart for business.
> To-day it is our pleasure to be drunk,
> And this our queen shall be as drunk as we.

It was the fate of "Tom Thumb" to be transformed—so far as it was possible to transform it—into a burlesque of Italian opera as well as of conventional drama. "Set to music after the Italian manner," it was brought out in 1733 as "The Opera of Operas," and had considerable vogue in the new guise thus given to it. It had been preceded in 1727 by Gay's "Beggar's Opera"; but that famous work was a social and political satire rather than a travestie of the exotic lyrical drama. It may be regarded as a species of prototype of the burletta or ballad opera of later days. Not even the transformed "Tom Thumb"[*] could be called an effective *reductio ad absurdum* of the Italian opera of those days. For that the public had to wait a short time longer.

Meanwhile, four years after the production of "Tom Thumb" came the "Chrononhotonthologos" of Henry Carey, author of "Sally in our Alley." This also is a burlesque tragedy, but the travestie is purely general. No individual play is directly satirised; the satire is aimed at a whole class of dramas—the same class as that which had suggested the composition of "Tom Thumb."

Carey says, in his prologue :—

> To-night our comic muse the buskin wears,
> And gives herself no small romantic airs ;
> Struts in heroics, and in pompous verse
> Does the minutest incidents rehearse ;
> In ridicule's strict retrospect displays
> The poetasters of these modern days,

---

[*] "Tom Thumb" was performed in 1740, with Yates as the ghost and Woodward as Noodle, Glumdalca (the giantess) being represented by a man. In 1745 Yates played Grizzle, Tom being enacted by a lady. The burlesque was seen at Covent Garden in 1828.

> Who with big bellowing bombast rend our ears,
> Which, stript of sound, quite void of sense appears ;
> Or else their fiddle-faddle numbers flow,
> Serenely dull, elaborately low.

"Chrononhotonthologos" is a short piece, in one act and seven scenes. It is described in its sub-title as "the most tragical tragedy that ever was tragedised by any company of tragedians," and it bears out the description tolerably well. When the curtain rises, there enter two courtiers of Queerummania—Rigdum-Funnidos and Aldiborontiphosco-phornio. Says the latter to the former :—

> Aldiborontiphoscophornio !
> Where left you Chrononhotonthologos ?

Chrononhotonthologos is the king, and we learn that he is in his tent, in a kind of waking slumber. Presently he enters, very much put out that he should be so inclined to doze, and very angry, consequently, with the God of Sleep. Says he :—

> Sport not with Chrononhotonthologos,
> Thou idle slumb'rer, thou detested Somnus ;

and "exits in a huff." Whereupon the two courtiers, who have retired, re-enter :—

> *Rigdum.* The King is in a most cursed passion ! Pray who is the Mr. Somnus he's so angry withal ?
>> *Aldi.* The son of Chaos and of Erebus,
>> Incestuous pair l brother of Mors relentless,
>> Whose speckled robe, and wings of blackest hue,
>> Astonish all mankind with hideous glare :
>> Himself, with sable plumes, to men benevolent
>> Brings downy slumbers and refreshing sleep.
> *Rigdum.* This gentleman may come of a very good family, for aught I know ; but I would not be in his place for the world.

Aldi. But lo l the king his footsteps this way bending,
His cogitative faculties immers'd
In cogibundity of cogitation.

Thereupon the king re-enters, followed almost immediately
by the captain of the guard, who informs him that
"th' antipodean pow'rs from realms below have burst the
entrails of the earth" and threaten the safety of the
kingdom. "This world is too incopious to contain them;
armies on armies march in form stupendous"—"tier on
tier, high pil'd from earth to heaven." The king, however,
is not alarmed. He bids Bombardinian, his general, draw
his legions forth, and orders the priests to prepare their
temples for rites of triumph :—

Let the singing singers,
With vocal voices, most vociferous,
In sweet vociferation, out-vociferise
Ev'n sound itself.

Happily the Antipodeans (who walk upon their hands) are
badly beaten, and all run away except their king, with
whom, alas ! Fadladinida, the wife of Chrononhotonthologos,
promptly falls in love. As she herself says to her favourite
maiden :—

Oh, my Tatlanthe ! Have you seen his face,
His air, his shape, his mien, his ev'ry grace?
In what a charming attitude he stands,
How prettily he foots it with his hands !
Well, to his arms—no, to his legs—I fly,
For I must have him, if I live or die.

Meanwhile, Bombardinian has invited the King to drink
wine with him in his tent. The King accepts, but, not
content with liquor, asks for something more substantial :—

Hold, Bombardinian, I esteem it fit,
With so much wine, to eat a little bit.

The cook suggests "some nice cold pork in the pantry," and is instantly slain by the irate monarch, who, deeming that Bombardinian is "braving" him, strikes him.　Whereupon the General :—

> A blow ! shall Bombardinian take a blow ?
> Blush ! blush, thou sun ! start back, thou rapid ocean !
> Hills ! vales ! seas ! mountains ! all commixing crumble,
> And into chaos pulverise the world ;
> For Bombardinian has receiv'd a blow,
> And Chrononhotonthologos must die.
>
> [They fight.　He kills the king.
>
> Ha ! what have I done ?
> Go, call a coach, and let a coach be call'd ;
> And let the man that calls it be the caller ;
> And, in his calling, let him nothing call,
> But coach, coach, coach !　Oh, for a coach, ye gods !
>
> [Exit, raving.

The doctor, pronouncing the king dead, is killed by the General, who then kills himself.　The Queen mourns her widowhood, and Tatlanthe proposes that she should wed Rigdum-Funnidos. [To this, however, Aldiborontiphoscophornio objects ; and so, to save discussion, the Queen will give no preference to either :—

> To make the matter easy,
> I'll have you both ; and that, I hope, will please ye.

Produced in 1734, "Chrononhotonthologos" was performed at intervals until 1815, when it was seen at Drury Lane, with Oxberry in the title-part and Dowton as the General.　After that it remained out of the theatrical repertory until 1880, when Mr. John Hollingshead revived

W. L.—V.

it, for one representation, at the Gaiety.* It is a slight piece of work, but contains some elements of comicality. It will always be esteemed by literary students, if only because the names of Rigdum-Funnidos and Aldiborontiphoscophornio struck the fancy of Sir Walter Scott, who bestowed them, in fun, upon the brothers Constable, the publishers. "Aldiborontiphoscophornio" is surely the perfection of mock-tragedy nomenclature.

It is to Carey that we owe, not only "Chrononhotonthologos," but the first really effective burlesque of Italian opera. In 1737 there was brought out at the Haymarket "The Dragon of Wantley," a "burlesque opera," of which Carey had written the dialogue and songs, and for which John Frederick Lampe had composed the music. Its object, according to the author, was "to display in English the beauty of nonsense, so prevailing in the Italian operas." The story was founded on the old ballad, with which, however, liberties were taken. In the first act, the natives of "that part of Yorkshire near Rotherham" are shown in much excitement, due to the ravages of the dragon, which has just entered the Squire's residence and consumed all the coffee, toast, and butter that was set out for breakfast. Says one Gubbins :—

> This Dragon very modish, sure, and nice is :
> What shall we do in this disastrous crisis ?

To which his daughter Margery replies :—

> A thought, to quell him, comes into my Head ;
> No Way more proper, than to kill him dead.

---

* The parts of Chrononhotonthologos, Bombardinian, Rigdum-Funnidos, Aldiborontiphoscophornio, Fadladinida, and Tatlanthe were then taken by Messrs. Murray, Shine, Soutar, Squire, Mrs. Leigh, and Miss Bella Howard respectively.

Not far hence lives "a valiant knight," named Moore, of Moore Hall, who may be trusted to destroy the dragon. Moore accordingly is approached, surrenders to the charms of Margery, and undertakes to do the deed. Meanwhile, Mauxalinda, an old flame of Moore's, becomes jealous of Margery, and seeks to slay her with a bodkin—a fate from which Moore happily rescues her. Mauxalinda is then threatened with quarter sessions; but she cries—

> O give me not up to the Law,
>   I'd much rather beg upon Crutches;
> Once in a Sollicitor's Paw,
>   You never get out of his Clutches.

Moore thereupon prepares to start for the Dragon's den:

> But first I'll drink, to make me strong and mighty,
> Six quarts of ale, and one of Aqua Vitæ.

Duly encountering the monster, Moore kills him (say the stage directions) with a kick in the rear, the Dragon crying "Oh, oh, oh! the Devil take your toe!" After that, Gubbins declares:—

> The Loves of this brave Knight, and my fair Daughter,
> In Roratorios shall be sung hereafter.
> Begin your Songs of Joy; begin, begin,
> And rend the Welkin with harmonious Din.

Thereupon there is this general chorus:—

> Sing, sing, and rorio
> An Oratorio,
> To gallant Morio,
>   Of Moore Hall.
> To Margereenia
> Of Roth'ram Greenia,
> Beauty's bright Queenia,
>   Bellow and bawl.

"The music," says the chronicler, "was made as grand and pompous as possible, to heighten the contrast between that and the words"—thus anticipating the comic method which has been utilised with so much success by Mr. Gilbert and Sir Arthur Sullivan.

From "The Dragon of Wantley," which, as might be expected, had a very considerable vogue, we come to "The Critic, or a Tragedy Rehearsed"—the last, and not the least, of Sheridan's dramatic works, produced in Drury Lane in 1779. Of so familiar a piece, what is there to be said? Is it not played with tolerable frequency at "benefits," for the sake of the "exceptional casts" it can supply? Have not all middle-aged playgoers seen and admired the younger Mathews as Sir Fretful Plagiary and Mr. Puff? Assuredly there are certain features of "The Critic" which everybody remembers. Everybody remembers Sir Fretful's famous lines on the plagiarists, who "serve your best thoughts as gypsies do stolen children—disfigure them to make 'em pass for their own"; as well as his special addendum about the "dexterous" writer who "might take out some of the best things in my tragedy and put them into his own comedy." Everybody remembers, too, Mr. Puff's no less famous catalogue of the varieties of *réclame*; his remark that "the number of those who undergo the fatigue of judging for themselves is very small indeed"; his explanation of the fact that he and Shakespeare had made use of the same thought; Lord Burleigh's shake of the head, which meant so much, and has become proverbial; the Spanish fleet, which could not be seen because it was not yet in sight; Tilburina, "mad in white satin"—and the like. It must be recollected, however, that "The Critic" as played and "The Critic" as written and printed are two very different things. In the acting version, the earlier scenes between Puff and Dangle and Sneer, as well as the latter portion of the "tragedy rehearsed," are very much compressed—no doubt with advantage to the public, for, clever as "The Critic" is as a whole, certain portions of it are out of date, and would not "go" well with a modern audience.

In glancing through the printed version, one is struck anew by the similarity that "The Critic" bears to "The Rehearsal," not only in form, but in detail. In both cases a dramatic author rehearses a tragedy in the presence of a couple of friends, who interject comments upon the performance. But the likeness does not end here—possibly because the theatrical world of 1779 was, in all essentials, very like the theatrical world of 1671. Bayes, in "The Rehearsal," says that he has "appointed two or three dozen" of his friends "to be ready in the pit" (at the *première* of his piece), "who, I'm sure, will clap." And so Sneer, in "The Critic," expects that he will not be able to get into Drury Lane on the first night of Puff's play, "for on the first night of a piece they always fill the house with orders to support it." Again, Bayes says that .

Let a man write never so well, there are, nowadays, a sort of persons they call critics, that, egad, have no more wit in them than so many hobby-horses; but they'll laugh at you, sir, and find fault, and censure things that, egad, I'm sure they are not able to do themselves.

In a similar spirit Sir Fretful stigmatises the newspapers as "the most villainous—licentious—abominable—infernal—— Not that I ever read them—no. I make it a rule never to look into a newspaper."

In one respect Sheridan's work is quite unlike the Duke of Buckingham's. It contains no direct travestie or parody of any kind. The burlesque is "at large" throughout. The satire embodied in the dialogue between Puff and his friends reflects upon all old-fashioned playwriting of the "tragic" sort. Puff opens the second scene of his "Spanish Armada" with a clock striking four, which, besides recording the time, not only "begets an awful attention in the audience," but "saves a description of the rising sun, and a great deal about gilding the eastern hemisphere." He makes his characters tell one another what they know already, because, although they know it, the audience do not. He hears the stage cannon go off three times instead of once, and complains, "Give these fellows a good thing, and they never know when to have done with it." "Where they do agree on the stage," he says, in another hackneyed passage, "their unanimity is wonderful." In the rehearsed tragedy itself the travestie is general, not particular. Here Sheridan satirises a different class of tragedy from that which Buckingham dealt with. As the prologue (not by Sheridan, however) says :—

> In those gay days of wickedness and wit,
> When Villiers criticised what Dryden writ,
> The tragic queen, to please a tasteless crowd,
> Had learn'd to bellow, rant, and roar so loud,
> That frighten'd Nature, her best friend before,
> The blustering beldam's company forswore.

The later "tragedy" took another tone :—

> The frantic hero's wild delirium past,
> Now insipidity succeeds bombast ;
> So slow Melpomene's cold numbers creep,
> Here dulness seems her drowsy court to keep.

Dulness, then, is what Sheridan is chiefly. girding at, but he has a keen eye also for the unconscious banalities of the *genre* he is dealing with. How truly comic, for instance, is the prayer to Mars offered up by Leicester and his companions !—

> Behold thy votaries submissive beg
> That thou wilt deign to grant them all they ask;
> Assist them to accomplish all their ends,
> And sanctify whatever means they use
> To gain them.

How delicious, too, in their absolute nonsense, are the lines given to the distraught Tilburina !—

> The wind whistles—the moon rises—see,
> They have killed my squirrel in his cage;
> Is this a grasshopper ?—Ha ! no; it is my
> Whiskerandos—you shall not keep him—
> I know you have him in your pocket—
> An oyster may be cross'd in love !—who says
> A whale's a bird ?—Ha ! did you call, my love ?—
> He's here ! he's there !—He's everywhere !
> Ah me ! he's nowhere !

For the rest, the text of the tragedy, as printed, is very dissimilar from the text as played. In representation, most of the fun is got out of intentional perversion of certain words or phrases. Thus, " martial symmetry " becomes " martial cemetery ";

> The famed Armada, by the Pope baptised,

becomes

> The famed Armada, by the Pope capsised;

" friendship's closing line " is turned into " friendship's clothes-line "; " My gentle Nora " into " My gentle Snorer "; " Cupid's baby woes " into " Cupid's baby clothes ";

"matchless excellence" into "matchless impudence," and so on. This is sorry stuff; and those who desire to appreciate Sheridan's travestie of the tragedy of his day must read "The Critic" in its published shape.

The next notable attempt at the burlesque of conventional tragedy was a return to the methods of "Chrononhotontho-logos." [In "Bombastes Furioso" (first played in 1816*) all satirical machinery was discarded; all that the author— William Barnes Rhodes—sought to do was to travestie his originals in a brief and telling story.] "Bombastes" is not now so often performed as it used to be; but not so very long ago it was turned into a comic opera, under the title of "Artaxominous the Great," and its humours are fairly well known to the public. Some of these the world will not willingly let die. [One still thinks with amusement of the "army" of Bombastes, consisting of "one Drummer, one Fifer, and two Soldiers, all very materially differing in size"; of the General's exhortation to his troops—

> Begone, brave army, and don't kick up a row;

and of the boastful challenge of the General, so promptly accepted by Artaxominous—

> Who dares this pair of boots displace
> Must meet Bombastes face to face.

And the piece bears re-perusal wonderfully well. Its literary merit is assuredly not less than that of "Chronon-hotonthologos": it is perhaps even greater. The opening colloquy between the King and Fusbos is genuinely divert-ing, embodying as it does one of those mock similes so dear

---

* The elder Mathews was Artaxominous; Liston, Bombardinian; and Miss H. Kelly, Distaffina. A few years later Munden played Bombardinian, and Farren, Fusbos.

to the satirists of old-fashioned tragedy. The King admits
to Fusbos that he is "but middling—that is, *so so!* " It is
not, however, either the mulligrubs or the blue-devils that
disturb him :—

> *King.* Last night, when undisturb'd by state affairs,
> Moist'ning our clay, and puffing off our cares,
> Oft the replenish'd goblet did we drain,
> And drank and smok'd, and smok'd and drank again !
> Such was the case, our very actions such,
> Until at length we got a drop too much.
> *Fusbos.* So when some donkey on the Blackheath road,
> Falls, overpower'd, beneath his sandy load,
> The driver's curse unheeded swells the air,
> Since none can carry more than they can bear.

By-and-by the King confides to Fusbos that his heart is not
wholly faithful to Queen Griskinissa—that he is also hope-
lessly in love with Distaffina, the acknowledged sweetheart
of Bombastes. Under the circumstances he asks for
Fusbos' advice :—

> Shall I my Griskinissa's charms forego,
> Compel her to give up the regal chair,
> And place the rosy Distaffina there ?
> In such a case, what course can I pursue ?
> I love my queen, and Distaffina too.
> *Fusbos.* And would a king his general supplant ?
> I can't advise, upon my soul I can't.
> *King.* So when two feasts, whereat there's nought to pay,
> Fall unpropitious on the self-same day,
> The anxious Cit each invitation views,
> And ponders which to take and which refuse :
> From this or that to keep away is loth,
> And sighs to think he cannot dine at both.

These, however, are not the best known of the mock
similes in "Bombastes." For those we have to look to the
scene in which the King, observing his General's above-

mentioned challenge, reviles Bombastes and knocks down his boots. Then we have the familiar lines :—

> *Bomb.* So have I heard on Afric's burning shore
> A hungry lion give a grievous roar ;
> The grievous roar echo'd along the shore.
> *King.* So have I heard on Afric's burning shore
> Another lion give a grievous roar,
> And the first lion thought the last a bore.

Next comes the fight between the monarch and the warrior; the King is killed, and then Fusbos kills Bombastes. Finally, the two deceased (despite the assertion of Fusbos that they are "dead as herrings—herrings that are red") come to life again, and all ends happily.

Of ordinary parody there is little in the piece, and what there is can scarcely be said to be of the best. There is a suggestion, in one ditty, of "Hope told a flattering Tale." But better than this is the song suggested by " My Lodging is on the Cold Ground," which is happy both intrinsically and as an imitation. Fusbos is the singer :—

> My lodging is in Leather Lane,
>   A parlour that's next to the sky ;
> 'Tis exposed to the wind and the rain,
>   But the wind and the rain I defy :
> Such love warms the coldest of spots,
>   As I feel for Scrubinda the fair ;
> Oh, she lives by the scouring of pots,
>   In Dyot Street, Bloomsbury Square.
>
> Oh, were I a quart, pint, or gill,
>   To be scrubb'd by her delicate hands,
> Let others possess what they will
>   Of learning, and houses, and lands ;
> My parlour that's next to the sky
>   I'd quit, her blest mansion to share ;
> So happy to live and to die
>   In Dyot Street, Bloomsbury Square.

> And oh, would this damsel be mine,
> No other provision I'd seek ;   ·
> On a look I could breakfast and dine,
> And feast on a smile for a week.
> But ah ! should she false-hearted prove,
> Suspended, I'll dangle in air ;
> A victim to delicate love,
> In Dyot Street, Bloomsbury Square.

[At this point, English stage burlesque suddenly takes a new departure, combining, with satire of the contemporary native " boards," satire not less keen of certain products of the foreign muse.   The incident came about in this way :— Just before the close of the eighteenth century, the English book-market had been flooded with translations of certain German plays, including Schiller's " Robbers " and " Cabal and Love," Goethe's " Stella," and Kotzebue's " Misanthropy and Repentance" ("The Stranger") and "Count Benyowsky." Canning, Ellis, and Frere, who were then bringing out *The Anti-Jacobin*, were struck by the absurdities contained within these dramas, and accordingly composed and printed (in June 1798) that well-known skit, " The Rovers, or the Double Arrangement."   In this the plays chiefly parodied are "Stella," "The Stranger," and "Count Benyowsky."   By " Stella " was suggested not only " the double arrangement " (by which Matilda and Cecilia share the affections of their lover Casimere), but the famous scene in which the two women, before they know they are rivals, become, on the instant, bosom friends.   Both admit that they are in love, and then—

Cecilia. Your countenance grows animated, my dear madam.
Matilda. And yours is glowing with illumination.
Cecilia. I had long been looking out for a congenial spirit ! My heart was withered, but the beams of yours have rekindled it.

Matilda. A sudden thought strikes me : let us swear an eternal friendship.

Cecilia. Let us agree to live together !

Matilda. Willingly.

Cecilia. Let us embrace.   (*They embrace.*)

"The Rovers," however, would hardly come within the scope of the present volume, were it not that, in 1811, at the Haymarket, there was produced, by Colman junior, a piece called "The Quadrupeds of Quedlinburgh, or the Rovers of Weimar," in which the adapter made use of the squib in *The Anti-Jacobin.* Colman's aim in this work was to ridicule not only the German plays, including Kotzebue's "Spaniards in Peru" ("Pizarro"), which had lately been brought before the English playgoer, but also the prevailing fancy for bringing animals upon the stage. At Astley's horses had figured both in "Blue Beard" and in "Timour the Tartar," and dogs had previously been seen in "The Caravan." To this, as well as to the unhealthy importations from Germany, allusion was made in the prologue :—

> To lull the soul by spurious strokes of art,
> To warp the genius and mislead the heart,
> To make mankind revere wives gone astray,

(a hit at "The Stranger"),

> Love pious sons who rob on the highway,
> For this the foreign muses trod our stage,
> Commanding German schools to be the rage. . . .
> Your taste, recovered half from foreign quacks,
> Takes airings now on English horses' backs ;
> While every modern bard may raise his name,
> If not on lasting praise, on stable fame.

"The Quadrupeds of Quedlinburgh" was not printed, and one does not know to what extent Colman took advantage of the text of "The Rovers." It is certain, however, that Casimere, Matilda, and Cecilia, as well as Rogero (a creation of the original parodists), all appeared in the burlesque, being enacted respectively by Munden, Mrs. Glover, Mrs. Gibbs, and Liston, Elliston taking the *rôle* of Bartholomew Bathos, a lineal descendant (no doubt) of Bayes and Puff. We read that, in addition to the travestie supplied by *The Anti-Jacobin*, fun was poked at the sentimental sentinel in "Pizarro," and the last scene of "Timour the Tartar" was closely imitated. The piece was acted thirty-nine times, and must therefore have been what, in those days, was accounted a success.

[We come now to a travestie of the old-fashioned tragedy which helps to connect the Old burlesque with the New, inasmuch as it was the production of James Robinson Planché. Of his "Amoroso, King of Little Britain: a serio-comick bombastick operatick interlude," played at Drury Lane in 1818, Planché was not particularly proud.] He was very young when he wrote it; he wrote it for amateur performance; and it got on to the stage of Drury Lane without his knowledge and consent. Harley, the comedian, appears to have seen or read the little trifle, and to have recommended it to the manager of "the national theatre." He himself represented Amoroso; Knight was Roastando (a cook); Smith was Blusterbus (a yeoman of the guard); Mrs. Bland was Coquetinda (the Queen of Little Britain), and Mrs. Orger was Mollidusta (a chambermaid). The piece was much applauded, and had the distinction of being quoted

in the *Times*.   It opens with the King being awakened by
his courtiers, to whom he angrily exclaims :—

> Leave at what time you please your truckle beds—
> But if you break my rest I'll break your heads.
>
> .   .   .   .
>
> I swear I'm quite disordered with this rout.
> Ahem !   My lords and gentlemen—get out !

The *Times* applied the last line to a Parliamentary
incident which had just occurred; and Planché admits
that he was flattered by the compliment.   But he would
not include "Amoroso" in the testimonial edition of his
burlesques and extravaganzas,—mainly, I imagine, because
the piece is so obviously an imitation of "Bombastes
Furioso," which it by no means equals in literary distinction.

The plot is simplicity itself.   Amoroso is in love with
Mollidusta, Mollidusta with Blusterbus, and the Queen
with Roastando.   "The King sees Roastando and the
Queen salute: he discharges Roastando.   The Queen sees
the King and Mollidusta together: she stabs Mollidusta.
The King stabs the Queen, Roastando stabs the King, the
King stabs Roastando."   In the end, all come to life again.
In the course of the play the King thus declares his passion
to Mollidusta :—

> When gooseberries grow on the stem of a daisy,
>   And plum-puddings roll on the tide to the shore,
> And julep is made from the curls of a jazey,
>   Oh, then, Mollidusta, I'll love thee no more.
>
> When steamboats no more on the Thames shall be going,
>   And a cast-iron bridge reach Vauxhall from the Nore,
> And the Grand Junction waterworks cease to be flowing,
>   Oh, then, Mollidusta, I'll love thee no more.

Amoroso also sings the following pseudo-sentimental ditty :—

> Love's like a mutton-chop,
>   Soon it grows cold,
> All its attractions hop
>   Ere it grows old.
> Love's like the colic sure,
> Both painful to endure,
> Brandy's for both a cure.
>   So I've been told !
>
> When for some fair the swain
>   Burns with desire,
> In Hymen's fatal chain
>   Eager to try her,
> He weds soon as he can,
> And jumps (unhappy man !)
> Out of the frying-pan
>   Into the fire.

Not to be outdone by the other lovers, the Queen and Roastando warble a duet, in which they confess their feelings for each other :—

> *She.* This morning I to Covent Garden went,
> To purchase cabbages was my intent,
> But, my thoughts dwelling on Roastando's looks,
> Instead of cabbages I asked for cooks !
>
> *He.* Last night, neglecting fricassés for stews,
> On Coquetinda's charms I paused to muse,
> And, 'stead of charcoal, did my man desire
> To put some Coquetinda on the fire.

Three months after " Amoroso " had been seen at Drury Lane, there was produced at the English Opera House a " serio-comic-bombastic-operatic interlude," written by George Daniel, and called " Doctor Bolus "—yet another burlesque of the old-fashioned drama, owing quite as much to " Bombastes Furioso " as did " Amoroso." In this piece the King, Artipadiades (Harley), is in love with Poggylina, a maid of honour, while the Queen, Katalinda (Miss Kelly), is enamoured of General Scaramoucho (Chatterley). The General revolts, and is defeated by the King. His amour is discovered, and, while the Queen is poisoned with one of Bolus's "infallible" pills, the General is stabbed by Artipadiades. The Queen, however, revives, and is thereupon stabbed by the King, who also stabs himself. But, in the end, as in " Amoroso," all the dead people are resuscitated. There are some gleams of humour in the dialogue, but not many. Bolus was played by John Wilkinson.

AFTER the production of "Amoroso," Planché remained silent, so far as travestie was concerned, till 1831, when he began in earnest his successful career as a burlesque writer. In the interval a new votary of travestie appeared in the person of Fox Cooper, of whose "Elbow Shakers" and "Ion" I shall have something to say by-and-by. Moncrieff and Buckstone, too, followed the example of T. Dibdin, in dealing more or less humorously with the subject of "Don Giovanni," while Buckstone also essayed to do the same with that of "Billy Taylor." None of these effusions, however, were burlesques in the ordinary acceptation of the word; [and 1831, therefore, may still be taken as the starting-point of the new theatrical era, of which Planché was the herald.

This era may be said to divide naturally into fairly balanced parts, the first extending from 1831 to 1865, the period covered by Planché's activity in the work; the second from 1865 to 1885, by which time Mr. Edward Terry and Miss Kate Vaughan had retired from the Gaiety. Within the former moiety are comprised the labours of four men who for many years shared with Planché the throne

of stage travestie. Need I say that I mean Gilbert Abbott
a'Beckett (with whom Mark Lemon so frequently col-
laborated), Francis Talfourd, and the Brothers Brough?
Planché's " Olympic Revels " (1831) was followed by
A'Beckett's " Son of the Sun " in 1834, by Talfourd's
" Macbeth " in 1847, and by the Brothers Brough's
" Enchanted Isle " in 1848. The " Joan of Arc " of
William Brough was seen in 1869; its writer had been
producing burlesque for over twenty years. Talfourd's
career as a dramatist was comparatively brief. Beginning
in 1847, it ended in 1860, but was brilliant while it lasted.

Modern burlesque was fortunate indeed in its founders
—all of them men of education and refinement, all of them
men of letters as well as playwrights. To the literary merit
of their products it is unnecessary to bear more than the
briefest testimony, for it is everywhere, and by everybody,
acknowledged. In the writings of these four men theatrical
burlesque was seen at its best. They came fresh to the
task, and made the most of their opportunities. They set
themselves really to travestie and to parody, and were
careful to present, amid their wildest comicalities, a
definite, intelligible story. They dropped naturally into
the decasyllabic couplet, and made free use of the pun;
but in neither case did they become mechanical or strained.
The verse of Planché and A'Beckett is smoothness itself, and
they do not descend to word-torturing. Talfourd and the
Broughs took more licence in this latter respect, but they
never sank into drivel. Above all, not one of these five
masters of burlesque permitted themselves to be vulgar
either in general treatment or in verbal detail.] They were
nice in their choice of subjects, and, like Mr. W. S. Gilbert

in the case of "The Princess," perverted them respectfully. One finds no horseplay in the fun of these genuine humourists. All their effects are made legitimately, and in decent fashion.

They were happy, too, in the good influence they exercised. The list of their colleagues during the period named is notable. One meets early with the names of Charles Selby and W. H. Oxberry. Then come those of Albert Smith, Kenny, and Shirley Brooks, Leicester Buckingham, and Andrew Halliday, by whom much excellent work was achieved in the 'forties and 'fifties. Of lesser note, in this particular department of endeavour, were Leman Rede, Stirling Coyne, and Tom Taylor, who were more distinguished in other fields. Selby and Oxberry had the knack of writing for the stage which so often results from experience in acting. Smith, Brooks, Buckingham, Halliday, Rede, Coyne, and Taylor, were men whose literary skill, acquired in other quarters, was of eminent service to the comic stage. Especially is it to be regretted that the genial and witty author of "Sooner or Later" did not devote more of his time and talent to the service of burlesque, of the qualities and possibilities of which he had so keen a sense.

But to turn now to the second moiety of the period above named—that extending from 1865 to 1885. We find that this, too, has had the good fortune to be domi-nated by some burlesque writers of very special capacity—to wit, Mr. F. C. Burnand, the late H. J. Byron, Mr. W. S. Gilbert, and Mr. Robert Reece. Mr. Burnand has been bringing out burlesques ever since 1855, when he wrote "Villikins and his Dinah" for the Cambridge A.D.C. His first London production was his "Dido," seen at the

St. James's in 1860.   His metropolitan career, therefore, has
covered more than thirty years.   Byron began at the Strand
in 1858, and ended at the Gaiety in 1879.   Mr. Gilbert's
labours as a producer of travestie in the ordinary sense
started early in the 'sixties with "Dr. Dulcamara," and
closed in 1870 with "The Princess."*   Mr. Reece opened
in 1865 with "Prometheus"; and work in which he had a
part was witnessed so recently as 1886.

Mr. Gilbert soon found that his true *métier* lay outside
the bounds of ordinary burlesque, and his "Princess" was
the stepping-stone to "The Palace of Truth," and, in due
course, to "H.M.S. *Pinafore*" and its successors.]   His
travesties of "L'Elisire d'Amore," "La Fille du Régiment,"
"The Bohemian Girl," "Norma," and "Robert le Diable,"
had, however, what all the best specimens of English
stage burlesque have had—a literary quality and an entire
absence of coarseness or suggestiveness ; and no doubt they
had, at the time, their due effect upon the public taste.
Meanwhile, the premier burlesque writers of the past thirty
years are Mr. Burnand, Byron, and Mr. Reece, whose
productions have been as notable for their multiplicity and
variety as for their technical excellence.   All three, like the
ablest of their predecessors, have written extravaganza as
well as travestie ; and, in travestie, they have gone far afield,
essaying and succeeding in all subjects and all styles.   They,
too, have favoured, in the main, the decasyllabic couplet and
the pun, bringing both of them to all the comic perfection
of which they were capable.   The pun, in particular, has

---

* In the preparation of "The Happy Land" (1873) Mr. Gilbert
had only a share, the scenario being his, but nearly all the writing
eing done by Mr. Gilbert Arthur a'Beckett.

reached its highest phase in the writings of these consummate jugglers with words.

Mr. H. B. Farnie had a considerable vogue in burlesque from 1870 to 1885, but never displayed the neatness or the spontaneity of the writers above mentioned. He was fluent, but that was all. Mr. Alfred Thompson at one time did good things in this direction, and so did Mr. Conway Edwardes. Mr. G. A. Sala composed one burlesque, but has not been induced to give it a successor. Mr. Herman Merivale has been content to write two : that he has not written more is to be regretted. Among other recent writers of travestie may be named—Mr. Gilbert Arthur à Beckett, Mr. Harry Paulton, Mr. F. W. Green, Mr. Arthur Matthison, Mr. Savile Clarke, Mr. W. Younge, Mr. Edward Rose, Mr. Alfred Murray, Mr. Albert Chevalier, Mr. George Dance, Mr. G. P. Hawtrey, Mr. Horace Lennard, Mr. Geoffrey Thorn, and Mr. Cecil Raleigh. In the provinces great successes have been made by Mr. J. McArdle and Mr. Wilton Jones. Of Messrs. Sims and Pettitt, Stephens and Yardley, "Richard Henry," and "A. C. Torr" and H. Mills, I shall have something to say when I come to consider "The New Burlesque," of which they have been the principal producers. If, within the last twenty years or so, travestie has been confined to a smaller number of theatres than before, and if it has been proportionately "depressed," that has been owing, chiefly, to the popularity of comic opera and farcical comedy, into the composition and exposition of which has been thrown, of necessity, very much of the talent which otherwise would have been devoted to the writing and acting of burlesque.

On the whole, the days between 1831 and 1885 were, for

burlesque, " palmy" days indeed.   They produced not only
many admirable writers of the *genre*, but many admirable
actors thereof.   Planché was generous in his praise of the
artists who helped so greatly to make his pieces " go " ; and
he did well to be so, for never, I suppose, was a comic
writer so fortunate in his interpreters.   During his first
years at the Olympic he had the aid of the incomparable
Vestris, of Rebecca Isaacs, of Miss Murray, of Mrs.
Macnamara, of Mrs. Honey, of John Brougham, of James
Bland, of James Vining, and of Charles James Mathews,—
all in the first rank of their art.   At Covent Garden, from
1840 to 1843, the company included, at different times, not
only Mme. Vestris, Mrs. Macnamara, Brougham, Bland,
and Vining, but Harley, Wm. Harrison, Morris Barnett,
Selby, Miss Fairbrother, Miss Priscilla Horton, Mrs. C.
Jones, and Mrs. Alfred Wigan.   At the Haymarket, during
the three years following, Planché had his ideas carried
out, not only by Bland and Miss Horton, and during one
year by Mme. Vestris and Charles Mathews, but also
by Caulfield, Widdicomb, Tilbury, Brindal, Braid, Julia
Bennett, Miss Reynolds, and Mrs. L. S. Buckingham.
Continuously lucky in this respect, Planché enjoyed—from
1847 to 1853, at the Lyceum—the services of Miss Fitz-
william, Julia St. George, Miss Oliver, John Reeve, Robert
Roxby, Basil Baker, and Mr. and Mrs. Frank Matthews, in
addition to Vestris and Mathews and many others of the
artists named above.   Finally, and best, when Planché
brought out, at the Olympic, his " Yellow Dwarf," his
" Discreet Princess," and his " Young and Handsome," his
chief comedian was the " great little Robson," the fame of
whose tragi-comic outbursts still lingers among us, and who

had for his successive supporters Horace Wigan, Emery, James Rogers, Julia St. George, Miss Maskell (Mrs. Walter Baynham), and Miss Swanborough.

What, meanwhile, had been the *personnel* at the other houses of burlesque? At the Strand in the 'thirties, the great favourites were W. J. Hammond, H. Hall, Mitchell, Oxberry, G. Cooke, Miss Daly, Miss Horton. At the Fitzroy one finds Miss Chaplin and W. Rogers; at the Victoria, Rogers and Mitchell; at the St. James's, Hall and Mme. Sala; at Sadler's Wells, Rogers and C. H. Pitt; at the Queen's, T. F. Matthews and Mrs. Selby; and at the Adelphi, O Smith, John Reeve, and Mrs. Stirling. Early in the 'forties we see Wright and Paul Bedford moving from the Princess's to the Adelphi, where Miss Chaplin and Miss Woolgar are also located. At the Strand we find Wigan, Hammond, and R. Romer. Later, we come across Keeley in burlesque at the Haymarket, along with Bland, Miss Reynolds, and Miss Horton. The second half of the century opens brilliantly at the Strand, where Reeve, Rogers, Romer, and Maskell are the male comedians, with Miss Marshall, Miss Romer, Miss Maskell, and Mrs. Horsman as their helpmates. Was not that a truly strong company? And was not the Adelphi fortunate, about the same time, in the possession of Miss Woolgar, Miss Mary Keeley, Keeley himself, and Paul Bedford? At the Haymarket were Buckstone and Mrs. Caulfield. Some of these may be names only to the uninstructed reader; but to the theatrical student they all convey a world of meaning, conjuring up a multitude of delightful associations.

When we come to 1856 we reach a landmark in the history of burlesque acting. William Brough's " Perdita " is "put up" by Charles Dillon at the Lyceum, and in the cast of it we find not only Miss Woolgar and the author, but that very youthful actress Marie Wilton, and that rising young comedian J. L. Toole. Here, then, is the beginning of the modern *régime.* Robson and Julia St. George are still playing at the Olympic; but the "palmy" days of the Strand Theatre are about to flash upon us. Marie Wilton stays for another year at the Lyceum, but in 1858 she is comfortably lodged at the little playhouse across the way, together with Bland and Poynter and Mrs. Selby, and Johnny Clarke, H. J. Turner, and Miss Ternan. In 1859 Charlotte Saunders is playing a mock Romeo to Marie Wilton's mock Juliet, and Eleanor Bufton and Maria Simpson and "Jimmy" Rogers are also members of the troupe —the one troupe which can regard itself as the legitimate successor to the Vestris-Mathews "combinations." In the year following, a new star arises at the Lyceum in the person of Lydia Thompson; at the St. James's are Nelly Moore and Cecilia Ranoe and Charles Young; at the Haymarket are Chippendale, Compton, and C. Coghlan. A few months more, and the name of Kate Terry appears on the burlesque bill at the St. James's. Fanny Josephs and E. Danvers have been added to the Strand establishment, which shortly welcomes Fanny Hughes and Ada Swanborough, Polly Marshall and George Honey.

Next comes the turn of the little Royalty. We are in 1863, and Mr. Burnand's "Ixion" is announced, with Jenny Wilmore in the title-part, David James as Mercury, Felix Rogers as Minerva, Mrs. Charles Selby as the Queen, and Ada Cavendish as Venus. Here, again, is a landmark, not to be left unnoted; here we have to record the first of many triumphs to come. Next year both David James and Thomas Thorne are in the troupe at the Strand, where they are destined to remain till they open the Vaudeville in 1870. In the year next again, the burlesque company at the Olympic is seen to include a young actress of the name of Ellen Farren, one day to become the chief tender of the "sacred lamp"; along with her are Amy Sheridan, Louisa Moore, Patti Josephs, and Mrs. Stephens. [Meanwhile, the Royalty has been running neck and neck with the Strand, and growing greatly in public favour. By 1866 it is ripe for another success—the most remarkable ever achieved on the burlesque boards—secured by the "Black-eyed Susan" of Mr. Burnand, with Fred Dewar as Captain Crosstree, Mr. Charles Wyndham as a Deal smuggler, Miss Oliver as Susan, Miss Nellie Bromley as Dolly Mayflower, and E. Danvers as Dame Hatley.] After this one notes the addition to the Strand troupe, first, of Miss Eliza Johnstone, Miss Elise Holt, and Miss Weathersby; and next, of Miss Lydia Thompson. At the New Queen's in 1868, Miss Kate Santley and Miss Henrietta Hodson are playing burlesque with W. H. Stephens and "Lal" Brough. In the same year the Gaiety Theatre is opened, by Mr. John Hollingshead with a new burlesque by Mr. W. S. Gilbert—"Robert the Devil," in which the leading character is undertaken by Miss Ellen Farren.

From this date onwards it is not necessary to do more than indicate a few salient points in connection with burlesque acting in this country. The opening of the Gaiety was the first step towards the expansion of the Old burlesque into the New. In the following year Mr. Edward Terry entered on an engagement at the Strand—

an engagement which lasted till 1877, and did as much
for the progress of stage travestie as did that of Miss
Farren at the other house.   In 1869 there was burlesque
at the Globe, with Edward Marshall and Miss Maggie
Brennan, and at the St. James's with Mrs. John Wood in
"La Belle Sauvage."*   In 1870 Harry Paulton went to
the Strand; and at the Royalty were Rachel Sanger, Arthur
Wood, and Alfred Bishop.   In 1871 there was burlesque
at the Court, with Mlle. D'Anka, Miss Oliver, Miss Kate
Bishop and Mr. Righton.   At the Vaudeville, next year,
Miss Nelly Power and Miss Marie Rhodes were supporting
Messrs. James and Thorne; while at the Royalty were
Miss Emma Chambers, Miss Kate Phillips, and Miss
Harriett Coveney.

In 1873 Mr. E. W. Royce goes to the Gaiety, and Miss
Lottie Venne is seen at the Court in "The Happy Land."
At the Folly, next year, Mr. Edouin takes the fancy of
the town as the Heathen Chinee in Mr. Farnie's "Blue
Beard;" Belmore, Mr. Odell, and Mr. Leonard Boyne all
essay to burlesque Mr. Irving as Hamlet; and Miss Pattie
Laverne plays the hero in Mr. Burnand's "Ixion Re-
Wheeled."   A "Robinson Crusoe," by Mr. Farnie, at the
Folly in 1876, brings to the front a droll Will Atkins in the
form of Mr. George Barrett.

In 1877, at the Gaiety, Edward Terry joins Miss Farren
and Mr. Royce, and in 1878 Selina Dolaro and G. W.
Anson are playing at the Folly in "Another Drink," while
Alma Stanley and Charles Groves are playing in "Venus"

---

* An adaptation of John Brougham's American burlesque, "Poco-
hontas."   Into this was introduced a travestie of the Bancroft's garden
scene in "School."   Mr. Lionel Brough played Captain John Smith.

at the Royalty. Miss Kate Vaughan, at the Gaiety, is already beginning to revolutionise stage dancing, making it at once graceful and decorous. At the Royalty, in 1880, are Miss Kate Lawler and Mr. Frank Wyatt; at the Gaiety are Mr. Dallas and Miss Gilchrist. In 1882, Mr. Toole, who has not been seen in burlesque for some time, takes part in a skit on rural melodrama. A year later Mr. Harry Monkhouse figures at the Gaiety; Mr. E. D. Ward and Miss Marie Linden first show, at Toole's, their talent for travestie; and Miss Laura Linden does the same thing at the Strand. In 1884 Mr. Willie Edouin and Miss Alice Atherton make, in "The Babes," their first joint success in London; and Mr. Edward Terry and Miss Kate Vaughan appear at the Gaiety for the last time in burlesque.

It is from this point that we may date the foundation of the New Burlesque, to which I shall return in my last chapter. In the chapters that immediately follow we shall be·able to see how numerous were the topics essayed by burlesque writers in the "palmy" days, and also with how much wit and humour those writers were able, for the most part, to charge the stories that they told and the pictures that they presented.

III.

"CLASSICAL" BURLESQUE.

PLANCHÉ was not only the founder of modern burlesque : he was the originator, in particular, of that
form of travestie which is commonly described as "classical"
—which deals with the characteristics and adventures of the
gods and goddesses, heroes and heroines, of the Greek and
Latin mythology and fable. It is true that comic pieces
on classical subjects had been played in England before
Planché brought out, at the Olympic, his "Olympic Revels"*
(January 1831).   But these pieces were not burlesques in
the present-century sense of the word.   Take, for example,
the "Midas" of Kane O'Hara, which, produced in 1762,
remained popular for so many years, and will always be
remembered as including the once famous ditty :—

> Pray, goody, please to moderate the rancour of your tongue :
>   Why flash those sparks of fury from your eyes ?
> Remember, where the judgment's weak the prejudice is strong,
>   A stranger why will you despise ?

The gods and goddesses are presented in "Midas" in a
light more or less ludicrous, and the dialogue, songs, and

---

* In "Olympic Revels," as in some other pieces, Planché had the
valuable assistance of Charles Dance.

choruses are flavoured with contemporary allusion, more or less humorous. But the form given to the work is that of the old-fashioned burletta.⟩ Indeed, the chief merit of "Midas," from a historical point of view, lies in the fact that it was its successful revival, with Mme. Vestris as Apollo, which, coupled with the publication of Colman junior's story, "The Sun-Poker," suggested to Planché the composition of his first "classical" burlesque. This had for subject the story of Prometheus and Pandora, and was remarkable, not only for the smooth flow of its versification and the general refinement of its tone, but also for the accuracy and consistency of the costumes, which were throughout "classical," and therefore in strong contrast to the haphazard, incongruous attire in which "classical" characters had hitherto been exhibited on the comic boards.

Prometheus and Pandora, I may note, figured later—in 1865—as the leading personages in Mr. Reece's "Prometheus, or the Man on the Rock," * in which the writer differed from his predecessor in admitting into his dialogue a large infusion of the punning element. In this direction Mr. Reece has always been proficient. Here are a few specimens of his work, picked out at random :—

> " Those steeds of yours will burn my house some day.
>   Fine animals."
>   " That leader came from Sestos;
>   Stands *fire* well, and so he counts *as best 'os.*"
>
> " What ! don't you think me handsome ? "
>   " Not very.
>   You've got *red hair* ! "
>   " Well, that's *hair-red-*itary."

---

* Byron also wrote a burlesque in which Prometheus figures— "Pandora's Box," seen at the Prince of Wales's in 1866.

"Why, darn your impudence!"
                    "There, stop your clatter.
With all your *darning* you'll not *mend* the matter."

"A couch that's made 'midst buttercups, he's shy on;
The verdant sward how could a *dandy lie on*?"

"You jeer at Pallas 'cos she's strict and staid.
With all your *railing* you'll need *Pallas' aid*!"

Planché's "Olympic Revels" proved so brilliantly successful that he was encouraged to follow it up, at the end of the year, with a companion composition—"Olympic Devils, or Orpheus and Eurydice." In this work, James Bland, the son of the lady who "created" Planché's Coquetinda, made his first appearance in burlesque, and among the female Bacchantes who took part in the groupings was a clever young girl, named Leonora Pincott, who was destined one day to be a great public favourite as "Mrs. Alfred Wigan." In "Olympic Devils" Planché's style is seen to excellent effect. Note, as an instance, the remarks addressed by Minos, Lord *Low* Chancellor, to the Fates :—

I vow you Fates are most industrious spinsters!
Miss Clotho there—man's destiny beginning—
Life's thread at tea, like a tee-totum spinning.
And then Miss Lachesis that same thread measures,
Taking great pains, but giving little pleasures.
Last comes Miss Atropos, her part fulfilling,
And cuts poor mortals off without a shilling.
The saddest sister of the fatal three,
Daughter, indeed, of *shear* necessity!
Plying her awful task with due decorum,
A never-ceasing game of "snip-snap-snorum"!
For help, alas! man pleads to her in vain—
Her motto's "Cut and *never* come again."

Elsewhere Orpheus says to Eurydice :—

> I am a lunatic for lack of thee !
> Mad as a March hare—oh, *ma chère* amie !

But Planché had a higher wit than that of punning. His satire and sarcasm have an agreeable, because not too pungent, cynicism—as in such little scraps of song as this (following upon the scene in which Orpheus, hearing that his wife is flirting with Pluto, cannot resist looking back at her and thus consigning her again to Pluto's tender mercies) :—

Orpheus. I have looked back—in your snare I am caught, sir—
> Pluto, thou'st cut a fond pair to the core !
> Oh, have I come all this way to be taught, sir,
> That folks who would thrive must keep looking before ?

Euryd. You have looked back—in the snare you are caught, sir—
> They who cheat him, faith, have none to cheat more !
> A man of the world—have you yet to be taught, sir,
> When your wife flirts behind you, to look straight before ?

In after years H. J. Byron wrote two burlesques on the legend of Orpheus and his wife, both of them produced at the Strand Theatre,* and it is notable that when Planché made, in 1865, at the Haymarket, his last appearance as a writer of extravaganza, it fell to his lot to treat once more of Orpheus and his surroundings.†

Planché's third classical burlesque was " The Paphian Bower, or Venus and Adonis," in which Benjamin Webster

* In 1863 and 1871.

† " Orpheus in the Haymarket." An opera buffo, founded on the French of Hector Cremieux. Performed, with music by Offenbach, by David Fisher, W. Farren, Louise Keeley, Nelly Moore, and Miss H. Lindley.

was seen for the first time in this class of histrionic work. Mme. Vestris, of course, was Venus, and in the course of the piece had to sing this eminently clever parody of " Sally in our Alley " :—

> Of all the swains that are so smart,
>   I dearly love Adonis ;
> And pit-a-pat will go my heart,
>   Till he bone of my bone is.
> No buckskin'd beau of Melton Mow-
>   bray rides so capitàlly.
> Oh, he's the darling of my heart,
>   And he hunts in our valley !
>
> Jupiter and the neighbours all
>   Make game of me and Doney ;
> But, notwithstanding, I with him
>   Contemplate matrimony.
> For he can play on the *cornet*,
>   And sing most musically ;
> And not a Duke in all the land
>   Can beat him at " Aunt Sally."

Venus and Adonis have always been great favourites with the producers of travestie. Among those who have made them the central figures of burlesque are Mr. Burnand, whose work was brought out in 1864, and Mr. Edward Rose, whose " Venus," written in collaboration with the Mr. Augustus Harris, and first performed at the Royalty in 1879 (with Miss Nelly Bromley as the heroine), was re-written for revival, and finally taken as the foundation of a third production in 1880.

In " The Deep, Deep Sea," brought out in 1833, Planché selected as the basis of his work the story of Perseus and Andromeda. He treated it with his usual reverence for the original legend. He represented Juno and the Nereids

as being angry with King Cepheus, and sending the sea-
serpent to devastate his shores. James Vining played the
Serpent, and his approach was announced to the monarch
in the following strain :—

> Mighty monarch, stir your stumps as if Old Nick were following :
>   A serpent with an awful twist has landed on your shore ;
> Our gallant soldiers, guns and all, by regiments he's swallowing ;
>   And munching up musicians and composers by the *score* !
>
> Of counsel learned in the law but *brief* work he is making—
> Apothecaries just as they were pills, sir, he is taking ;
> He snaps the parson right in two, as well as his oration ;
> And ere the beadle bolts the door, he bolts the congregation !
>
> Mighty monarch, stir your stumps, for court and caravansary
>   Are emptied of inhabitants all crazy with affright ;
> The monster he is longer far than any suit in Chancery,
>   And beats the Court of Aldermen, by chalks, for appetite !

The Serpent, when he arrives, introduces himself to the
king in an engaging fashion :—

> All bones but yours will rattle when I say
> I am the sea serpent from America.
> Mayhap you've heard that I've been round the world ;
> I guess I'm round it now, mister, twice curled. . . .
> Of all the monsters through the deep that splash,
> I'm "number one" to all immortal smash.
> When I lie down, and would my length unroll,
> There ar'n't half room enough 'twixt pole and pole.
> In short, I grow so long that I've a notion
> I must be measured soon for a new ocean.

The exaggeration which is so characteristic of American
humour is here happily satirised. In another passage,
Perseus, addressing himself to Andromeda, sings a neatly
turned parody of " We met—'twas in a Crowd " :—

W. L.—V.

We met ! 'twas at the ball,
  Upon last Easter Monday ;
I press'd you to be mine,
  And you said, " Perhaps, one day."
I danced with you the whole
  Of that night, and you only ;
Ah, ne'er " cavalier seul "
  Felt more wretched and lonely.
For when I squeezed your hand,
  As we turned one another,
You frown'd and said, "Have done !
  Or I'll speak to my mother ! "

They called the Spanish dance,
  And we flew through it fleetly—
'Twas o'er—I could not breathe,
  For you'd blown me completely.
I led you to a seat
  Far away from the dancers ;
Quadrilles again began,
  They were playing " the Lancers " ;
Again I squeezed your hand,
  And my anguish to smother .
You smiled, and said, " Dear Sir,
  You may speak to my mother."

In 1861 Perseus and Andromeda reappeared upon the comic stage at the instance of William Brough, who made them the hero and heroine of a burlesque at the St. James's.

The story of Telemachus was the subject which engaged the attention of Planché immediately after he had done with Perseus. Fénelon's tale had become extremely familiar to the British schoolboy, who at that time was not thought to have " grounded " himself sufficiently in French until he had read the narrative in the original. Hence Planché's " Telemachus, or the Island of Calypso," * concerning which

---

* Played at the Olympic in 1834.

the author took credit to himself once more for having "preserved the well-known plot with the most reverential fidelity." Ten years later the same subject was treated in the "Telemachus" of Stirling Coyne, played at the Adelphi with Miss Woolgar in the title-part, Wright as Calypso (a ballet-dancer!) and Paul Bedford as the hero's Mentor or "tor-Mentor." In 1863 the story of the parents of Telemachus proved attractive to Mr. Burnand, whose "Patient Penelope" made her curtsey at the Strand, to be followed at the St. James's, two years later, by the same writer's "Ulysses."

Still tracing the course of Planché's labours in burlesque, we come next to the production, at the Haymarket in 1845, of "The Golden Fleece"—perhaps, on the whole, the most delightful of the series. In this ingenious and brilliant piece, the two parts of which were entitled respectively "Jason in Colchis" and "Medea in Corinth," Planché had taken the narrative of Apollonius Rhodius and the tragedy of Euripides, and had built upon them a composition in which he sought less to cast ridicule upon the legends selected than to travestie what he called "the *modus operandi* of the classical period, which really illustrates the old pro- verbial observation that there is but one step from the sublime to the ridiculous." He brought again upon the stage the ancient Chorus, incarnated in a single person, who explained the action of the piece as it went on, not hesi- tating even to interrupt it when the humorous opportunity occurred. Charles Mathews undertook the part, heralded by a jocose announcement on the "bills" to the effect that "The lessee has, regardless of expense, engaged Mr. Charles Mathews to represent the whole body of the chorus, rendering

at least fifty-nine male voices entirely unnecessary." In the
opening scene, the Chorus thus described his functions :—

> Friends, countrymen, lovers, first listen to me :
> I'm the Chorus ; *whatever* you hear or you see
> That you don't understand, I shall rise to explain—
> It's a famous old fashion that's come up again,
> And will be of great service to many fine plays
> That nobody can understand nowadays ;
> And think what a blessing if found intervening,
> When the author himself scarcely knows his own meaning.
> You may reap from it, too, an advantage still further :
> When an actor is bent upon marriage or murther,
> To the Chorus his scheme he in confidence mentions,
> 'Stead of telling the pit all his secret intentions ;
> A wondrous improvement you all will admit,
> And the secret is just as well heard by the pit.
> *Verbum sat.*—To the wise I'll not put one more word in,
> Or instead of a Chorus, they'll think me a *burden.*

Later in the piece, announcing the approach of King Æetes
(Bland), the Chorus interposed with :—

> Æetes comes, looking as black as thunder,
> And when you hear the cause you'll say " No wonder " ;
> For Jason, aided by Medea's spell,
> Has done the trick, and done the King as well.
> You'll think, perhaps, you should have seen him do it,
> But 't isn't classical—you'll hear, not view it.
> Whatever taxed their talents or their means,
> These sly old Grecians did *behind* the scenes ;
> So, fired with their example, boldly we
> Beg you'll suppose whate'er you wish to see.

Elsewhere occurred this famous bit of badinage between
King and Chorus :—

> *Chorus.* Be calm, great King—'tis destiny's decree.
> *Æetes.* How dare you talk of destiny to me !
> What right have you with such advice to bore us ?
> *Chorus.* Sir, I'm the Chorus.
> *Æetes.*   Sir, you're indecorous.

In the course of the piece Mathews sang, among other
things, an excellent ditty, to the tune of "The Tight Little
Island":—

> 'Twas very ungrateful, you'll say, sir,
> But, alas! of the world it's the way, sir,
> When all a friend can, you have done for a man,
> He'll cut you quite dead the next day, sir.

But perhaps the most successful parody in "The Golden
Fleece" was that on "The Fine Old English Gentleman,"
assigned to Mme. Vestris as Medea. This is worth
quoting in full:—

> I'll tell you a sad tale of the life I've been led of late,
> By the false Bœotian Boatswain, of whom I am the mate:
> Who quite forgets the time when I pitied his hard fate
> And he swore eternal constancy by all his gods so great;
>> Like a fine young Grecian gentleman,
>> One of the classic time!
>
> Now he lives in a fine lodging, in the palace over there,
> Whilst I and his poor children are poked in a back two-pair;
> And though he knows I've scarcely got a second gown to wear,
> He squanders on another woman every farthing he's got to spare,
>> Like a false young Grecian gentleman,
>> One of the classic time.
>
> He leaves me to darn his stockings, and mope in the house all day,
> Whilst he treats her to see "Antigone," with a box at the Grecian play,
> Then goes off to sup with Corinthian Tom, or whoever he meets by
>   the way,
> And staggers home in a state of beer, like (I'm quite ashamed to say)
>> A fine young Grecian gentleman,
>> One of the classic time.
>
> Then his head aches all the next day, and he calls the children a
>   plague and a curse,
> And makes a jest of my misery, and says, "I took him for better or
>   worse";

And if I venture to grumble, he talks, as a matter of course,
Of going to Modern Athens, and getting a Scotch divorce !
    Like a base young Grecian gentleman,
    One of the classic time.

" Medea," it will be remembered, was the title and subject of a burlesque by Robert Brough, brought out at the
Olympic in 1856, with Robson in the title-part, Emery as
Creon (King of Corinth), and Julia St. George as Jason.
Medea (" the best of mothers, with a brute of a husband,"
as the sub-title has it) was one of Robson's most impressive
rôles, being charged at more than one point (notably in the
closing scene, which was played by all the characters in
serious fashion) with real tragic intensity. In the lighter
vein were such episodes as the duet with Jason (to the air
of " Robinson Crusoe "), which I quote as illustrative of the
neatness and humour with which Brough constructed such
trifles :—

Medea. I have done for this man
        All that tenderness can,
I have followed him half the world through, sir ;
        I've not seen him this year,
        And the first thing I hear
Is " he's going to marry Creusa."
        Going to marry Creusa,
        Going to marry Creusa,
        Ting a ting ting !
        Ting a ting ting !
All I can say, sir, is, *do*, sir.

Jason. If you'll take my advice,
        You'll pack up in a trice,
Nor of time to pack off be a loser ;
        For the popular wrath
        Will be likely to froth
'Gainst a foe to myself or Creusa.

> I am going to marry Creusa,
> And, believe me, the best thing for you's a
> Fast ship to bespeak,
> And some desert isle seek,
> Like a sort of she Robinson Cruiser.

[The last of Planché's classical burlesques was produced at the Lyceum in 1848.] It was on the subject of " Theseus and Ariadne," and was fortunate in the services of Charles Mathews as Dædalus. In this character Mathews sang a song which Planché had written for private performance and had brought " down to date" for the occasion. It is one of the happiest *mélanges* ever put together, beginning—

> I'm still in a flutter—I scarcely can utter
>   The words to my tongue that come dancing—come dancing ;
> I've had such a dream that I'm sure it must seem
>   To incredulous ears like romancing—romancing.
> No doubt it was brought on by that Madame Wharton,
>   Who muddled me quite with her models—her models ;
> Or Madame Tussaud, who in waxwork can show
>   Of all possible people the noddles—the noddles.

[The only song, of the kind, worthy to compare with this, is the description of the Heavy Dragoon sung by Colonel Calverly in the " Patience" of Mr. Gilbert, who, as a master of light badinage and intricate rhythm and rhyme, is the lineal descendant of the author of " Theseus and Ariadne."]

[After Planché, the most notable of the deceased writers of " classical" burlesque is undoubtedly Francis Talfourd.] Planché's knowledge of the Greek mythology and drama was admittedly derived from translations and from dictionaries ; Talfourd was a university man, and had an at-first-hand acquaintance with the masterpieces which he so skilfully travestied. The marks of this are visible in all his "classical" pieces, and notably in the first of them— "Alcestis, the Original Strong-minded Woman, being a most Shameless Misinterpretation of the Greek drama of Euripides." This was played at the Strand in 1850. The " argument" prefixed to it is an excellent bit of punning :—

Admetus, being due to Death, and as such totally unprepared to take himself up, is about to betake himself down, according to previous arrangement, when Orcus, who had meanwhile been trying his mean wiles on Alcestis (Admetus' very much better half), expresses himself willing to receive her as a substitute; her husband, friends, and relations not feeling quite so disposed to be disposed of. Alcestis, however, consents, packs up her traps, and then obligingly goes packing down those of Orcus. At this melancholy juncture, Hercules chances to be passing through Thessaly, on his return from his provincial engagements, and, having a knack of turning up a trump at a *rub*, plays his club so judiciously as to retake the queen, in spite of the deuce, and restores her to her family and friends.

In the dialogue of "Alcestis" we have such quips as these :—

> E'en like a detonator down he goes
> To pay the *debt o' natur* which he owes.

> To curb my rising love I idly tries,
> I *eyes the idol* that I *idolise!*

> I may be captivating ; but Death, stronger,
> Will not be *kept-a-vaiting* any longer.

> I'd no time to aggravate Mamma,
> Or make my *Pa* my *foe* by a *faux pas!*

In one place Alcestis, apropos of the marriage which is being forced upon her, cries bitterly :—

> Why was I ever *saddled* with this *bridal*?

Phædra sings a parody on "I'm afloat, I'm afloat!":—

> I'm a flirt, I'm a flirt, yet on thirty's bright side,
> And numbers have offer'd to make me their bride ;
> Yet, though suitors don't flag in attention to me,
> I'm a flirt, I'm a flirt, and my hand is yet free !

In 1851 came "Thetis and Peleus," in which Talfourd had a collaborator. In 1857 he produced, at the Haymarket, "Atalanta, or the Three Golden Apples," inserting in the "bill" a comic note to the effect that "Lest he should be accused of murdering a good subject, the Author begs to state that it was FOUN' DED from unknown causes many years ago." Miss Oliver was the Atalanta, and Miss Wilton the Cupid. Among the other characters is Mississarris, Atalanta's duenna, "the Guard of the Old Greek Stage, with, in this instance, an eye to the Males, subsequently attached to the old Coach, Paidagogos," played by Compton. One of the cleverest scenes in the piece is designed and written in parody of the balcony scene in "Romeo and Juliet." Hippomenes, the hero, is seen climbing "over the garden wall," guitar in hand. Descending, he soliloquises :—

> He jests at scars who ne'er in climbing hit upon
> A place with spikes and broken glass to sit upon.
> But soft, a light !—where lights are there's a liver.
> 'Tis she ! I'll try a gentle hint to give her
> Upon my mandoline, though I'm afraid
> I'm somewhat too hoarse for a serenade.
> This night air is too musical by far,
> And on my chest has struck a light *catarrh*. . . .
> Ah, see ! The window opens—it is she,
> More fair than ever in her *robe de nuit*.
> (*Atalanta appears on balcony above.*)

> She speaks—yet nothing says ! She's not to blame,
> Members of Parliament do much the same.
> Her mouth rests on her hand—I'm not above
> Wishing I were upon that hand a glove.
> Gladly the storms of Poverty I'd weather,
> So we might live from hand to mouth together !

Elsewhere Hippomenes delivers himself of a superexcellent pun. Some one says to him, referring to his studies,—" But think of your degree " ; to which he replies :—

> I do—and see
> 'Tis a *degree* too *far-in-height* for me.

After " Atalanta " * came Talfourd's " Pluto and Proserpine, or the Belle and the Pomegranate," played at the Haymarket in 1858, and his " Electra in an Electric Light," performed at the Haymarket the year following. In " Pluto and Proserpine," as in his other pieces, the original myth is followed closely. One passage supplies a happy parody of the famous " palace-lifting-to-eternal-summer " speech in " The Lady of Lyons." Pluto has appeared to Proserpine as a young man, and has laid siege to her heart in proper form. He is careful not to disclose his identity. At last Proserpine says :—

> But I must know at least, sir, where you lodge.
> *Pluto (aside)*. I'll try the popular Claude Melnotte dodge.
> (*Walks her across the stage, as Claude does Pauline.*)
> If, therefore, dearest, you would have me paint
> My residence exactly (*aside*) as it ain't,
> (*Aloud*) I would entreat you, Proserpine, to come where
> A palace lifting to eternal—somewhere—
> Its marble halls invites us.

---

* Of recent years Atalanta has been made the heroine of a burlesque by Mr. G. P. Hawtrey. Of this I give some account in my final chapter on " The New Burlesque."

Proserp.   By-the-bye,
Where is this place?
    Pluto (embarrassed). In the Isle of Skye.
Thy days all cloudless sunshine shall remain,
For on our pleasure we will ne'er draw *rein ;*
At noon we'd sit beneath the vine-arched bowers,
And, losing all our calculating powers,
Think days but minutes—reckoning time by *ours ;*
Darkness shall be at once with light replaced,
When my hand lights on that light taper waist ;
Our friends shall all true constant lovers be
(So we should not be bored with company) ;
Love's Entertainments only would we seek,
And, sending up to Mudie's once a week,
No tales that were not Lover's we'd bespeak,
No sentiments in which we were not sharers
(Think what a lot of rubbish that would spare us). . . .
Dost like the picture, love, or are you bored ?
    Proserp. Beautiful !
    Pluto (aside).   'Tis a copy after *Claude.*

" Pluto and Proserpine " has the usual supply of puns, as
in the following couplet :—

> *Diana.* You never weigh a word, dear, you're so wild.
> *Proserp.* You used to call me such a *wayward* child.

But Talfourd, like Planché, could rise above mere *jeux
d'esprit,* and furnish, when necessary, bits of persiflage
which deserve to linger in the memory. Thus, in one of
the scenes, Pluto addresses Cerberus in a fashion intended
to suggest Launce's colloquy with his dog in " The Two
Gentlemen of Verona " :—

> You've yet to learn the notions of propriety,
> Observed by dogs in upper-air society ;
> So I'll exhibit in a bird's eye view
> Th' ordeal well-bred puppies must go through.

Your thoughts you show too openly—on earth
They oft are saddest who display most mirth ;
You must by no means growl to mark resentment,
Or wag your tail in token of contentment ;
When most you're doing wrong, be most polite,
And ne'er your teeth show *less* than when you bite,
So may you still enjoy, when youth is past,
The sunshine of your dog-days to the last.

I have already referred to three classical burlesques by
H. J. Byron. A fourth exists in the "original classical
pastoral" called "Pan," which first saw the light at the
Adelphi in 1865. Pan, it may be recorded, was impersonated
by Mr. J. L. Toole. He had a good deal to say, and much
of it was in the form of *jeux de mots*. Take, for example,
the passage in which Pan discovers that Syrinx, whom he
loves, is in love with Narcissus. He calls down thunder
from the skies ; and then follows this tirade :—

Narcissus. What means this sudden dreadful change, I wonder?
Pan. It means, great Pan is outraged !
Omnes.   Pan !
Pan.   Ah, Pan !
Beware his hate and jealousy, young man.
Blight shall o'erwhelm ye ! See, your native corn
Turns into ashes with my withering scorn.
Your wheat shall shrink and shrivel, every sheaf;
Your cattle swell the *cattle*logue of grief;
With murrain all your sheep rot in their pens,
The pip shall finish all your cocks and hens ;
Dry rot shall spoil your flails, your ploughs, and harrows,
Break up your waggons ; even your *wheel*-barrows
Shall come to *woe.*
Your land shall grow so hard, in vain you tills.
Like lazy volunteers, with weakish wills,
It will object to being *bored* by *drills.*
Your turnip-tops shan't spring up from the roots,
Your rye shall grow awry, your corn shan't shoot,

Your peas, towards which the Arcadian feeder leans,
Become things of the *past*, and all turn *beans*.
Ha, ha! the prospect cuts you to the core,
Probes, punctures, penetrates.—Pour, torrents, pour!
Descend, ye hailstones, bumpers, thumpers, fizzers;
It cuts you like a *knife*, doesn't it, Nar-*scissors*?

This is a very fair specimen of Byron's rather careless
method; and another is at hand in the following lines,
which are spoken after the Carian captain has shown to
Pan a jar of wine :—

Captain. That's wine.
Pan.   What's wine?
Captain.   A fluid very rare;
It's unknown here; we bring it from afar;
Don't speak a word of thanks—there, hold your *jar*. . . .
 Pan. The jar's a most uncommon sort of shape,
(*Smells it*) Oh, oh! may I be shot if it ain't grape!
                         [*Tastes it, and smacks his lips.*
Gollopshus! (*drinks*). More gollopshus than the first!
It quenches, yet somehow increases, thirst.
(*Drinks*) Talk about nectar. These celestial fellers
Have no such drink as this stuff in their cellars.
I must bid Ganymede to earth to fly—
Ganymede, brin-*g an immed*-iate supply.
                [*Drinks, and becomes gradually elevated—hiccups.*
Nectar celestial drink's supposed to be;
It's called divine—this is *de vine* for me!
(*Sings*) We'll drown it in the bowl! (*Staggers*) I see two bottles!
I only wish I'd got a pair of throttles!
My, everything's in two! As for that there tree,
It was a single tree, it's now a *pair* tree.
That bay I thought Arcadian—but, I say,
It seems to me, my friend, you're *Dublin* bay.
Fact, 'tis a pair of bays. The earth seems reeling,
While this is still so gently o'er me stealing.

To the burlesques by William Brough already mentioned
may be added "Endymion, or the Naughty Boy who cried

for the Moon" (St. James's, 1860), and "Pygmalion, or the
Statue Fair" (Strand, 1867). The former,* of course, has
to do with the fabled fondness of Diana for Endymion, and
vice versâ. The goddess sees the youth lying asleep upon
Mount Latmos, and, descending, kisses him :—

> Strange weakness—thus my beams so bright to dim !
> I should *be more* myself—not *beam o'er* him.
> The gods all mock my silvery splendour paling ;
> Not silvery, but irony, *their* railing.
> Paling and railing !—what dread fears that calls up,
> Their *bitter raillery* suggesting *All's up!*

Before Endymion has seen Diana, he is asked by Actæon
whether he is in love; to which he replies :—

> Oh, no ! We men of fashion
> Have long ago forsworn the tender passion.
> We can't afford it.
>   *Actœ.*   Why not?
>   *Endym.*   Well, a wife
> May suit folks in the lower walks of life ;
> But in our station, what girls seek in marriage
> Is not a *walk* in life ;—they want a carriage.
> Then, what with dress and crinoline extensive,
> The sex which should be *dear* becomes *expensive.*
> Once hearts were trumps ;—that suit no more we follow ;
> Since a good suit of diamonds beats them hollow.

Here he drops into a parody of " Our Hearts are not our
Own to Give " :—

> Our hearts we've not alone to give,
>   When we to wed incline ;
> In lowly cots on love to live,
>   In poetry sounds fine.

---

* Miss Herbert was Diana, and Miss Kate Terry one of the
nymphs attending on her. Charles Young was Actæon ; Belmore,
Pan.

> But folks to live on love have ceased ;
> Our hearts when we'd bestow,
> Some hundreds sterling, at the least,
> Should with the fond hearts go.

When, again, Actæon asks Endymion whether he ever shoots, he replies, " No, I don't care about it ":—

> *Actæ.* Not care for shooting, man ? What's life without it ?
> All nature shoots. Say, what's the earliest thing
> Boys learn at school ? Why, shooting in the ring.
> The seed you sow must shoot before it grows ;
> We feel the very corns shoot on our toes.
> We shoot our bolts, our game, our foes—what not ?
> We're told where even rubbish may be shot.
> The stars shoot in the sky—nay, I've heard say,
> Folks sometimes shoot the moon on quarter-day.

Among the *personæ* in the piece is Pan, whom we find addressing the fauns in this punning style :—

> Oh long-ear'd, but short-sighted fauns, desist ;
> To the great Pan, ye little pitchers, list ;
> Pan knows a thing or two. In point of fact,
> He's a deep Pan—and anything but cracked.
> A perfect oracle Pan deems himself ; he
> Is earthenwarish—so, of course, is *delfy*.
> Trust, then, to Pan your troubles to remove ;
> A warming-Pan he'll to your courage prove.
> A prophet, he foresees the ills you'd fear ;
> So for them all you have your *Pan-a-seer*.

In " Pygmalion " * we are asked to suppose that Venus is indignant with the sculptor for his lack of susceptibility to female charms. Cupid therefore undertakes to punish him by making him fall in love with his new statue,

* Miss Raynham was the hero ; Mr. David James, his apprentice Cambyses ; Mr. Thomas Thorne, the Princess Mandane ; Miss Ada Swanborough, Venus ; Miss Elsie Holt, Cupid ; and Miss Eliza Johnstone, Mopsa.

Galatea.   To this statue Venus, at Pygmalion's request,
gives life ; but she withholds the power of loving.   Galatea,
therefore, is for ever slighting the sculptor's affection.
Here is the opening of their first interview, which the
curious may compare with the similar situation in Mr.
Gilbert's " Pygmalion and Galatea : "—

Pygmal. My beautiful—my own ! (*embracing her*).
Statue.   Oh ! don't, sir, please ;
I'm sure I'm much too soft to stand a squeeze.
Pygmal. Too soft !   What mean you?
Statue.   Nay, I hardly know.
I was so firm and hard an hour ago ;
Suddenly I grew soft——
   Pygmal.   Nay, speak no farder.
You're getting softer but renews my (h)*ardour* ;
Unrivalled maid !
   Statue.   You rivals talk about,
Who've done your best yourself to cut me out;
With chisel—mallet—sir, 'tis my conviction,
Your mallet ought to have my *mallet*-diction.
   Pygmal. Your sculptor, *amorous,* implores you madly.
   Statue. Yes ! sculptors (h)*ammer-us* poor statues sadly ;
Yet I ne'er felt it till an hour ago ;
I *stood, heigho !* there in your *stud-i-o,*
Within a niche !
   Pygmal.   Speak on, oh form bewitching !
   Statue. Standing the *niche-in,* straight I felt *an itching* ;
Throughout my frame a feeling seemed to tingle,
Bade me go forth with human kind to mingle.
   Pygmal. Oh, joy ! 'twas life ! and life you must go through
      with me.
   Statue. Well, having made me, what d'ye mean to do with me ?
Of course I can't *disparage* what you've done ;
But say, can I *dis parish* claim upon ?
Or must I trust of casual wards the mercy?
Have I a settlement, or *vice versy ?*
   Pygmal. Come to my arms !

Statue.   Nay, as the matter stands,
It's not your arms—I'm left upon your hands.
What's to be done with me? I never sought
Into a human figure to be wrought.
You're great at figures ; I, a wretched sad stone,
Know nought of figures—I'm far from a Glad-stone !

In the end, Psyche infuses soul into Galatea, and she and the sculptor understand each other.

In 1883 Mr. H. P. Stephens submitted to Gaiety audiences a one-act piece which he called " Galatea, or Pygmalion Re-versed." In this Galatea was the sculptor, and Pygmalion the statue ; and with Miss Farren as the former, and Mr. Edward Terry as the latter, the result was eminently laughable. Cynisca, by the way, was turned into a man (Cyniscos), and was played by Elton.

Two mythological burlesques stand to the credit of Gilbert Abbott a'Beckett—"The Son of the Sun, or the Fate of Phaeton," played at the Fitzroy Theatre so long ago as 1834 ; and " The Three Graces," a two-act piece, seen at the Princess's in 1843, with Oxberry, Wright, and Paul Bedford in the cast. Both of these travesties are very smoothly and gracefully written, with fewer puns than the author afterwards permitted himself. " The Three Graces," moreover, is not very prolific in contemporary allusion ; though here and there, as in the following passage, between the heroines—Aglaia, Thalia, and Euphrosyne— there is some gentle satire :—

Agl. Euphrosyne, we shall be miss'd by Venus.
Eup. With her we easily can make our peace,
If something, her attractions to increase,
We take from earth.
Agl.   Why, yes, that's very true,
If we could only meet w th something new.

L.—   5

    Eup. That mixture for the hair, what is it call'd ?
It's advertised as "solace for the bald."
    Agl. I'll take her some of that.
    Eup.   Or what's that's stuff—
For which, I saw the other day a puff?
Something to be upon the features sprinkled,
And offering "Consolation to the wrinkled."
    Tha. Venus don't want such aids.
    Eup.   That's very true ;
Want them, indeed ! the ladies never do ;
But when such little purchases are made,
Of course 'tis only to encourage trade.
    Agl. They've got on earth a very odd idea
Of what the Graces really are, I fear.
    Eup. They have indeed : I chanced one day to go
Into a first-rate milliner's *depôt,*
That is *par excellence*—the first of places
To meet with earthly notions of the Graces.
    Agl. That's very true—and there what did you see ?
    Eup. Things unbecoming either of us three.
    Agl. What wear they on their heads ?   I think I've known
Mortals who've dress'd them something like our own.
    Eup. Bonnets they lately wore, but oh, so small,
They nearly dwindled into none at all.

In "The Son of the Sun" there is an episode which
helps to illustrate the condition of the drama in London
at that period (1834).   Apollo is questioning the Muses
who have just returned from London to Olympus :—

    Apol. Euterpe, Music's Muse, I understand
That you had lodgings somewhere in the Strand.
    Eut. Oh ! the Lyceum !   Yes ; I had a bout of it
For a short time, until they burnt me out of it.
    Apol. Melpomene, Thalia,—still remain
Your temples, I suppose, near Drury Lane ?
    Thal. Our temples !   Yes ; as usual they stand,
Extensively superb, and coldly grand.
But, oh ! the worship's wholly chang'd !   Ah me ! it is
A cruel thing—they've turn'd out us poor deities.

F. C. BURNAND

Eup. That mixture for the hair, what is it call'd?
It's advertised as "......... for the bald."
Agl. I'll take care never of that.
Eup.   Or what's that's stuff—
For which, I see no ...... dare a puff?
                              .... wrinkled,
                              ... the wrinkled."

                              That's very true;

... across the water screenage trade.
Agl. They ..... go ..... earth a very odd idea
Of what the Graces really are, I fear.
Eup. They have indeed: I chanced one day to go
Into a first-rate milliner's *depôt*,
That is *par excellence*—the first of places
To meet with earthly notions of the Graces.
Agl. That's very true—and there what did you see?
Eup. Things unbecoming either of us three.
Agl. What wear they on their heads? I think I've known
Mortals who've dress'd them something like our own.
Eup. Bonnets they lately wore, but oh, so small,
They nearly dwindled into none at all.

In "The Son of the Sun" there is an episode which
helps to illustrate the condition of the drama in London
at that period (1834). Apollo is questioning the Muses
who have just returned from London to Olympus:—

Apol. Euterpe, Music's Muse, I understand
That you had lodgings somewhere in the Strand.
Eut. Oh! the Lyceum! Yes; I had a bout of it
For a short time, until they burnt me out of it.
Apol. Melpomene, Thalia,—still remain
Your temples, I suppose, near Drury Lane?
Thal. Our temples! Yes; as usual they stand,
Extensively superb, and coldly grand.
But, oh! the worship's wholly chang'd! Ah me! it is
A cruel thing—they've turn'd out us poor deities.

F. C. BURNAND.

My friend Melpomene's dagger, and her bowl,
Are in the clutches of a noisy soul
With Madame Melodrama for her name.
Apol. That's downright usurpation.
All.   Shame ! oh, shame !
Thal. And as for me, my place—a pretty pass !—
Is taken by a vulgar thing, called Farce.
Apol. But where is Shakspeare ?
Thal.   Bless me, don't you know ?
Shakspeare is trampled on.
Apol.   By whom ?
Thal.   Ducrow.

Mr. Burnand has written more "classical" burlesques than
any man living or dead. A university man, like Talfourd,
he has displayed complete mastery of mythologic themes,
submitting them to ingenious perversion, and adorning them
with a wealth of pun and parody of which it is impossible, in
these brief limits, to give more than a few samples. He has
shown special interest in the legends connected with the
siege of Troy,* producing three burlesques more or less
connected with that event. First, in 1860, came "Dido," at
the St. James's, with Charles Young as the heroine; next,
in 1866, "Paris, or Vive Lemprière," at the Strand ; † next,
in 1867, "The Latest Edition of Helen, or Taken from the
Greek," at Liverpool.‡   Helen of Troy, I may note, *en
parenthèse*, had been the heroine of two other travesties : one
by Vincent Amcotts—"Fair Helen" (Oxford, 1862) ; the
other by Mr. Robert Reece—"Our Helen" (Gaiety, 1884).

* "The Siege of Troy," by the way, was the title and subject of a
burlesque by Robert Brough (Lyceum, 1858).

† Paris, Miss Raynham ; Œnone, Mr. Thomas Thorne ; Castor, Mr.
David James ; Orion, J. D. Stoyle ; Venus, Miss A. Swanborough ;
Juno, Maria Simpson ; Jupiter, Miss Eliza Johnstone.

‡ Paris, Miss Raynham ; Helen, Miss Furtado. "Helen" is
described by the writer as a "companion picture to 'Paris.'"

In "Dido," Mr. Burnand's genius for word-play is agree-
ably manifested.   I take some lines at random :—

> " Æneas, son of Venus, sails the sea,
>   Mighty and *high*."
>   " As *Venus' son* should be."
>
> On the sea-shore, dear, I've just come from walking,
> Studying my fav'rite poets.   Need I tell ye
> The works I read were those of *Crabbe* and *Shelley*?
>
> It is the Queen—of life she seems aweary ;
> And mad as *Lear*, looking just as *leary*.
> A riddle strikes me : " Why's she thus behaving,
> Just like a bird of night ? "   " 'Cos she's a *raving*."
>
> Mad as a March hare.   It is the fate
> Of *hares* to be then in a *rabid* state.
>
> " I ne'er shall move as heretofore so gaily,
>   I feel quite ill and dizzy."
>   " *Dizzy ?   Raly ?* "

Æneas comes on first as a begging sailor, with " I'm
starving " inscribed on a paper suspended from his neck.
He strikes up a song, but soon stops it :—

> What ? no one here ?   Thy singing vain appears.
> Land may have *necks* and *tongues*—it has no *ears*.
> None to be done, and nothing here to do.
>   [*Takes off begging paper.*
> " I'm starving."   Ah, it happens to be true !
> On air I cannot feed, howe'er one stuffs,
> Not even when it comes to me in *puffs*.
> I wonder what's become of our small party,
> Who, yesterday, were sailing well and hearty ?
> I saw our shipwrecked crew sink in the *bay* ;
> 'Twould be a subject fit for *Frith*, R.A.
> And if the shore last night they failed in gaining,
> I am the only *Landseer* now remaining.
> Being no gambler, I'll ne'er trust again
> My fortunes to the chances of the *main*.

In 1863 Mr. Burnand brought out, at the Royalty, " Ixion, or the Man at the Wheel," * which proved to be one of the happiest of his efforts. This he followed up, at the same theatre, two years later, with " Pirithous," in which the adventures of Ixion's son were as humorously depicted. In the interval he had produced at the Olympic " Cupid and Psyche " (December, 1864), a burlesque on an ever-popular subject. Years before—so early as 1837—a piece called " Cupid," written by Joseph Graves, had been represented at the Queen's and Strand, with Wild and Miss Malcolm at the one house and Hammond and Miss Daly at the other as the God of Love and his beloved. In " Cupid," however, there was little verbal wit. The god figured as a gay deceiver, who had promised marriage to Psyche, but had refused to "implement" the undertaking. Whereupon Jupiter decides that Cupid shall be shot dead by Psyche ; but she, using the god's own arrows, does but transfix him with the love she yearns for. Cupid sings, early in the piece, a parody of " The Sea ! the Sea ! " beginning—

> Psyché ! Psyché ! my own Psyché,
> The pretty, fair, and ever free !—

But, otherwise, Graves's " book " is not particularly brilliant, though smoothly written and fairly brisk in action.

In " Cupid and Psyche " Mr. Burnand made Psyche the daughter of a king, who, because she will not marry and thus relieve him of the anxiety caused by a certain prophecy, chains her to a rock on the sea-shore. To this he is incited by Venus, who regards Psyche as her rival

* See p. 40. Eleven years later, Mr. Burnand wrote for the Opera Comique his "Ixion Re-Wheeled," the cast of which included, beside Miss Laverne, Miss Amy Sheridan and Miss Eleanor Bufton.

in beauty.   Psyche is duly rescued and espoused by Cupid,
who (as in the old myth) remains invisible to her until
her curiosity gets the better of her prudence ; and, in the
end, Venus abates her enmity, and the union of the pair
is duly recognised.   In one place, Psyche, entering, distractedly, in search of Cupid, cries :—

> A river ! I debate with myself wedder
> I'll end my *tale* with a sensation *header*
> From a small boat.   It could not clear the reèds ;
> One cannot make a*n oar way* through these *s(weeds)*.
> Why should I live ?   Alas, from me forlorn
> Each lad turns on his *heel* to show his (s)*corn* !
> The county lads to me make no advances ;
> The county girls avert their *county-nances.*
> Counties ! (*struck with an idea*) I'll drown myself,—
> > Down hesitation !
> Nor men, *nor folk,* shall stop my *suffoc*-ation !

Elsewhere Mars says to Cupid :—

> Stop, you ill-bred little pup !
> Is this the way an 'Arrow boy's brought up ?
> Your conduct would disgrace the lowest Cretan.
> *Bacchus.* " An 'Arrow boy ! "—egad, that joke's a n*eat 'un.*

At another point Cupid himself says that

> A *yawn*, however gentle,
> Is to the face not ver*y orn*amental.

At the very end of the piece, there is a skilful bit of
rhyming.   Psyche " comes down," and says :—

> Now, stupid—
> Why don't you speak the tag and finish, Cupid ?
> *Cupid.* Because I'm in a fix, my charming friend.
> *Psyche.* How so ?
> *Cupid.*   The piece with your name ought to end ;
> And, though I should give all my mind and time to it,
> I know that I shan't get a word to rhyme to it.

King (*cleverly*). There's Bikey.

Bacchus (*as if he'd hit it—rather*). Dikey!

Zephyr (*suggestively*). Fikey!

Venus (*authoritatively*). Likey!

Cupid (*who has shaken his head at each suggestion*). Pooh!

Chrysalis. Oh! (*every one interested, as if she'd got it now*) Crikey! (*every one disgusted*).

Psyche. Ma'am, that's vulgar, and won't do.

Grubbe (*calmly and complacently*). Ikey!

Cupid. Absurd. I yield it in despair. Come—the finale; I'll commence the air (*sings two very high notes— all shake their heads*).

Mars. Oh no! we cannot sing in such a high key.

Cupid (*joyfully to Psyche, catching the rhyme at once*). That's it. (*takes her hand—to audience*). Pray smile on Cupid.

Psyche. And on Psyché.

Among other "classical" burlesques may be mentioned Mr. Burnand's "Arion," seen at the Strand in 1871, with Mr. Edward Terry, Mr. Harry Paulton, and Miss Augusta Thomson; and H. B. Farnie's "Vesta," produced at the St. James's in the same year, with Mr. John Wood and Mr. Lionel Brough. Mr. Burnand's "Sappho" (1866), and "Olympic Games" (1867), also call for mention. John Brougham's "Life in the Clouds" belongs to 1840; Tom Taylor's "Diogenes and his Lantern" to 1849; the Brothers Brough's "Sphinx" to the same year; William Brough's "Hercules and Omphale" to 1864; and Mr. Reece's "Agamemnon and Cassandra, or The Prophet and Loss of Troy," to 1868.

IV.

BURLESQUE OF FAËRIE.

AS Planché was, in effect, the Father of Classical
Burlesque, so was he also, even more irrefragably,
the Father of the Burlesque of Faërie—of the fairy tales of
the nursery, and especially of those derived from French
sources. Memorable, indeed, was the production of
Planché's "Riquet with the Tuft*"; this piece was the
precursor of something like twenty others from the same
pen, all written on the same principle and in the same
vein. Planché had been to Paris, and had there seen
Potier playing in "Riquet à la Houppe." He came home
and straightway wrote his own version of the story, partly in
verse, partly in prose, having in Charles Mathews a Riquet
not equal indeed to †Potier, but with obvious merits of his
own. Vestris was the Princess Emeralda, and James Bland
Green Horn the Great—Rebecca Isaacs, then only a little
girl, being the Mother Bunch. The result was complete
success, carrying with it great encouragement to the
dramatist to persevere in the new path on which he had
entered.

These fairy pieces of Planché's were not burlesques quite

* At the Olympic in 1836.

in the sense in which his classical pieces were, but they belong, nevertheless, to the burlesque *genre*. Each treats lightly and humorously a story already in existence; each includes parodies of popular lyrics, as well as songs written to the airs of popular ditties; and the burlesque spirit animates the whole. Every now and then, the writer, rising superior to parody, produces a lyric which has a definite accent of its own. Here, for example, in " Riquet with the Tuft," is a song accorded to the grotesque and misshapen hero. It has genuine wit as well as genial philosophy:—

> I'm a strange-looking person, I am,
>   But contentment for ever my guest is;
> I'm by habit an optimist grown,
>   And fancy that all for the best is.
> Each man has of troubles his pack,
>   And some round their aching hearts wear it;
> My burden is placed on my back,
>   Where I'm much better able to bear it.
>
> Again, tho' I'm blind of one eye,
>   And have but one ear that of use is,
> I but half the world's wickedness spy,
>   And am deaf to one half its abuses;
> And tho' with this odd pair of pegs,
>   My motions I own serpentine are,
> Many folks blest with handsomer legs
>   Have ways much more crooked than mine are!
>
> Nature gave me but one tuft of hair,
>   Yet wherefore, kind dame, should I flout her?
> If one side of my head must be bare,
>   I'm delighted she's chosen the outer!
> Thus on all things I put a good face,
>   And however misshapen in feature,
> My heart, girl, is in the right place,
>   And warms towards each fellow-creature!

The origin of " Riquet with the Tuft " is to be found in
Perrault's " Contes de ma Mère l'Oye." Planché went to
the same source for his " Puss in Boots : an original,
comical, *mews*-ical fairy burletta " (Olympic, 1837), in which
Charles Mathews was an incomparable Puss, with Bland as
Pumpkin the Prodigious, Vestris as the Marquis of Carabas,
and Brougham as a very Irish ogre. In this there was a
good deal of prose dialogue, of which the following scene
between Puss and the three maids-of-honour may be taken
as a diverting specimen :—

Chatterina. You're in the army, I presume?

Puss. No, ma'am.

Chatt. Why, you wear moustaches.

Puss. Yes, ma'am, yes ; but that's because—because I can't help it,
you see. I belong to a club, and all the members are obliged to wear
them.

Chatt. What club ?

Puss. It's a sort of Catch Club.

Arietta. What, musical?

Puss. Very.

Ari. And where do you meet ?

Puss. We meet alternately upon each other's roof.

Skipperella. Upon each other's roof?—that's quite a new step.

Puss. I beg pardon, did I say *upon ?* I meant *under.*

Ari. You can sing, then?

Puss. I can squall a little, *à la* Cat-oni.

Ari. Who taught you?

Puss. Cat-alani.

Skip. And dance, too?

Puss. I remember the time when I would have run anywhere after
a ball.

Skip. What is your favourite dance?

Puss. The Cat-alonian Cat-choucha.

Chat. Well, never mind about singing and dancing ; suppose we fix
upon some game to pass away the time, at which we can all play?

Ari. I'm content.

Skip. And I.

Puss. And I. What shall it be ?

Chat. " Puss in the Corner."
Puss. No, no, I don't like that.
Chat. Choose one yourself, then.
Puss. My favourite game is " Cat's Cradle."
All. Oh no, we can't bear that !
Chat. Come, name another from your catalogue.
Puss (aside). Cat-alogue ! They grow personal !

The subject of " Puss in Boots " was afterwards handled by H. J. Byron.* In this case we find the monarch of the piece called Noodlehead IX. ; the Princesses are named Biddi, Coobiddi, and Chickabiddi ; and there are two woodcutters called Gnarl and Knot. The puns in the dialogue on the word *cat* are even more numerous than in the older piece, and somewhat more varied. As thus :—

Will. What ! left his youngest child, a cat !
Bob.   It's true.
Will. Well, that's a *feline* sort of thing to do.

Again :—

Cat. I am, as you perceive, sir, an I-*tale*-ian,
But never scratch my friends, though I'm an n*ailey'un* ;
It's only foes that ever raise my fur.
Will. Well, really you're a charming *furry*-ner.

Once more :—

Will. What can you do ?
Cat.   My pictures folk applaud ;
They say they're scratchy, but resemble *Claude.*
I'm not much of a linguist, my good friend,
But I've a-*talion* at my finger's end ;
I can't dance well amongst young ladies, yet
I come out very well in a *puss-et.*
I sing at times like any *cat-a-lani.*
Will. Your favourite opera is——
Cat.   The *Purr*-itani.

---

* At the Strand in 1862, with Rogers, Clarke, Miss A. Swanborough, Miss C. Saunders, Miss F. Josephs, and Miss F. Hughes in the principal parts. The full title of the piece was " Puss in a New Pair of Boots."

In the course of the piece King Noodlehead sings a song
in which some fun is made of the conventionalities of
Italian opera :—

> At the Opera, and at Covent Garden as well,
> I have always observed that the expiring swell,
> Tho' you'd fancy just there he'd be shortest of breath,
> Sings a difficult song just before his own death.
>> Such as diddle, diddle, diddle,
>> Chip chop ri chooral i day,
> That's how they arrange things at the Operay.

> And I've likewise remarked that the young hero-ine
> Walks about in a low dress of thin white sat-in,
> Defying the fog, and the cold and the damp,
> And also rheumatics, and likewise the cramp.
>> With a diddle, diddle, diddle, etc.

> I've remarked that the peasants who come on the scene,
> Are, p'raps, awkward, but still most offensively clean,
> They lay monstrous stress on the *"whens"* and the *"whats,"*
> And sing—" Oh, joy "—together like mere idi-ots.
>> With a diddle, diddle, diddle, etc.

One of the prettiest and wittiest of Planché's adaptations
from Perrault's store was " The Sleeping Beauty in the
Wood," seen at Covent Garden in 1840. The Beauty was
the Princess Is-a-Belle—of course, Mme. Vestris ; the
inevitable King—Thomas Noddy of No-Land—was the
inevitable Bland ; James Vining was Prince Perfect ; and
Brougham was a woodcutter—one Larry O'Log. But the
most whimsical character in the piece was played by Harley
—the Baron Factotum, " Great-Grand-Lord-Everything,"
who may be compared with Pooh-Bah in Mr. Gilbert's
" Mikado." In " The Mikado," Ko-Ko is " Lord High
Executioner of Titipu," and Pooh-Bah is " Lord High
Everything Else "—he is " First Lord of the Treasury,
Lord Chief Justice, Commander-in-Chief, Lord High

Admiral, Master of the Buckhounds, Groom of the Back-
stairs, Archbishop of Titipu, and Lord Mayor, both acting
and elect, all rolled into one." The Baron Factotum is
even more embarrassed with offices and duties. As he
says at one juncture :—

> I shall go crazy. Ye who sigh for place,
> Behold and profit by my piteous case.
> As Lord High Chamberlain, I slumber never;
> As Lord High Steward, in a stew I'm ever !
> As Lord High Constable, I watch all day ;
> As Lord High Treasurer, I've the deuce to pay ;
> As Great Grand Cupbearer, I'm handled queerly ;
> As Great Grand Carver, I'm cut up severely.
> In other States the honours are divided,
> But here they're one and all to me confided ;
> They've buckled Fortune on my back—until
> I really feel particularly ill !
> Young man, avoid the cares from State that spring,
> And don't you be a Great Grand anything.

He then sings, to the tune of " Where the bee sucks ":—

> Who would be a Great Grand Lord High,
> All the blame on him must lie ;
> Everywhere for him they cry,
> Up and downstairs he must fly—
> After all folks, verily !
> Verily, verily ! Few would live now
> Under the honours beneath which I bow.

The programme of the "The Sleeping Beauty" bore the
following notice :—

In strict accordance with the Modern School of Melodramatic
Composition, Eighteen years are to be supposed to have elapsed
between the First and Second Parts ; One Hundred years between
the Second and Third Parts ; and considerably more than One Hundred after the piece is over.

Planché went again to Perrault—directly or indirectly—

for his " Blue Beard " (1839) and his " Discreet Princess "
(1855). The last named (from " L'Adroite Princesse ")
was notable as including in its cast Robson as Prince
Richcraft, and Emery as Gander the Stupendous. In " Blue
Beard " Bland played the Baron Abomelique (the hero),
Mme. Vestris the heroine (Fleurette), and John Brougham,
the actor-dramatist, an Irish character—the O'Shac O'Back.
How often has this fascinating subject been dealt with
since ! Dozens of pantomimes have had it for a basis;
the burlesques founded on it are not quite so numerous.
The best known are those by H. J. Byron (1860) and
Mr. Burnand (1883); there are also two others by H. T.
Arden and Frank Green.

But it was to the " Contes des Fées " of Madame
D'Aulnoy that Planché was most largely indebted for his
fairy stories. The list (extending from 1842 to 1854) is
quite an imposing one. First came " Fortunio, and his
Seven Gifted Servants," based on " Belle-Belle, ou le
Chevalier Fortuné." Next, " The Invisible Prince, or the
Island of Tranquil Delights," taken from " Le Prince
Lutin." " Le Rameau d'Or " suggested " The Golden
Branch," and " The King of Peacocks " * had its origin in
" La Princesse Rosette." From " Le Serpentin Vert " was
derived " The Island of Jewels "; from " L'Oiseau Bleu,"
" King Charming, or the Blue Bird of Paradise "; from
" La Grenouille Bienfaisante," " The Queen of the Frogs ";
from " La Biche au Bois," † " The Prince of Happy Land,

---

* This, first played at the Lyceum in 1860, was afterwards revived
at the St. James's with Miss Kate Terry as the Princess.

† Other versions of this tale have been written by Maddison Morton
(at Drury Lane), and by Mr. Burnand (at the Holborn in 1868,
under the title of " The White Fawn ").

or the Fawn in the Forest"; from "La Princesse Carpillon,"
"Once upon a Time there were Two Kings"; and from
"Le Nain Jeune," "The Yellow Dwarf and the King of
the Gold Mines." "Beauty and the Beast" was taken from
a tale by Mme. le Prince de Beaumont; but Planché
claimed that the treatment was wholly new. He had
Vestris for his Beauty, Harrison the tenor for his Beast,
and Bland for his Sir Aldgate Pump, the father of Beauty.
"The Good Woman in the Wood" was from a story by
Mme. de la Force; and "Young and Handsome" from
a faërie by the Countess de Murat. "Graciosa and
Percinet" likewise had a French origin.

It was, however, in each case only for the fable that
Planché had to give thanks: everything else—even in most
instances the nomenclature—was his own. And that nomenclature was often very ingenious and amusing. Thus, in
"Fortunio," we have an impecunious noble called Baron
Dunover (played by Morris Barnett). In "The Invisible
Prince" the name of the Queen of Allaquiz is Blouzabella;
her son is the Infante Furibond;* and among her courtiers
are the Marquis of Anysidos, Count Palava Torquemova
(who introduces the ambassadors), and Don Moustachez
de Haro y Barbos (Captain of the Guard). In the same
piece, the Princess of the Island of Tranquil Delights is
called Xquisitelittlepet, and her ladies in waiting are Toxaloto-
tittletattle and Itsaprettipetticoat. Soyez Tranquille (with
a clever suggestion of Soyer) is the *chef de cuisine* in "The
King of the Peacocks," in which there is also an Irishman,

---

* This part, originally played (in 1846) by James Bland, was
played by Mr. Toole at the Adelphi in 1859, and afterwards by
George Honey at the Princess's.

The O'Don't Know Who, and a German, the Baroness Von Huggermugger. Planché's kings and queens have mostly comic names. There is Giltgingerbread the Great, with Tinsellina, his consort, in " The Island of Jewels." There is Henpeckt the Hundredth in " King Charming "; there is Fulminoso the Pugnacious in " The Queen of the Frogs "; there is Periwigulus the Proud in " Once upon a Time there were Two Kings." Henpeckt, again, has a valet called Natty, and a porter called Nobby. Elsewhere we come across an usher named Antirumo, an Indian named Tan-tee-vee (of the tribe of Tal-hee-ho), and an evil genius named Abaddun. The Yellow Dwarf is christened, very appropriately, Gambogie.*

" The Yellow Dwarf," it may here be chronicled, is the title of a burlesque by Gilbert Abbott a'Beckett and by Mr. Robert Reece; A'Beckett's being produced in 1842, Planché's in 1854, and Mr. Reece's in 1882. " Beauty and the Beast" has been made the subject of travestie by Mr. Burnand. The " Fortunio " of Planché was also rivalled in the " Lady Belle Belle, or Fortunio and his Seven Magic Men " of H. J. Byron (Adelphi, 1863).† This last was in a thoroughly H. J. Byronic vein, with a Count Collywobbol among its characters and the usual supply of puns and

---

* The part of the Yellow Dwarf was first played (Olympic, 1854) by Robson, of whose performance Planché says that " So powerful was his personation of the cunning, the malignity, the passion and despair of the monster, that he elevated extravaganza into tragedy." At one point his delivery of the lines moved Thackeray almost to tears. " It is not a burlesque," he exclaimed: "it is an idyll."

† Byron was indebted to Mme. D'Aulnoy for the idea of his "Orange Tree and the Humble Bee, or The Little Princess who was Lost at Sea " (Vaudeville, 1871).

parodies. Here are a few of the best óf the puns. The Princess Volante is a very Atalanta in her fondness for race running :—

I'll run a race
With any living ped, through wind or rain ;
Some like what's handsome—I prefer the *plain.*
I have this morning run a spanking heat,
Two miles in just ten minutes.
    King.   Wondrous *feat* !
    Prin. Everything pedal has its charms for me.
I'd have gone miles the great Miss *Foote* to see.
My tastes are visible e'en at my meals ;
My favourite fish, of course, are *soles* and *eels.*
Pota*toes* I consider are *A-oners,*
Though I've a preference for scarlet-*runners.*
And when at children's parties I am present,
I think a game at four-*feits* very pleasant.

"The White Cat," by Planché (1842), has among its *personæ* Wunsuponatyme, King of Neverminditsnamia ; Prince Paragon ; and Jingo, a Court fool. In "The Fair One with the Golden Locks" (1843), the King is called Lachrymoso,* and the woman of the bedchamber Mollymopsa. Finally, there is "The Seven Champions of Christendom" (1849), in which Charles Mathews played Charles Wag, Esq., "in attendance on" St. George of England. With this ends the list of Planché's compositions of this kind—a remarkable contribution to the stage literature of wit and humour.

From Planché's "Seven Champions of Christendom" to the "St. George and the Dragon" of Gilbert Abbott a'Beckett (1845) and the "Sir George and a Dragon, or We

---

* Lachrymoso was played by Mr. Toole at the Adelphi so recently as 1860.

W. L.—V.

                                  6

are Seven" of Mr. Burnand (1856) is a natural and easy
transition.   In A'Beckett's piece, Kalyba, the sorceress, has
stolen St. George when a child, in order that he might fall
in love with her, and so rescue her from prophesied destruc-
tion.   Getting rid of her with a wave of her own wand, he
turns up with his fellow Champions at Memphis, where
King Ptolemy is in a state of impecuniosity, the Dragon
having swallowed up all his resources.   The monster demands the King's daughter Sabra, but St. George contrives
to trick him out of the legal securities he holds, and eventually destroys him by the power of the steam press.   There
is a vein of allegory running through the piece, which has,
however, its share of *jeux de mots*.   Thus, Kalyba's hand-
maid says to her :—

> Your hair, my lady, 's getting rather dry,
> Some of the Russian balsam shall I try ?
>   *Kaly.* Well, p'raps you may—yet no—upon the whole,
> Anything Russian 's hurtful to the *Pole*.
> The very thought my nervous system shocks,
> O ! would that mine were like Chubb's—safety locks !
> Should I turn grey, I'd bid the world good-bye.
>   *Maid.* If you turn grey, it would be time to *dye*.

Elsewhere there is some sarcasm at the expense of the
newspapers.   St. George says to Sabra :—

> These evening papers, blow the horn and cry them ;
> Inviting every one to come and buy them.
> This is the way the sort of thing is done—
> (*Crying*) Se-cond edition here ! the *Memphis Sun*,
> Wondrous intelligence ! for here you have in it
> The sudden resignation of the Cabinet.
>   *Sab.* The Cabinet resigned !
>   *St. G.*   No, that's mere vapour !
> You must say something, just to sell the paper.

In Mr. Burnand's version, which is the longer of the two, there is much more story, and there are many more puns. St. George has not so prominent a place in the action, which is more elaborate and varied; while the dialogue is in the writer's most rollicking mood. Take, for example, these lines of Kalyba's, addressed to her sirens :—

1st Siren. Madame, there is a four-oared boat in view without a steerer.

> *Kalyba* (using pince-nez).   P'raps the Harvard crew.
> No, they don't row *half hard* enough for that ;
> Take care ! they'll go ashore upon the flat.
> They don't row well, but with uncommon pluck ;
> The stroke wants art—p'raps he's a stroke of luck.
> I wonder where they come from ! maybe Dover !
> A crab ! as sure as *eggs* is *eggs* they're *ova* !
> Attract them here ; you must not let them pass ;
> Some visitors—give me my looking-glass (*they offer telescope*).
> Not that (*they give her a hand-mirror*).
> Now sing, as Sirens did before us ;
> We *lure all* here with tooral *looral* chorus.
> To practise bathing arts we've our diploma.
> (*All have by this time produced the hand-mirrors and combs.*)
> To attitudes ! (*All pose themselves combing hair, etc.*)
> We're in a state of *comber.*

Here, again, is a specimen of daring pun-making :—

> *Vizier.* Sultan of Egypt, this pathetic tear
> Proves you've one faithful *Vizier* left—*viz. here.*
> *Sultan.* My star is set.
> *Vizier* (*looking at star on Sultan's breast*).   With honour
> you have borne it.
> Stop ! if your *star is set* in diamonds, pawn it.
> *Sultan.* The real one—this sham one's rather tasty—
> Is gone : so *requiescat*—sir—*in pastey.*

A popular subject with the writers of burlesque for Christmastide has been the time-honoured one of

Cinderella. The first travestie of any importance was by Albert Smith and Kenny, seen at the Lyceum so long ago as 1845. Next came H. J. Byron's version at the Strand in 1860, followed by Mr. Green's in 1871, Mr. Wilton Jones's (at Leicester) in 1878, and Mr. Reece's (at the Gaiety) in 1883. A provincial burlesque on this topic was called "Done-to-a-Cinderella," and in America there has been a "Cinder-Ellen." Mr. Reece's piece was called, simply, "Our Cinderella"; Mr. Jones's, "Little Cinderella." Byron's was christened "Cinderella, or the Lover, the Lackey, and the Little Glass Slipper." It has been a great favourite with the public ever since it was first played with Maria Simpson as Cinderella, Miss Oliver as the Prince (Popetti), Miss Charlotte Saunders as his valet Dandino, John Clarke as the Baron Balderdash, and Rogers and Miss Lavine as Clorinda and Thisbe. Over and over again has this clever piece of work served as the basis of pantomime "openings" both in town and country.

Following the traditional story closely enough, it bristles with the puns in which Byron revelled, and which he poured forth with singular and somewhat exhausting lavishness. Thus, we find Dandino saying:—

> As I've made my bed so I must lie.
> Continuing *bed* metaphor, sir—I,
> When quite a child, the blackest draught would drain,
> And took my *pill*—oh! on *account o' pain!*
> And as my youthful feathers all unfurled
> Seemed formed to make a *bold stir* in the world,
> Little dreamt I I should appear a valet as,
> For I seemed born to reign in royal *palliasse*;
> But suddenly the future seemed to frown;
> Fortune gave me a quilt, an' *I'd a down.*

A little farther on **Dandino** and the **Prince**, who are about to exchange characters for the nonce, have the following little contest in pun-making :— .

> *Dandi.* But I must have a change of toggery :
> This coat, you will admit, is not the best cut,
> And neither is my waistcoat quite the *West cut.*
> I must di*vest* myself of that affair :
> These buckles ain't the thing for *Buckley* Square.
>   *Prince.* You shall be decked in gems of vast expense,
> And be a gem-man in a double sense.
> Your servant, I will wait, clean boots, wash glasses ;
> Thus serve a nob, a*n' ob-serve* all that passes.
>   *Dandi.* Then you'll obey me till you've found La Donna ?
> You *pledge* your princely word?
>   *Prince (shaking his hand heartily).* *A-pawn* my honour.

An even better instance of Byron's tendency to run a pun to death is to be found in this colloquy between the Prince and Cinderella. The latter says :—

> *Cind.* Cinders and coals I'm so accustomed to,
> They seem to me to tinge all things I view.
>   *Prince.* That fact I can't say causes me surprise,
> For *kohl* is frequently in ladies' eyes.
>   *Cind.* At morn, when reading, as the fire up-burns,
> The print to stops—to semi-*coaluns*—turns.
> I might as well read Coke.
>   *Prince.*   Quite right you are,—
> He's very useful reading at the *bar.*
> (*Chaffingly*) Who is your favourite poet ?—Hobbs?
>   *Cind.*   Not quite.
> No, I think, *Cole*-ridge is my favourite ;
> His melan-*coally* suits my situation ;
> My dinner always is a *coald coal*-lation,
> Smoked pictures all things seem, whate'er may be 'em,
> A *cyclorama,* through the " *Coal I see 'em.*"

More acceptible in pantomime than in travestie, " Little

Red Riding Hood" has nevertheless been the heroine of at least one burlesque which has made its mark—namely, that which Leicester Buckingham brought out at the Lyceum just thirty years ago, under the auspices of Edmund Falconer. He had Miss Lydia Thompson for his Blondinette (Red Riding Hood), and Miss Cicely Nott for the young lady's lover, Colin. The fairy element was freely introduced, and instead of the wolf of the original there was a Baron Reginald de Wolf ("the would-be abductor of Blondinette, who finds he is sold when she 'ab duck'd herself to escape him "). Here and there one gets in the " book " a glimpse of parody ; as in—

> My protegè—my protegè,
>   Ah ! never look so shy,
> For pretty girls seem ugly
>   When a gloom is in their eye.

Or, again, in—

> They say the peasant's life is sweet,
>   But that we know all trash is, O ;
> He very little gets to eat,
>   For often scarce his cash is, O.
>
> Teeth then he gnashes, O,
>   Gnaws his moustaches, O ;
> But jolly are the hours he spends
>   When plentiful the cash is, O.

Passing over " Jack the Giant Killer," which H. J. Byron made the subject of a burlesque, and " Jack and the Beanstalk," which was treated in the same vein by the late Charles Millward, we come to the travesties suggested by stories in the " Arabian Nights' Entertainments." These are fairly numerous. We may note, in particular, some of the versions of the tales of Aladdin, Ali Baba, Prince

Camaralzaman, and Abon Hassan, which seem to have offered most attractions to our comic writers.

The first "Aladdin" of importance was that given to the world by Gilbert Abbott a'Beckett in 1844. This was entitled "The Wonderful Lamp in a New Light," and had Wright for its Aladdin and Paul Bedford for its Magician. Next in order of time comes H. J. Byron's "Aladdin, or the Wonderful Scamp,"* which has shared the fate of his "Cinderella" as a basis for pantomimes. In this his fondness for *jeux de mots* is as patent as ever, as well as the ease (without conspicuous finish) with which he fitted words to the songs of the day. Of direct parody there is little in this "Aladdin," which, however, opens with a brief suggestion of "The sea, the sea," sung by the Vizier :—

> The tea ! the tea !
>   Refreshing tea.
> The green, the fresh, the ever free
>   From all impurity.
> I may remark that I'll be bound
> Full shillings six was this the pound—
> Full shillings six was this the pound.
> I'm on for tea—I'm on for tea !
> For the savour sweet that doth belong
> To the curly leaf of the rough Souchong,
> Is like nectar to me, nectar to me, nectar to me.
> Let others delight in their *eau de vie*—
> What matter, what matter? I'm on for tea.

During the last twenty years there have been four other notable burlesques on the "Aladdin" subject—Mr. Alfred

---

* In this the original Aladdin was Miss Marie Wilton ; the Princess Badroulbadour, Miss Bufton ; Widow Twankay, Rogers ; Abanazar, Clarke ; The Sultan, Miss Charlotte Saunders ; and Pekoe, Miss Fanny Josephs (Strand, 1861).

Thompson's (1870), Mr. Green's (1874), Mr. Reece's (1881), and Mr. Geoffrey Thorn's (1890). With Mr. Reece's are associated pleasant memories of the bright "street boy" of Miss Farren, Mr. Edward Terry's whimsical magician, and the grace and refinement of Miss Kate Vaughan's Badroulbadour.

Second only to "Aladdin" in acceptability both to authors and to public, is the story of "Ali Baba, or the Forty Thieves." Here, again, A'Beckett is (with Mark Lemon) to the fore with the travestie called "Open Sesame, or a Night with the Forty Thieves." This was produced at the Lyceum Theatre, and had Mr. Frank Matthews for its Ali Baba, Mrs. Alfred Wigan for its Ganem, Wigan himself for its O'Mustapha (he was an Irish Mussulman), the beautiful Miss Fairbrother for its Abdallah, Keeley for its Hassarac, Miss Georgina Hodson for its Cogia, and Mrs. Keeley for its Morgiana. *There* was a cast for you! How many burlesque casts of our own time could lay claim to so much talent and beauty? Cassim, in this piece, had to make one admirable pun :—

> Such heaps of gems I never saw before :
> E'en Mortimer can't boast of such a Storr.

Elsewhere, O'Mustapha, who was a shoemaker, had to say :—

> Business is dreadful bad—what's to be done?
> Where I sold fifty boots, I don't mend one.
> No longer Wellingtons are all the go :
> High-lows alone are worn by high and low.
> In vain upon my door this bill I fix—
> " Five thousand Bluchers, all at 8s. 6d.,
> Strong boys' at 3s. 9d."—folks once would use,
> But now it's quite another pair of shoes.

A'Beckett, however, did not lay himself out for punning in and out of season. His chief merit is the neatness of his style and the pervading nature of his wit.

The most famous of all the Ali Baba travesties was that "joint-stock" burlesque, "The Forty Thieves," written by members of the Savage Club, and performed by the authors themselves at the Lyceum, in 1860, for the benefit of the families of two literary men just then deceased. Planché wrote the prologue for this piece, and it was at once so brilliant and so admirably delivered by Leicester Buckingham that it nearly obtained the extraordinary honour of an encore. It was followed, three years later, by H. J. Byron's " Ali Baba, or the Thirty-Nine Thieves (in accordance with the author's habit of taking one off!)." * Abdallah, the captain of the thieves (played by Miss Ada Swanborough), was here depicted as a rascal of the quiet, elegant order, in sharp contrast to the Surrey-side villainy of his lieutenant, Hassarac. A colloquy between these gave Byron an opportunity of satirising the melodramatic criminal of the " good old times " :—

> *Abdal.* From all you say, my friend, you see it's plain
> That vulgar violence is on the wane ;
> Therefore become more polished in your style,
> And, like King Richard, murder when you smile.
> I go into society, and none
> Know I'm a thief, or could conceive me one ;
> I start new companies—obtain their pelf,
> And, having started them, I start myself ;
> Swindle the widow—the poor *orphan* do—
> And then myself become an *off 'un* too.

* Miss P. Marshall, Ganem ; George Honey, Hassarac ; Miss Bufton, Cogia ; Miss F. Hughes, Zaide ; Miss C. Saunders, Morgiana (Strand, 1863).

Hassarac. Bother ! that's not of villainy my notion ; ·
Give me the tangled wood or stormy ocean—
A knife—dark lantern—lots of horrid things,
With lightning, every minute, at the wings ;
A pistol, big enough for any crime,
Which never goes off at the proper time ;
Deep rumbling, grumbling music on the drums—
A chord whenever one observes " She comes " ;
An opening chorus, about '' Glorious wine '' ;
A broadsword combat every sixteenth line ;
Guttural vows of direst vengeance wreaking,
And thunder always when one isn't speaking.
That was the style—exciting, if not true,
At the old Cobourg ;
    Abdal.   Oh, *coburg*lar, do—(*crosses to R.*)
You're horrifying me !
    Hassarac (*draws*). Spoon ! sappy ! duffer !
Ha, ha ! lay on, you milk-and-water muff-a,
And *hem'd* be he who first cries hold enough-a !

In 1872 Mr. Reece wrote for the Gaiety a piece called
" Ali Baba à la Mode " ; in 1880 he prepared for the same
theatre another version called " The Forty Thieves." * This
latter, if I remember rightly, was the first of the burlesques
in three acts. It presented in Mr. Terry (Ali Baba),
Miss Farren (Ganem), Mr. Royce (Hassarac), and Miss
Vaughan (Morgiana), a quartett which is specially well
remembered for the *verve* and vivacity of its performance.

The fortunes of Prince Camaralzaman have been pictured
on the burlesque stage by the Brothers Brough, by Messrs.
Bellingham and Best, by H. J. Byron, and by Mr.
Burnand.† " Camaralzaman and Badoura, or the Peri
who loved the Prince," was the Broughs' title, and they

---

* A burlesque on the subject of " Ali Baba " was written by Mr.
Gilbert Arthur a'Beckett.
† In the years 1848, 1865, 1871 and 1884 respectively.

had the assistance of Mrs. Keeley, of Keeley (as a Djinn), of Bland (as the Emperor Bung), of Miss Reynolds (as Badoura), and of Miss Horton (as the hero). Dimpl Tshin was the name given to one of the characters, and Skilopht that of another. The original story was followed in the main. Camaralzaman declines to marry at his father's request, and is incarcerated. In that position he soliloquises :—

> 'Tis now the very witching time of night,
> Which, were I free, would bring with it delight ;
> Now could I drink hot grog, hear comic songs,
> Or join the gay Casino's gladsome throngs,
> Or drain, 'midst buzzing sounds of mirth and chaff,
> The foaming stout, or genial half-and-half ;
> But here a prisoner condemned to stop,
> I can indulge in neither malt nor "hop."
> O, cruel Pa ! to place me in this state,
> Because I would avoid your own sad fate.
> Dear mother, though a model of a wife,
> Gave me a slight distaste for married life.
> Better be thus than free, and have to stand
> " An eye like Ma's, to threaten and command."

Camaralzaman then breaks out into the following little bit of vocal parody :—

> The Pope he leads a happy life,
> Because he hasn't got a wife ;
> And one to take he's not so flat,
> He knows a trick worth two of that.
> No shrill abuse his ear affrights
> For stopping out too late at nights ;
> No curtain lectures damp his hopes :
> A happy lot must be the Pope's.

The Broughs were always ingenious in their word-plays. Says one of the characters in this burlesque :—

> Soon, I feel, with passion and disgust,
> Within this *bosom* there will be a *bust.*

Again :—

> I wonder how he'd look with a moustache ;
> He's got none yet, though, thanks to sorrow's growth,
> He feels a little *down about the mouth.*

Says Badoura to a suitor whom she does not favour :—

> I may be handsome, but I'll now be plain ;
> So, I'll not have you, sir—you kneel in vain ;

to which he replies :—

> Can one so fair thus speak to her adorer ?
> Your form a *Venus,* but your words a *Floorer.*

In the piece by Messrs. Bellingham and Best—" Prince Camaralzaman, or the Fairies' Revenge " *—we find, amid many well-conceived and well-executed puns, a rather successful adaptation of the " To be, or not to be " soliloquy, possessing the merit of being quite in keeping with the character of the matrimony-scorning Camaralzaman :—

> To wed or not to wed—that is the question
> Which weighs me down like midnight indigestion.
> Whether it is nobler in a man to bear
> The stings and taunts of an outrageous fair,
> Or to take arms against a married life,
> And, by opposing, shun it ? To wed a wife—
> No more ; for by a wife we say we end
> The undarned stockings laundresses won't mend,
> The buttonless shirts and all the botheration
> That single flesh is heir to—a consummation
> Devoutly to be wished—forswear the club
> And wed, perchance, a flirt,—ay, there's the rub ;
> For in our married lives what rows there would be,
> If all were not precisely as it should be !

---

* These authors were happy in having Miss Ellen Farren to represent their hero, Miss Henrietta Lindley being the Badoura, W. H. Stephens and Mrs. Stephens the King and Queen, and Mr. Soutar the Skidamalink (King of the Isle of Ebony) (Olympic, 1865).

And who would bear a scolding vixen's tongue,
Backed by a mother-in-law, not over young ;
The cook, who, when annoyed, the dinner burns,
The insolence of Buttons, and the spurns
That patient masters from their servants take,
When one a quiet house might always make
By keeping single ?   I'll not change my lot,
But rather bear the ills that I have got
Than fly to others that I yet know not.

In another passage, the " spiritualistic " craze is satirised in a so-called " chant " :—

Abracadabra, mystic word, come down to us from the cosmogony,
'Tis the spell that binds the spirits beneath Mr. Home's mahogany ;
You've been to a *séance,* of course, when darkness baffles the searcher,
And a spectral hand rises quivering—sceptics hint that it's gutta-percha.
When ghostly fingers are tickling some foolish old fellow's fat dumpy
    knee,
And the medium floats as easily as a modern bubble company ;
'Tis then that the spirits are working—to asses the men they trans-
    mogrify
By spells that have nothing in common with the generally received
    orthography.

Two of the burlesques on "Arabian Nights" topics are from the pen of Francis Talfourd.   First came—in 1852, at the Olympic—"Ganem, the Slave of Love" (with Miss Fanny Maskell as Fetnah, the caliph's favourite) ; and later —in 1854, at the St. James's—"Abon Hassan, or the Hunt after Happiness" (with Mr. Toole as Haroun-al-Raschid). In the former piece the wealth of felicitous punning is remarkable.   Thus, in his very first speech, Ganem, coming in intoxicated, says :—

All things around me seem involved in doubt,
I only know that I've been dining out.
I've made some blunder, sure—but how I've made it
Is from my dizzy pate quite dissipated.

A light upon my understanding breaks—
I must be drunk ! Or what is it thus makes
My head to stoop and butt the ground incline,
Unless the butt of beer or stoop of wine ?
Now, to go on—so—Ganem, my boy, steady—
I can't go far.—I'm too far gone already.
Ah ! could I swarm this lime, I might, *sans doute,*
Learn from its friendly branch my proper route.

In other places we read :—

A needlewoman's life's, at best, but *sew-sew*

(which is as true as it is witty) ;

> *Alkalomb.* He had the freedom, sir, to squeeze me.
> *Giaffar.*   Yes,
> You wouldn't check the freedom of the *press.*
> *Caliph.* In his affections I stand no competitor
>   (*squaring up*),
> And for that *belle's life* you'll find I'm a *head-hitter.*
>
> *Malevola.*   I'm her abettor in the plucky course.
> *Caliph.* You couldn't, ma'am, *abet her* in a *worse.*

" Abon Hassan " is less freely endowed with verbal
pleasantry, but it has its fair share of puns, and the songs
are numerous and bright. At the close, the hero, addressing the audience, allows himself to drop into the
reflective mood :—

> In mine, read a too common history—
> How many an unfortunate, like me,
> With feverish haste the cup of pleasure begs,
> To find experience in its bitter dregs !
> The wretched man sips at the draught now hated.
> Unless, like me, he gets *a-man-sip-hated.*
> Beware, then, how you mix and make your cup,—
> I'll give you a receipt for it : boil up
> In a clean vessel—say your own clay crock—
> As much good humour as will form your stock ;

Throw in to others' faults a modest blindness,
Adding a quart of milk of human kindness ;
Scrape up a few acquaintances, but you
Had better take care they're your wife's friends too :
Omit the mother-in-law, if you've the power,
As apt to turn the milk aforesaid sour !
Skim off bad habits from the surface : you'll
Then let it stand—'tis better taken cool ;
Or, should you be in love a far-gone coon,
Stir the whole gently with a virtuous " spoon " ;
In which case, flavour with a dash of sentiment,
Garnish with smiles, and drink it with contentment ! *

On German faërie our comic dramatists have not drawn
at all largely. Such pieces as Gilbert Abbott a'Beckett's
" Knight and the Sprite, or the Cold-Water Cure," with
Ondine as its heroine; H. J. Byron's " Nymph of the
Lurleyburg, or the Knight and the Naiads," based on
the Lurline legend ; and Mr. Burnand's " Rumpelstiltskin,
or the Woman at the Wheel," founded on one of the
Brothers Grimm's narratives, are exceptional incursions
in this field. The first was seen at the Strand in 1884,
with Mrs. Walter Lacy as Sir Hildebrand, and with Hall
and Romer in other parts. "The Nymph of the Lurleyburg " has often done duty for the purposes of Christmas
extravaganza. When it was first performed—in 1859
—Miss Woolgar was the Sir Rupert the Reckless, Mr.
Toole the Seneschal, and Paul·Bedford the Baron Witz, the
locale being the Adelphi. Mr. Burnand introduced into

* Another burlesque on the same story, entitled " Abon Hassan, or
An Arabian Knight's Entertainment," was brought out at the Charing
Cross Theatre in 1869. The author's name was Arthur O'Neil, and
the cast included Miss Emily Fowler as the hero, and Mr. Flockton as
Haroun Alraschid.

"Rumpelstiltskin" (Royalty, 1864) a few modifications of the German tale, inventing and importing new characters. In one of the scenes he furnished a diverting suggestion of the situation in "The Ticket of Leave Man," when there comes the sudden and effective revelation of "Hawkshaw the Detective!" Among the *personæ* are King Tagarag the Tremendous, Prince Poppet, Baron Higgle-de-Piggle, Wriggleletto (the court spy), Jolinosio (a miller), and Fraulein Splitaharter (the belle of the village). Miss Ada Cavendish was the Princess Superba.

"The Vampire"—a burlesque by Mr. Reece, which was played at the Strand in 1872—appears to have owed its origin about equally to the German legend, the romance which Lord Byron wrote on the subject, and the play which Dion Boucicault founded on the topic in 1852. As, however, the legend was the inspiration alike of romance, play, and travestie, the travestie may be mentioned here. Mr. Reece had drawn the Vampire as a being so fond of "blood," that he sought to possess it in the shape of the notebooks of two "sensation"-novelists, one of whom, Lady Audley Moonstone, was admirably represented by Mrs. Raymond.* The following specimen of the dialogue has been handed down to us. Some one says to a Welsh corporal :—

> On Monday and on Tuesday you were queer :
> Why drink on Wednesday?
> *Corporal.*   'Cause I'm *Thursday*, dear.

In the realm of Spanish legend there have been still fewer explorers. Albert Smith took one of Washington

---

* Mr. Edward Terry was the Vampire himself, and other parts were taken by Harry Cox, Miss Rose Cullen, and Miss Topsy Venn.

Irving's tales of the Alhambra, and fashioned it into "The Alhambra, or The Beautiful Princess," played at the Princess's in 1851, with the Keeleys, Wigan, Harley, Flexmore, and Miss Vivash. H. J. Byron afterwards went to the same source for "The Pilgrim of Love," in the first cast of which—at the Haymarket in 1860—we find the names of Mrs. Buckingham White as the Pilgrim, Chippendale as his tutor, Compton as the King of Toledo, Rogers as the King of Granada, and C. Coghlan as Mafoi, a Frenchman : a rather notable collocation of distinguished players.

The Fables of Æsop have inspired at least one travestie —"Leo the Terrible," by Stirling Coyne and Francis Talfourd. In this piece (brought out at the Haymarket in 1852) all the characters but four wore the heads of beasts or birds—a lion (Bland), a wolf (Buckstone), a fox, an owl, a ram, a poodle, a cat (Miss Maskell), and so on. The four exceptions were Sir Norval de Battersea, Timoleon Sindbad Potts (Keeley), Æsop, and Gay ; and the play opened with a *rencontre* between the two last-named worthies. Æsop began with a vocal parody on "The Light of other Days" :—

> To write in other days as Gay did,
>   The world is grown too fast ;
> The rage for La Fontaine has faded—
>   The stream run dry at last.
> On me the world has turned the tables
>   And turned to bad, I guess ;
> For they who thus can spurn my Fables
>   Must care for morals less.
> Stop ; who comes here? If I to judge am able,
> 'Tis Gay, the worthiest son of modern Fable.
>   *Enter* Gay *dejectedly.*
> How dull and sad he seems !

W. L.—V.

Gay (*soliloquising*). My old dominion
On earth is gone.
 Æsop (*rising*). Gad ! that's just my opinion.
 Gay. Æsop ! What brings you here? Why thus, by Styx,
Are you, your staff and luggage, in a fix?
As downcast as a 'prentice runaway.
 Æsop. Am I? Well, *you* look anything but Gay,
But tell me—whither have you wandering been?
 Gay. About the world. Such changes now I've seen—
Such altered views of virtue and rascality ;
There's not a fable left—'tis all reality.
 Æsop. Reality ! Why, bless your simple soul,
The world's a fable now from pole to pole !
Pills, politics, or projects made to cram one,—
What we called fables once are now called gammon.

In the end, the various animals express repentance for
the wrong they have committed; and Æsop, in recog-
nition thereof, restores them to the shapes they formerly
presented.

V

BURLESQUE OF HISTORY.

IN this department the artists in travestie have not done so much as might have been expected. Even when we include in the word "history" such things as myths, legends, and traditions, we find that the historical, in comparison with the other fields open to the parodists, has been quite "second favourite." Particularly little has been achieved in the burlesque of foreign persons and events; and, in the case of our own celebrities, the only really familiar figure on the comic stage has been that of "Bluff King Hal." King Arthur, Alfred the Great, Elizabeth, Oliver Cromwell, have made rare appearances in motley. In the by-paths of history, general and local, the burlesque writers have devoted themselves most frequently to popular personages like Herne the Hunter, the Lady Godiva, Robin Hood, Dick Whittington, Guy Fawkes, Claude Duval, and Richard Turpin.

The story of Rome has supplied subjects for two of the most notable burlesques of the past twenty years—the "Romulus and Remus" of Mr. Reece, and the "Field Marshal Julius Cnæsar" of Mr. Burnand. The former was played at the Vaudeville in 1872, and had for its chief interpreters Messrs. James and Thorne, who had not yet wholly surrendered burlesque for comedy. Mr. James was Romulus, and Mr. Thorne was Remus; and they came on in the first scene as children, dressed in pinafores and socks, and carrying toys. The pair begin by quarrelling as to which of them was born first. Remus rests his claim on his superior size :—

> Nature, perceiving "true grit " and "no shoddy,"
> Made me thus "double stout" with " extra body."

To which Romulus replies :—

> Though at our birth (when both kicked up a shine)
> His cry was *stout*, mine was the *elder whine* !
> Hence this thin body, wise folks say who've been here,
> " We're sure you are the *elder*, now we've *seen yer*."

When the two grow up (as they do between the first scene and the second), the question is, which is to be King of Rome—a question decided eventually by personal combat, in which Remus falls. Ultimately the pair decide to be partners in the throne—an obvious allusion to the position held by the two actors in reference to the Vaudeville Theatre.

The date of the production of " Romulus and Remus " (1872) could be fixed by the aid of a brief passage introduced in travestie of a scene between Cromwell and the King in Mr. Wills's " Charles I.," then " running " at the Lyceum. Early in the piece we have these lines :—

> *Remus.* The public will have (though to me it's pills)
> The classic drama. Well, they have their *Wills.*
> *Apollo.* One manager this line keeps without swerving—
> *Baccharia.* And he succeeds !
> *Romulus.*   But not without des-*erving.*

Later, Remus says to Romulus :—

> I can't express to you the pain I suffer
> In saying it; but, brother, you're a duffer!
> I am the happy man! Pride has a tumble!
> Your hopes of reigning, sir, are *all of a crumble*!
>> *Rom.* You dare to scoff at me, rebellious thing! (*knocks his hat off*)
> Uncover in the presence of your king!
> (*To audience*) That's historical!
>> *Rem.* What! strike me, dare you?
> (*Quietly*) Give me an earldom, and perhaps I'll spare you!
>> *Rom.* Your base insinuation I resent.
> I go in for king and parliament.
>> *Rem.* Your parliament's all gingerbread! (How nice!)
> I am a patriot and will have my price.
>> *Rom.* Defied! (*blows trumpet*). What, ho! my faithful guards, where be 'em?
>> (*Enter, from various entrances, all the characters, and supers. Tableau as in " Charles I."*)
> (*To audience*) I say! They can't beat *that* at the Lyceum.

In this piece Apollo (Miss Nelly Power) figures as a sort of Chorus, commenting on the action and interposing in it; while Baccharia (Miss Maria Rhodes) is represented as the sister of Tatius and a husband-huntress. The burlesque has all Mr. Reece's ingenuity in *jeu-de-mot* work. For instance :—

> *Tatius.* This is too much!
> *Baccharia.* To boast of deeds audacious.
> *Tatius.* Too callous!
> *Romulus.* *Calais!* Don't be *Ostend-Tatius!*

Mr. Burnand's " Julius Cnæsar " made the walls of the Royalty resound with laughter in the autumn of 1870. In the spring of 1869 William Brough had brought out at the Strand his version of the tale of Joan of Arc, whom he represented as the leader of a troop of Amazons, extremely interested in Woman's Rights. She comes, as in history, to the French king's assistance; but, falling in love with a young English soldier, is captured by the invaders and condemned to resume female attire,—a sentence which in the end she manages to evade. A leading part is played by the Duke of Burgundy, who is for ever uncertain on which side he shall fight, and whose name provides frequent opportunity for punning. Thus :—

> *Dunois.* See, Burgundy comes !
> *King.*   Is he indeed with me ?
> As a rule Burgundy ne'er yet agreed with me.
> He says he is my friend !
> *Duchatel.*   Well, that's a thumper !
> The name of Burgundy suggests a bumper !
> *La Hire.* He comes !
> *King (looking off).* With what a swagger, too !   It's clear
> Burgundy doesn't think himself small beer !

Again :—

> *Lionel.* Then, my lord, Burgundy, with all his train,
> Will join our ranks.
> *Talbot.*   My plans are changed again !
> He'll lick the foe in no time—if not quicker !
> Burgundy's such a very potent *licker !*
> Strengthened by him, war's hardest blows we'll mock—
> With a strong Burgundy, despise a kn*ock.*

Here, too, is a clever bit of word-play :—

> *Burgundy.* The *proffer'd table* I must needs refuse ;
> My time I can more *profitably* use.
> I can't *dine nicely* while with projects vasty
> My mind is filled for changing the *dy-nasty.*

On this occasion Joan was impersonated by Mr. Thomas Thorne, Mr. David James being the Duke of Burgundy,

Miss Eleanor Bufton the King, Miss Bella Goodall the Dunois, and Miss Amy Sheridan the Lionel. In the present year Joan of Arc has again become the subject of "respectful perversion,"—this time by Messrs. J. L. Shine and "Adrian Ross," and after a fashion to which I shall draw attention in my final chapter.

Of foreign notabilities, the only other subject of burlesque worth mentioning is Christopher Columbus, who gave the title to, and was the principal character in, a piece written by Mr. Alfred Thompson, and performed at the Gaiety two-and-thirty years ago. He was also the hero of a travestie by John Brougham, played in America.

The first English personage in burlesque, in point of historical order, is the legendary King Arthur, who was the chief figure in an "extravaganza" produced at the Haymarket in 1863.* Of this the author was William Brough, who owed considerably more to Malory than to Tennyson. There was a scene in which, as in the "Idylls," Vivien makes Merlin the victim of his own spell; but otherwise the laureate's withers were unwrung. Arthur (Miss Louise Keeley) becomes King of Britain by virtue of his power to draw the magic sword from the stone in which it is embedded. He is looking forward to wed Guinevere (Miss Wright), when suddenly she is captured by Cheldric, the Saxon invader, from whom, however, she is successfully re-captured by the aid of Vivien (Miss Romer) as the wielder of Merlin's wand. Sir Launcelot (Miss Lindley) is exhibited less as the lover of Guinevere than as a warrior; another prominent knight is the cowardly Sir Key, represented by Compton. Of direct parody, as I have said, the

* "King Arthur, or the Days and Knights of the Round Table."

piece has little; of punning, as usual, it is all compact.
Vivien says to Merlin :—

> Teach me your art.   In magic I'd excel;
> In studies deep I'd plunge, a *diving belle*.

And again,—

> Now for my lesson.   It's a curious thing,
> But knowledge is *increased* by *lessoning*.

Arthur says to Guinevere :—

> Fortune us has made alike ;
> I've acted like a *spoon*—while you act *ladle*-like !

Also, when he has lost his *ladle*-love :—

> My Guinevere made prisoner, Merlin too !
> Both I've to rue, if 'tis indeed *ter-rue*.
> To cope with all these horrors can I hope?
> What evil stars affect my horrors-cope !
> No one can I, the slightest aid to lend, see ;
> I'm in a frenzy since I can no *friend see*.
> My wits, unstrung, hang loose my head inside,
> What should be Christmas feels like *wits-untied*.

Guinevere, on her part, is equally afflicted with the
punning mania.   While immured in Cheldric's castle, she
soliloquises :—

> Shall I endure this state of things unjust?
> I, Arthur's destined spouse?   I *spouse* I must.
> How *sad a loss* is mine ! regrets are idle !
> A *saddle 'oss*, including *reign* and *bridal*.
> My star uprising side by side with his'n,
> No more uprising now, my fate's *a-prison*.
> This roomy kingdom, mine in expectation—
> Now I have nought but my own *room-i-nation*.
> Kept by the Saxon in this den of his,
> I'm numbed with cold—no doubt the *room-it-is*.

In Australia, twenty-three years ago, there was produced a burlesque called " King Arthur, or Launcelot the Loose, Gin-ever the Square, and the Knights of the Round Table, and other Furniture"; the perpetrator's name was W. M. Akhurst: Of recent years, the only prominent travestie of the subject has been that produced in 1889, by Messrs. Richard Butler and Henry Chance Newton ("Richard-Henry"), who entitled their work "Launcelot the Lovely, or the Idol of the King." Here, again, Tennyson and Malory were both very loyally and lightly treated, and, though Mr. Arthur Roberts as Launcelot was eminently funny, the prepossessions of the audience were in no way shocked.

The romantic tale of the loves of Fair Rosamond and His Majesty Henry II. has naturally attracted the notice of the travestie writers. In one instance, I regret to record, it fared very ill at the hands of the "dramatist." One T. P. Taylor brought out at Sadler's Wells in the 'thirties a one-act piece which he called "Fair Rosamond according to the History of England," in which the story was at once modernised and degraded. Henry became a Mr. Henry King—"a ruler, having been a stationer"; the Queen necessarily figured as " Mrs. Ellinor King." Rosamond herself was transmogrified into "a black girl, fair yet faulty," talking in "darkey " patois, and furnished with a father, black like herself, who combined the profession of fiddler and boot-black. The piece appears to have been successful in its day, but, to read, it is both vulgar and without a spark of wit.

Happily, the subject was taken up in our own time by Mr. Burnand, whose " Fair Rosamond, or the Maze, the

Maid, and the Monarch," seen at the Olympic in 1862, is among the most vivacious of his productions.* Here the writer boldly breaks away from historical tradition. He makes Henry in love with Rosamond, it is true; but Rosamond (Miss Hughes), on her side, has given her heart to Sir Pierre de Bonbon (Horace Wigan)—a Frenchman, as his name betokens. As Rosamond sings in the *finale* :—

> Hist'ry says that Rosamond
> Of King Hen-e-ry was fond ;
> Thus my character was wronged,
>   By a base aspersion ;
> To old stories don't *you* trust,
> Covered up with ages' dust.
> For the truth henceforth you must
>   Take our Wych Street version.

Rosamond, therefore, being innocent, it stands to reason that it would not be fair to poison her, as in the story; and so the Queen (played originally by Robson) is made to excuse her clemency in not forcing the girl to accept the " cup " she offers her :—

> Why's Rosamond not killed at all ?   You see,
> She isn't poisoned as she ought to be !
> Because, in deference to modern ways,
> No poisoned heroines can end our plays ;
> Besides, the brimming cup she held this minute,
> Like the objection, friends, has nothing in it.
> You'll say, with history we freedom use ;
> Well, don't historians write to suit their views ?
> We answer to the critical consistory,
> That we have made *our* views to suit our history.

---

* Mr. Frederick Langbridge has printed a burlesque on this subject, with a title somewhat similar.

One of the most amusing scenes in the burlesque is that in which Ellinor meets Henry for the first time after hearing of his infidelity :—

> Q. *Ellinor* (*coming down close to Henry*). Ahem !
>
> K. *Henry.* You spoke. (*Aside*) I see with rage she's brimming.
>
> Q. *Ellin.* (*aside*). I gave a "hem"—now I'll begin my trim-
> ming.
> False man !
>
> K. *Hen.* Pooh, pooh ! the epithet's beneath
> Contempt—I cast it in your false teeth.
>
> Q. *Ellin.* False teeth !
>
> K. *Hen.*   False hair !
>
> Q. *Ellin.*   Your speech, sir, is too blunt.
> *False hair !* I will not put up with affront,
> I'd rather dye.
>
> K. *Hen.*   For my consent don't wait ;
> *Die early !* on this subject don't *di-late.*
>
> Q. *Ellin.* Dost thou remember once a foreign land,
> Dost thou remember lovers hand in hand,
> Dost thou remember those soft murmuring lispers,
> Dost thou remember 't was the hour of *Vispers,*
> Dost thou remember, as I think you must,
> *Dost* thou——
>
> K. *Hen.* Oh ! do not kick up such a *dust.*
> I really cannot stand and listen to it,
> Thank goodness, no one but yourself *du'st* do it.
>
> Q. *Ellin.* Treat me with scorn—that's right. Oh, ne'er was seen
> A *suv'rin* King with such a *suff'rin* Queen !

Following the stream of time, we arrive next at a travestie of the insurrection, in the reign of Richard II., in which Wat Tyler was the prime mover. Tyler deserves celebration in the history of burlesque as the hero of the only work of this kind produced by Mr. George Augustus Sala. This well-known *littérateur* came out as a writer of travestie at the Gaiety in 1869, but has not been tempted to repeat the achievement. The fact is to be regretted, for his "Wat Tyler, M.P." had many strokes of wit and satire. Wat, being named Tyler, naturally became, in a piece of this *genre*, a hatter. He is portrayed as aspiring to Parliament, succeeding in his candidature, resisting payment of a tax upon chignons, heading a revolt against the powers that were, penetrating triumphantly into the royal palace, there getting drunk, and being, in the end, overpowered by the forces of the King. In his address to the electors from the hustings, there is a pleasant amalgam of pun and sarcasm. Tyler (who was impersonated by Mr. Toole) begins by saying :—

> A poor industrious hatter I stand here (*cheers*),
> And standing now proceed to take that *cheer.*
> You know me !
> > *Crowd.*   Sartainly.
> > *Wat.*   Am I a fool ?
> > *Crowd.* No !
> > *Wat.*   Was I ever base corruption's *Toole* ?
>
> Patriots, potwallopers, and townsmen dear,
> Voters unbribable and pure, look 'ere.
> Your sympathy my warmest thanks evokes,
> For you I'd brave the very *block*—my *blokes* !
> Tho' yonder dandy may treat me with scorn,
> I was of poor but honest parents born.
> Just twenty years ago, in ragged gown
> And soleless shoes, I trudged into this town,
> With one-and-ninepence and two plated spoons
> Within the pockets of my pantaloons.
> > *Beaumanners.* Where did you get the spoons from ?
> > *Wat.*   See how malice
>
> Ever conspires to drug the poor man's chalice !
> Where did I get the spoons from ? Well, so far
> As I remember—from my grandmamma !
> But you, my friends, my whole career have seen.
> People of Essex, both these hands are clean (*holds out his hands*).
> > *Oldest inhabitant.* They ain't.

Wat.   They is ! Who's that ? Some tyrant's minion.
Gag him ! and vote for freedom of opinion.
      (*Inhabitant is hustled off the stage.*)
Few are the promises you'll hear from me.
Send me to Westminster as your M.P.,
And you shall see——
      Crowd.   What ?
      Wat.   Here's what you shall see :
Wealth, splendour, carriages and four—that's what ;
The strongest ale a halfpenny a pot,
Taxes abolished, grievances amended,
And all the theatres' free lists ne'er suspended,
Washing for nothing, pickles, pastry, fun,
And Wallsend coals at eighteenpence a ton.
Give me your votes, and by next Michaelmas quarter
Each man shall have the moon who owns a pail of water.
Then a bold peasantry, their country's pride,
Shall live on eggs and bacon neatly fried.
The workhouse poor shall feed on buttered crumpets,
And eat roast mutton to the sound of trumpets ;
The beggar smoke the best Bengal cheroots,
And have another man to clean his boots.
      Beaumanners. Suppose to this the other makes objection?
      Wat. You hear my honourable friend's reflection.
In such a case, deny it if you can,
It's plain that we must hang the other man.
I've said my say ; the Commons are my goal ;
I am a hatter—let me head the poll.

Beaumanners, who is in love with Tyler's daughter Ellen
(Miss Constance Loseby), was represented by Miss Ellen
Farren,* to whom Mr. Sala assigned the delivery of some
of his best puns—as, for instance :—

> It seems to me the business of a *pa*
> Is simply all his children's bliss to *mar.*

---

* The cast was particularly good, including Miss Rose Coghlan as
the King, Miss Litton as the Queen, Maclean as Walworth, Mrs. Leigh
as Mrs. Tyler, Miss Tremaine, and J. B. Rae.

Jane Shore has been the heroine of a burlesque written by Mr. Wilton Jones, and brought out in the provinces eleven years ago. Messrs. " Richard Henry " have also composed a travestie of her story, as handed down by chroniclers. In Mr. Jones's piece reliance was placed, as of old, upon humorous situation and ear-splitting pun. I give an example of both qualities. Jane has denounced Richard, Duke of Gloucester, as the murderer of the Princes in the Tower, and he now proclaims her doom :—

> *Gloucester.* Policemen, hear the sentence on Jane Shore —
> (*Reading from scroll*) She's never to have dinner any more ;
> No breakfast, tea nor supper—that's her fate—
> No matter how much she may *supper*-licate.
> She'll starve to death for being over pert.
>   *Jane* (*feebly*). No *dinner*?
>   *Gloucester.*   No, ma'am ; only your *desert.*
> High treason is her crime, and I repeat
> No one shall give her anything to eat ;
> She'll have the fields, the roads to rest her knees on,
> And if she likes can even sleep *high trees on* ;
> But take good care no pity she arouses—
> And mind you keep her from the public-houses !
>   *Jane* (*aghast*). And is that *all* the sentence ? I shall drop !
>   *Gloucester.* Yes—there the sentence comes to a *full stop.*
>   *Jane.* Then for the sentence I had best prepare.
> Will some one kindly let down my back hair ?
>   (*Catesby and Hastings let her back hair down.*)
>   *Jane.* Well, if you won't remove this dreadful ban,
> I'll die as picturesquely as I can !

In three well-known travesties, Henry VIII. plays the most conspicuous part—in William Brough's " Field of the Cloth of Gold " (1868, Strand), in Mr. Burnand's " Windsor Castle " (Strand, 1865), and Mr. Conway Edwardes' " Anne Boleyn " (Royalty, 1872). I name these in the order in

which they deal with historical events. In "The Field of
the Cloth of Gold" Katherine of Arragon is Queen, with
Anne Boleyn (Miss F. Hughes) as maid of honour and
(as Her Majesty suspects) a rival. To this suspicion Anne
makes reference in the following lines :—

> Queen Katherine ! her I'm quite afraid of ;
> She vows it isn't *honour* that I'm *maid* of ;
> Declares King Henry loves me—as for me,
> I am no better than I ought to be ;
> Such language she employs, I'm grieved to state
> Queen *Kate* gets daily more *in-daily-Kate.*
> If I remonstrate, or to her appeal,
> Katherine goes off like a Katherine wheel.

In "Windsor Castle" the King is in love, more or less,
with Anne (Mr. Thomas Thorne), but inclined to let his
vagrant fancy wander after Mabel Lynwood (Miss Ada
Swanborough), who turns out to be Anne's sister. Anne, it
is recorded, sang like a siren, and was especially addicted
to a few French ditties. Of these Mr. Burnand makes her
sing a diverting parody, printed, in "the book of the play,"
in French "as she is pronounced." The song is called

CHARNSUNNETTE D'ANNE BOLEYN,

Arngtitulay

"LER SHEVALIAY AY SAR BELLAY."

I.

Le Sh'valiay ay sar Bellay,
  Ker deetial Sir Grong Mossoo lar ?
Avec lespree der Jernessay
  "Commongvoo portayvoo?"
Parley voo frarngsay ?
Parley voo—Tra-la-la-la-la-la.
    (*Refrang*). Parley voo, etc.

" O Sh'valiay," dit sar Bellay,
   " Cumbeang ler caffy newaur lar ? "
" Ay p'tee tas o der veeay ? "
   Toot sweet o reservoir.
Jenner comprong par
Jenner com—Tra-la-la-la-la.
   (*Refrang*). Jenner com, etc.

Morale.

Kong Johnteyomme L'Onglay say
   Daymarnd lay pomme de tare lar
Partong poor lar Syreeay
   Ay Veve lar Lester Square !
Charnsong ay finny
O sey ay finny mong tra-la-la-la.

In " Anne Boleyn," again, Anne (E. Danvers) is at
last Queen, but with her life embittered by King Henry's
flirtations with Jane Seymour (Miss Harriet Coveney). Thus,
in one place, Anne exclaims :—

Again he slights me !   Bubbling heart, be still !
Keep Henry from that girl I must, and will !
She hinted I—in language far from vague—
Like *Xantippe*, was *sent to be* a plague ;
Openly told that corpulent barbarian
I'm his " grey mare," and also no *grey-mare-ian* ;
Said I'm a vixen, and in manner rude
Told him he wasn't *wise* to be so *shrew'd*.
My happiness she's marred, my heart she's wrung
With *hideous hints* from her (h)insidious tongue.
She would ke-rush me !—ah !   But soft—no riot !
Now, bubbling heart, oblige me, and lie quiet.

The King himself describes the course of his feelings
towards Anne in the following ditty :—

When I courted Anne Boleyn, with love I was drunk,
Oh, I cannot remember the thoughts that I—*thunk*,
I know I winked at her, and she at me—*wunk*,
   With my itheremyky, kitheremyky,
   Katheremyku-etty cum, fol de rol liddle de ray.

I said, " Let me kneel at your feet," and I—*knole*,
And I asked her upon me to smile, and she—*smole*,
Then I said, " I feel happier than ever I—*fole*,"
    With my, etc.

She murmured, " My waist do not squeeze," but I—*squoze*,
And remained at her feet till she told me to—*rose*,
For she wanted to sneeze, and softly she—*snoze*,
    With my, etc.

For a time I continued to woo, yes, I—*wode*,
Then I asked her to go to the church, and we—*gode*,
Having made up our minds to be tied, we were—*tode*,
    With my, etc.

Time winged his swift course, yes, his swift course Time—*wung*,
And this was the thing he was bringing, and—*brung;*
Dislike for Anne Boleyn, I wish she was hung !
    With my, etc.

"The Field of the Cloth of Gold" (which was revived
in London, with only tolerable success, a year or two ago)
has to do mainly with the meeting of Henry VIII. and
Francis I. (Mr. David James) on that historic spot—an
event which is here surrounded with the most ludicrous
circumstances possible. There is a sub-plot which deals
with the loves of Constance de Grey (Miss A. Swanborough)
and the Earl of Darnley (Miss Lydia Thompson), as interrupted and jeopardised by the pretensions and machina-
tions of Sir Guy the Cripple (Mr. Thomas Thorne). The
comic incidents are somewhat pantomimical, and the main
merit of the piece lies in the humour of its dialogue, which
is always sparkling. One of the puns in this burlesque is
among the very best ever perpetrated, and is, indeed, a
historical possession. Need I quote it? The King has
crossed over from Dover to Calais on a stormy day, and
arrives in a very "indisposed" condition :—

W. L.—V.
                                                     8

> *Henry.* I am ill.
> *Suffolk.*   Nay, sire, cheer up, I pray.
> *Henry.* Yesterday all was fair—a glorious Sunday,
> But this *sick transit* spoils the *glory o' Monday.*

But the piece is full of quips almost equally good.   Mark
the puns that the two kings fire off at each other when they
foregather on the Field of the Cloth of Gold :—

> *Henry.* Pshaw !   Bluff King Hal fears not to make advances
> So long as the great King of *France is Francis.*
> *Francis.* With pride I this alliance look upon,
> While *Hal be on* the throne of *Albion.*
> *Henry.* The English Harry 'd flattery despise,
> He deems *all truths* here uttered by *al-lies.*
> Of good old racy stock, he scorns hypocrisy.
> *Francis.* We've heard much of the English *Harri-stock-racy.*

After this, one thinks comparatively little of such sallies
as :—

> " You an *exile* here are *rated.*"
>   " Yes,
> It's not *exile-a-rating,* I confess."
>
> So, sire, I on the Tuesday ran away,
> To 'scape the *wedding* on the *Wedding's day.*
>
> " Oh, mind ! my hair you out in handfuls pull."
> " Why so much cry about a little wool ? "

At one point we have :—

> *De Bois.* Your Majesty, we've sought you everywhere.
> Your absence much alarm has been creating,
> Even the royal dinner's been kept waiting
> Till you came home.
> *Francis.*   So you regret, I see,
> The *missing dinner*—not the *absentee.*

Surrey, in " Windsor Castle," is represented not only
as poet but as composer, and in the combined characters
puts together a love song addressed to his Geraldine.

Unfortunately, when he comes to sing it to her, he finds he has forgotten some of the words :—

> *Surrey.* Well ! the *refrain* which I composed as well,
> Is no " Fol de riddle lol," made in my cell ;
> Where, 'stead of idly *lolling* all the day,
> My time I fol de riddle *lolled* away,
> I cannot somehow call each verse to mind,
> But substitutes for words I soon can find ;
> Toodle um, or something of that sort ;
> I'll sing the air ; 'tis very sweet and short.
>
> (*Sings.*)
> Oh my Geraldine,
> No flow'r was ever seen so toodle um.
> (*Fondly*) You are my lum ti toodle lay,
> Pretty, pretty queen
> Is rum ti Geraldine and something teen,
> (*Rapturously*) More sweet than tiddle lum in May.
> Like the star so bright,
> That something's all the night,
> My Geraldine !
> (*With intensity*) You're fair as the rum ti lum ti sheen,
> *Boleyn* (*without*). What, ho !
> *Surrey* (*speaks impressively*). This is impromptu.
> Hark ! there is what—ho !
> From something-um, you know,
> Dear, what I mean.
> (*With deep feeling*) Oh ! rum ! tum ! ! tum ! ! ! my Geraldine.

"Anne Boleyn" is particularly prolific in good puns, in the making of which the author showed himself an adept. It would be a pleasure to quote a few of them, but I give instead some lines in which, speaking through the mouth of one of his characters, the writer satirises the methods of the old-fashioned drama :—

> *Mine* were the " palmy days" when, I declare,
> A little table and two chairs, sir, were
> Thought furniture sufficient for a scene ;
> When a baize drugget—generally green—

Covered the stage where'er the place was laid,
Serving alike for palace, cot or glade ;
When, in a drawing-room, a servant-maid
Would sing a duet with the comic man ;
When dramas only for a few nights ran ;
When a rhymed tag to every piece was tacked ;
When most plays had a dozen scenes an act ;
When bucket boots and ringlet wigs were worn,
" Acting's a lost art," sir, since *you* were born ;
Those are the days which I look back upon,
Of broadsword combats with—" Ha, ha ! Come on ! "

Good Queen Bess was added to Mr. Burnand's gallery
in 1870, when his " E-liz-a-beth, or the Don, the Duck,
the Drake, and the Invisible Armada," was brought out at
the Vaudeville, with Mr. Thorne as the Queen, Mr. David
James as Whiskerandos, and George Honey as Drake.
The " Maiden Queen " has not been greatly tantalised by
the burlesque writers, who, on the other hand, have made
very free with a gentleman who much disturbed her successor—Guy Fawkes. Mr. Burnand handled him in 1866
(at the Strand) ; H. J. Byron followed suit at the Gaiety in
1874 ; last year we had the " Guy Fawkes, Esq." of Messrs.
" A. C. Torr " (Fred Leslie) and H. F. Clark ; and I believe
that Mr. Wilton Jones, too, has written a travestie on the
subject.   Charles II. was burlesqued by Mr. Gilbert Arthur
a'Beckett in 1872, the *locale* being the Court Theatre,
and the full title of the piece " Charles II., or Something
like History."   In this, as in Mr. Reece's " Romulus
and Remus," there was some parody of the Lyceum
" Charles I."—Mr. Righton, as Cromwell, imitating both
Mr. Irving and George Belmore, besides indulging in the
cancan ! W. J. Hill was the King, and Mme. Cornèlie

D'Anka the Queen (Catherine of Braganza). Pepys, Rochester, and Lily the Astrologer also figured in the piece. Cromwell was afterwards the leading personage in the " Oliver Grumble " of Mr. George Dance (Novelty, 1886).

About the names of such heroes and heroines as the Lady Godiva, Dick Whittington, Robin Hood, Herne the Hunter, and those distinguished footpads Claude Duval and Dick Turpin, there hangs a good deal that is clearly mythical. Still, some myths have more real vitality than absolute fact ; and who does not believe firmly that the Lady Godiva rode round Coventry "clothed on " with nothing but her chastity, and, by taking away a grinding tax, " built herself an everlasting name "?   Her adventuré has been burlesqued at least twice—once by Francis Talfourd and a collaborator, at another time by Mr. H. Chance Newton.   The Talfourd piece was called " Godiva, or Yᵉ Ladye of Coventrie and Yᵉ Exyle Fayrie " and produced at the Strand in 1851. Mr. Newton christened his work " Giddy Godiva."   In the earlier burlesque, "yᵉ exile fayrie " Ignota (Miss Romer) is introduced merely as a *dea ex machinâ* in the interests of the heroine (Miss Marshall), who, in a passage of Shakespearean reminiscence, discusses the undertaking to which she has been incited by her husband :—

> To be, or not to be, at his suggestion,
> A pose plastique, is yet a doubtful question !
> To bare my arms against a sea of troubles,
> And by a pose to end them !   Each day doubles
> The people's wrongs, the proud Earl's heavy tax ;
> To help to ease them I would not be lax ;
> But then to ride—riding, by some low scrub
> Perhaps be seen !—Ah, bother—there's the rub !

> The fear that still my courage may be less
> When I have shuffled off this mortal dress,
> Must give me pause.

A prominent character in the piece is Our Own Reporter, "Y^e Specyall Commyssionere and Correspondente of y^e *Busie Bee*" (John Reeve), who would fain play the part of Peeping Tom, and who, early in the play, sings a song wittily descriptive of his ordinary avocations :—

> *Rep.* I'm a mercantile man, and my living is got
> By selling of articles——
>   *Leofric and Godwin.* What? what? what?
> *Rep.* They're white and black, they're short and long,
> And some of them sometimes go for a song ;
> And during my time, of labour by dint,
> I've set up many a column of——
>
> | | |
> |---|---|
> | *Leo.* | Granite ? |
> | *Godwin.* | Iron ? |
> | *Leo.* | Gutta Percha ? |
>
> *Rep.* No, no; that's not the sort of thing to make up the business that I do !
>
> *Rep.* I'm a military man, for I often have a shot
> At public foes with——
>   *Leofric and Godwin.* What? what? what?
> *Rep.* If I fire at you 'twill be no joke,
> For you'll hear the report, but see no smoke ;
> And my charge is prepared with what do you think?
> By a devil and steam, of paper and——
>
> | | |
> |---|---|
> | *Leo.* | Sulphur and brimstone ? |
> | *Godwin.* | Gunpowder ? |
> | *Leo.* | Gun-cotton ? |
>
> *Rep.* No, no; that's not the sort of thing to make up the business that I do !
>
> *Rep.* I'm a literary man, and I can put a blot
> On a proud snob's scutcheon——
>   *Leofric and Godwin.* Hey ! what? what? what?

Rep. And if I mention the people's woes,
And show you up, why down you goes;
And the flow of language that I possess
Will open the tide of the Public——
    Leo.   Water Companies?
    Godwin.   Baths and Washhouses?
    Leo.   I have it—Press!
    Rep. Just so! Now you know the sort of thing that makes up
      the business that I do!

Three burlesques have been devoted to the life and adventures of Sir Richard Whittington. There was, first, the "Whittington Junior, and his Sensation Cat," of Mr. Robert Reece (Royalty, 1870); next, the "Young Dick Whittington" of Mr. Wilton Jones (Leicester, 1881); and next, the "Whittington and his Cat" of Mr. Burnand (Gaiety, 1881). Mr. Reece had Miss Henrietta Hodson (Mrs. Labouchere) for his Whittington, while Miss Farren was Mr. Burnand's. Robin Hood has had at least as many burlesque biographies as Whittington. A travestie, written by Stocqueler, Shirley Brooks, and Charles Kenny, and produced at the Lyceum in 1846, with the Keeleys, Wigan and Frank Matthews, was followed in 1862, at the Olympic, by one from the pen of Mr. Burnand. Mr. Reece wrote one, called "Little Robin Hood," which was seen at the Royalty in 1871, and this was revived—in three-act form—at the Gaiety in 1882, with Mr. Arthur Williams as a particularly droll Richard I. Robin Hood, it may also be noted, was a prominent character in Mr. Barnand's "Hit or 'Miss,'" at the Olympic in 1868. Herne the Hunter (who has a place in Mr. Burnand's "Windsor Castle") was made the leading personage in, and gave the title to, a travestie composed by Messrs. Reece and Yardley, and performed at the Gaiety

in 1881.   Five years later, at the Folly, we had " Herne
the Hunted," in which Mr. H. P. Stephens had a hand,
as well as Messrs. Yardley and Reece.   Claude Duval was
turned into a burlesque hero by Mr. Burnand, and strutted
his hour upon the stage at the Royalty in 1869; followed
longo intervallo by Turpin—here called " Dandy Dick
Turpin, the Mashing Highwayman,"—whom Mr. Geoffrey
Thorn (Charles Townley) made the chief personage of a
travestie performed in London in 1889.

VI.

BURLESQUE OF SHAKESPEARE.

TRAVESTIE of the drama and things dramatic has naturally played a large part in the history of English stage burlesque. Side by side with the producers and interpreters of tragedy, melodrama, and plays of sentiment, have been the possessors of the humorous spirit, who —whether as writers or as actors—have been quick to see the points in which works of serious plan and treatment have been open to the shafts of ridicule and raillery. As we have seen, most of the earliest efforts in English stage burlesque were directed against the extravagant tragedies of the seventeenth and eighteenth centuries. As time went on, and the limits of the serious drama became more extended, so did the limits of burlesque expand, and, from the days of John Poole downwards, the large variety of serious dramatic production has co-existed with a corresponding variety in the subject and style of the travesties submitted to the public.

Among those travesties a prominent place has been taken by the pieces devoted to the burlesque of Shakespeare —not because they have been particularly numerous, for they have not been so—nor because they have been

uniformly successful, for the earlier specimens were sin-
gularly weak—but because of the general daring of the
attempts, and because also of the genuine sense of
fun exhibited by such baiters of "the Bard" as Gilbert
a'Beckett, Francis Talfourd, Stirling Coyne, William
Brough, Andrew Halliday (Duff), F. C. Burnand, H. J.
Byron, and W. S. Gilbert. [The business of burlesquing
Shakespeare has never, so far as I can see, been taken
up in a wholesale or an intentionally irreverent spirit.
The seventeenth and eighteenth-century satirists left "the
Bard" severely alone, and it was not until 1810 that the
first formal travestie of Shakespeare—Poole's "Hamlet
Travestie"—saw the light.* The author then made all
due apology for his temerity, at the same time pointing
out the absurdity of the idea that any amount or kind of
burlesque could possibly sully the fame of the dramatist.
Two years later, in the course of his preface to the fourth
edition of his work, Poole ironically congratulated "those
who, on its first appearance, were apprehensive for the
reputation of Shakespeare," upon the fact "that, notwith-
standing Three Editions already before the public, he is
neither expelled from our libraries, nor banished from our
stage."

The truth is, a brilliant burlesque does harm to nobody;
and a bad burlesque does but recoil upon the head of its
author and his exponents. Poole's "Hamlet Travestie" is

---

* It was performed at Covent Garden in 1813, with Mathews as
Hamlet, Blanchard as the King, Liston as Ophelia, and Mrs. Liston
as the Queen. It was revived in 1874 on one occasion with Mr. Odell
as Hamlet, and shortly afterwards with Mr. Leonard Boyne as the
Prince, both actors indulging in an imitation of Mr. Irving's performance.

marked by the best intentions, but, as a whole, it makes dreary reading. The opening colloquy between Hamlet, King Claudius, and Queen Gertrude will give, to those who have not already perused the piece, a notion of the quality of the dialogue :—

King (*to* Hamlet). Cheer up, my son and cousin, never mind—
Ham. A little more than kin, and less than kind.
King. Why hang the clouds still on you ? Come, have done.
Ham. You're out, my lord ; I'm too much in the sun.—
Queen. Come, Hamlet, leave off crying ; 'tis in vain,
Since crying will not bring him back again.
Besides, 'tis common : all that live must die—
So blow your nose, my dear, and do not cry.
Ham. Ay, madam, it is common.
Queen.　　　　　　　　　　　If it be,
Why seems there such a mighty fuss with thee ?
Ham. Talk not to me of seems—when husbands die,
'Twere well if some folks seem'd the same as I.
But *I* have that within, you can't take from me—
As for black clothes—that's all my eye and Tommy.
King. Cheer up, my hearty ; though you've lost your dad,
Consider that your case is not so bad :
Your father lost a father ; and 'tis certain,
Death o'er your great-grandfather drew the curtain.
You've mourn'd enough ; 'tis time your grief to smother ;
Don't cry : you shall be king some time or other.
Queen. Go not to Wittenburg, my love, I pray you.
Ham. Mamma, I shall in all my best obey you.
King. Well said, my lad ! Cheer up, no more foul weather :
We'll meet anon, and all get drunk together.

It was part of Poole's method to put the soliloquies into the form of songs, and so we find the lines beginning " O that this too too solid flesh would melt !" appearing in the following form :—

A ducat I'd give if a sure way I knew
How to thaw and resolve my stout flesh into dew !
How happy were I if no sin was self-slaughter !
For I'd then throw myself and my cares in the water.

Derry down, down, down, derry down.

How weary, how profitless,—stale, and how flat,
Seem to me all life's uses, its joys, and all that :
This world is a garden unweeded ; and clearly
Not worth living for—things rank and gross hold it merely.

Derry down, etc.

Two months have scarce pass'd since dad's death, and my mother,
Like a brute as she is, has just married his brother.—
To wed such a bore !—but 'tis all too late now ::
We can't make a silk purse of the ear of a sow.

Derry down, etc.

The time-honoured " To be or not to be " is sung in this version to the tune of " Here we go up, up, up " :—

When a man becomes tired of his life,
    The question is, "to be, or not to be?"
For before he dare finish the strife,
    His reflections most serious ought to be.
When his troubles too numerous grow,
    And he knows of no method to mend them,
Had he best bear them tamely, or no ?—
    Or by stoutly opposing them, end them ?

Ri tol de rol, etc.

To die is to sleep—nothing more—
    And by sleeping to say we end sorrow,
And pain, and ten thousand things more,—
    Oh, I wish it were *my* turn to-morrow !
But, perchance, in that sleep we may dream,
    For we dream in our beds very often—
Now, however capricious 't may seem,
    I've no notion of dreams in a coffin.

Ri tol de rol, etc.

W. S. GILBERT.

'Tis the doubt of our ending all snugly,
  That makes us with life thus dispute;
Or who'd bear with a wife old and ugly,
  Or the length of a chancery suit?
Or who would bear fardels, and take
  Kicks, cuffs, frowns, and many an odd thing,
When he might his own quietus make,
  And end all his cares with a bodkin?
                  Ri tol de rol, etc.

The " annotations" appended to the text of the burlesque
are in parody of the performances of the commentators,
who at least are fair game for chaff of this sort, and on
whom Poole, in his preface, lavishes some excellent indignation.

Of subsequent burlesques of " Hamlet" there have not
been many, but some of them have been really clever and
commendable. There was, for instance, Talfourd's, published at Oxford in 1849; there was the " Hamlet à la
Mode " of Messrs. G. L. Gordon and G. W. Anson,
performed at Liverpool in 1877; there was the " Very
Little Hamlet" of Mr. William Yardley, seen at the Gaiety
in 1884; and last, but assuredly not least, we have had the
" Rosencrantz and Guildenstern " of Mr. Gilbert, which,
written avowedly without thought either of public or of
private representation, has been enacted at a benefit
matinée during the present year.

In " Rosencrantz and Guildenstern," which is an unpretentious little " skit," covering only some sixteen or
seventeen printed pages, Mr. Gilbert supposes that Hamlet
is the son (not the nephew) of Claudius. " Rosencrantz is
a lover of Ophelia, to whom Hamlet is betrothed, and they
lay their heads together to devise a plan by which Hamlet

W. S. GILBERT.

'Tis the doubt of our ending all snugly,
    That makes us with life thus dispute;
Or who'd bear with a wife old and ugly,
    Or the length of a chancery suit?
Or who would bear fardels, and take
    Kicks, cuffs, frowns, and many an odd thing,
When he might his own quietus make,
    And end all his cares with a bodkin?
                  Ri tol de rol, etc.

The "annotations" appended to the text of the burlesque are in parody of the performances of the commentators, who at least are fair game for chaff of this sort, and on whom Poole, in his preface, lavishes some excellent indignation.

Of subsequent burlesques of "Hamlet" there have not been many, but some of them have been really clever and commendable. There was, for instance, Talfourd's, published at Oxford in 1849; there was the "Hamlet à la Mode" of Messrs. G. L. Gordon and G. W. Anson, performed at Liverpool in 1877; there was the "Very Little Hamlet" of Mr. William Yardley, seen at the Gaiety in 1884; and last, but assuredly not least, we have had the "Rosencrantz and Guildenstern" of Mr. Gilbert, which, written originally without thought either of public or of private representation, has been enacted at a benefit *matinée* during the present year.

In "Rosencrantz and Guildenstern," which is an unpretentious little "skit," covering only some sixteen or seventeen printed pages, Mr. Gilbert supposes that Hamlet is the son (not the step-son) of Claudius. "Rosencrantz is a lover of Ophelia, to whom Hamlet is betrothed, and they lay their heads together to devise a plan by which Hamlet

may be put out of the way.   Some Court theatricals are in
preparation."   Now, once upon a time, Claudius had written
a tragedy, which was damned, and to which no one is
allowed to make reference on pain of death.   "Ophelia
and Rosencrantz persuade Hamlet to play his father's
tragedy before the king and court.   Hamlet, who is unaware
of the proscription, does so ; and he is banished, and
Rosencrantz happily united to Ophelia."

In the first act, Rosencrantz, who has never seen Hamlet
(apparently, because the former has been abroad), asks
Ophelia what the Prince is like, and that gives Mr. Gilbert
an opportunity for some characteristic satire.   Ophelia says
of Hamlet that he is " alike for no two seasons at a time " :—

> Sometimes he's tall—sometimes he's very short—
> Now with black hair—now with a flaxen wig—
> Sometimes an English accent—then a French—
> Then English with a strong provincial " burr."
> Once an American and once a Jew—
> But Danish never, take him how you will !
> And, strange to say, whate'er his tongue may be,
> Whether he's dark or flaxen—English—French—
> Though we're in Denmark, A. D. ten—six—two—
> He always dresses as King James the First !
>   *Guild.* Oh, he is surely mad !
>   *Oph.*   Well, there again
> Opinion is divided.   Some men hold
> That he's the sanest far of all sane men—
> Some that he's really sane, but shamming mad—
> Some that he's really mad, but shamming sane—
> Some that he will be mad, some that he *was*—
> Some that he couldn't be !   But, on the whole
> (As far as I can make out what they mean),
> The favourite theory 's somewhat like this :
> Hamlet is idiotically sane
> With lucid intervals of lunacy.

In the second act, the Queen, observing that Hamlet is about to soliloquise, urges Rosencrantz and Guildenstern to "prevent this, gentlemen, by any means" :—

> Anticipate his points,
> And follow out his argument for him ;
> Thus you will cut the ground from 'neath his feet,
> And leave him nought to say.

The result is as follows :—

Enter Hamlet ; *he stalks to a chair, throws himself into it.*

Ham. To be—or not to be !

Ros. (R. *of chair*)   Yes—that's the point !
Whether he's bravest who will cut his throat
Rather than suffer all—

Guild. (L. *of chair*) Or suffer all
Rather than cut his throat ?

Ham. (*annoyed at interruption, resumes*) To die—to sleep——

Ros. It's nothing more—Death is but sleep spun out—
Why hesitate ?   (*Offers him a dagger.*)

Guild.   The only question is
Between the choice of deaths which death to choose.

     (*Offers another.*)

Ham. (*in great terror*) Do take these dreadful things away. They make
My blood run cold. (*Resumes*) To sleep, perchance to——

Ros.   Dream.
That's very true. I never dream myself,
But Guildenstern dreams all night long out loud.

Guild. With blushes, sir, I do confess it true !

Ham. This question, gentlemen, concerns me not.
(*Resumes*) For who would bear the whips and scorns of time——

Ros. (*as guessing a riddle*) *Who'd* bear the whips and scorns ? Now le t me see.
Who'd *bear* them, eh ?

Guild. (*same business*) Who'd bear the *scorns* of time——

Ros. (*correcting him*) The *whips* and scorns.

Guild.   The whips and scorns, of course.

                    (*Hamlet about to protest*)

Don't tell us—let us guess—the *whips* of time?

Ham. Oh, sirs, this interruption likes us not.

I pray you give it up.

Ros.   My lord, we do.

We cannot tell *who* bears these whips and scorns !

The third act opens with a passage in which the turns
and rhythm of Shakespearean prose are happily imitated :—

Enter King *and* Queen, *meeting* Rosencrantz.

Queen. A fair good morrow to you, Rosencrantz. How march the
Royal revels ?

Ros. Lamely, madam, lamely, like a one-legged duck. The Prince
has discovered a strange play. He hath called it "A Right Reckoning
Long Delayed."

Claud. And of what fashion is the Prince's play?

Ros. 'Tis an excellent poor tragedy, my Lord—a thing of shreds and
patches welded into a form that hath mass without consistency, like an
ill-built villa.

Queen. But, sir, you should have used your best endeavours to wean
his phantasy from such a play.

Ros. Madam, I did, and with some success; for he now seeth the
absurdity of its tragical catastrophes, and laughs at it as freely as we
do. So, albeit the poor author had hoped to have drawn tears of
sympathy, the Prince hath resolved to present it as a piece of pompous
folly intended to excite no loftier emotion than laughter and surprise.

After Poole published his "Hamlet,"* Shakespearean
burlesque slumbered until 1834, when Maurice G. Dowling

* In "Hamlet Improved," by Colonel Colomb, a Mr. Mendall is
supposed to have revised the last act of "Hamlet" in accordance with
modern notions. Polonius is alive, having been only wounded by
Hamlet; Hamlet's father also is alive, having only pretended to be dead.
At the close, the King, Queen, Laertes, and Ophelia, all come to life
again. Hamlet is represented by a stuffed figure, the actor chosen for
the part having refused to enact it.

produced at Liverpool his "Othello Travestie." In this dull production, the Moor of Venice figures as "an independent nigger from the Republic of Hayti," and talks in "darkey" dialect (as does the same writer's Clifford in "Fair Rosamond"). Here, for example, is this Othello's address to the Senate (written and sung to the air of "Yankee Doodle") :—

Potent, grave, and rev'rend sir,
Very noble massa—
When de maid a man prefer
Den him no can pass her.
Yes, it is most werry true,
Him take dis old man's daughter;
But no by spell, him promise you,
But by fair means him caught her.

'Tis true she lub him berry much,
'Tis true dat off him carry her,
And dat him lub for her is such,
'Tis werry true him marry her.
All dis be true—and till him dead,
Him lub her widout ending—
And dis, my massa, is the head
And tail of him offending.

Dis old man once him lub me too,
Do' now in rage before ye,
And often say, "Come Othello,
And tell us pretty story,
About der time when yon young child,
(You naughty lilly child ye),
And when you 'bout de wood run wild,
And when you sold for slavey."

Den ebery day him tell all dis,
And sometimes lilly lie, too,
And him look in de eye of miss.
And den him hear her sigh, too,

W. L.—V.

Den missee meet him all alone,
    And den him ax her wedder,
Him make de both two hearts in one,   ,
    Den off dey run togedder.

W. J. Hammond played Othello in this piece, both at
Liverpool, and afterwards at the Strand Theatre, where
popular Miss E. Daly was the Desdemona and H. Hall
the Iago.   What can these presumably capable actors have
thought of their *rôles*?   The text of the burlesque is almost
wholly without humour, of which, however, there is a gleam
in the complaint made by Cassio that he has been ruined
by a pint of beer :—

My reputation's lost—my reputation !
I'm bother'd, sir—I'm bother'd quite with thinking ;
I've lost my reputation, sir, for drinking.
I, who to good brown stout ne'er yet turn'd tail,
Drunk and bedevil'd with a mug of ale !
Was ever man in such a situation ?
My reputation, sir—my reputation !

H. J. Byron's "Rival Othellos" (played at the Strand
in 1876) was not a travestie of the tragedy; but it
gave opportunity for some clever burlesque of tragic
acting.

We come now to the first (and, so far as I know, the only)
travestie of "King John," which happily was essayed by the
capable pen of Gilbert Abbott a'Beckett.   The year was
1837, the *locale* the St. James's Theatre, and Hall the
representative of the title-part, with Mme. Sala as Lady
Constance.   The play was lucky in being dealt with by so
deft a workman.   The subject was not very promising, and
all was done with it that was possible.   The scene in which

the King incites Hubert to get rid of Arthur was thus
travestied :—

> Hubert, my friend, I had a thing to say.
> But let it pass—the sun is shining bright :
> To suit my purpose, it had needs be night,
> If where we stand could be a railroad tunnel,
> As if we looked at Tartarus through a funnel ;
> If you could only scent what I propose,
> Yet let it not smell rankly in your nose,
> If you could, or if I—— Hubert, my lad,
> Who made that coat ?—indeed, the cut's not bad.
>   *Hub.* Great king, you know I always lov'd you well,
> Then why not in a word your wishes tell ?
> Why roll your troubled eye about its socket?
> My lord, your heart is in your breeches pocket.
> Though it would cost my life, what is't you need ?
> I'll do your bidding—
>   *K. John.*   You're a friend indeed !
> But Hubert, Hubert, Hubert, throw your eye
> On that young lad, that now is standing by ;
> I'll tell you what, my friend : that boy, I feel,
> Is, in my path, a piece of orange peel,
> And wheresoe'er I tread he'll throw me down,
> And if I fall, you know, I crack my crown.
>   (*Taking out his snuff-box.*)   ·
> You are his keeper—are you up to snuff?
>   *Hub.* I am ! I'll keep the urchin safe enough.
>   *K. John.* Remove him——
>   *Hub.* He shall die !
>   *K. John.* Egad, I feel
> So merry, Hubert, I could dance a reel.
> What shall I give thee ?
>   *Hub.*   What you please.
>   *K. John.* Then let it—
> Stand over, gentle Hubert, till you get it.

Here, again, is the perversion of the famous scene between
Hubert and the boy :—

Arth. Hubert,.good Hubert, how are you to-day?

Hub. I must not listen to his childish chatter,
For if I do he'll melt my heart like batter.
(*Aside*) Look here, young Arthur (*gives warrant*): can you understand
This paper, written in a large text hand?

Arth. Oh, can I read it?—oh, unhappy youth !
Must you with pinchers then take out my tooth?

Hub. Young boy, I must.

Arth.   And will you?

Hub.   Yes, I will.

Arth. Oh, it's too bad—when you were taken ill,
Who was it to the chemist's ran full gallop,
To get a penny dose of salts and jalap !
And when I've seen you, after dining out,
When you've made free at some hot drinking bout,
Have I not always been extremely willing
To give for soda-water my last shilling?
And you'll take out my tooth? If you will, come—
I'll not resist,—here is my tooth, by gum !

Hub. Young boy, I've sworn to do it—do not flinch :
These instruments must help me at a pinch.
Come forth ! (*Stamps.*)

                Enter Ruffian, *with a pewter basin, towel*, etc.

(*To* Ruffian). Do as I bid you.

Arth.   Hubert, stay :
My tooth is out—do send that man away.   (Ruffian *seizes* Arthur.)

Hub. Now for the pinchers—now for one bold tug.

Arth. Why be so boisterous ? I will hold my mug.
For Heaven's sake, Hubert,. send that man away,
And not a word against it I will say.
Hubert, thy word indeed shall be my law ;
My tooth is out : see, I will hold my jaw !

Hub. (*to Ruffian*). Go, stand without ; I by myself will do it.

Ruffian. Indeed 'twould make me ill were I to view it.

                                [*Exit* Ruffian.

Elsewhere King John sings, to the air of "The Light of other Days," this excellent parody :—

The robe of other days has faded,
   Its gloss has from it pass'd ;
For dust with little specks has shaded
   The stuff too fine to last.
The robe of velvet made of cotton,
   For wear much better pays ;
But, alas ! how shabby this I've got on,
   The robe of other days !

The coat that is not worth a stiver,
   An old and worn-out thing,
When touch'd with black and blue reviver,
   Like a new one up will spring.
You may dye the coat of one that's needy,
   Of stuff as coarse as baize ;
But the robe is done for when 'tis seedy,
   The robe of other days.

The first burlesque of " Romeo and Juliet " was brought
out at the Strand in the same year as that which saw
the birth of A'Beckett's " King John." The author was
Maurice G. Dowling, who succeeded in producing something worthy to rank with his " Othello." In his " Romeo
and Juliet " Montagu and Capulet are rival basket-makers,
" Mr." Mercutio being foreman to the former, who also has
" Mr. Ben Volio " in his employ. Tybalt is a fireman and
ratcatcher to the Duke of Mantua ; " Mr." Friar Laurence,
a " black-and-white-smith " at Gretna Green. Romeo talks
in illiterate fashion, and at one point sticks a pin into Paris's
back ! Miss Daly was the Juliet, and she and Hammond
(as Romeo) had to speak, in the balcony scene, such lines
as these :—

Enter Romeo *over wall.*

Rom. He just knows nothing who's been scratched with pins,
Unless he's felt the pain of broken shins.
     (Juliet *appears at balcony with lantern.*)
Oh my ! what light is that upon the wall
Rising like yeast ? Crikey, if she should fall !

Come down, my duck : the moon can't stand no chance—
You'll easy stare her out of countenance.
You're prettier far than she— I'm not in joke,
Miss ; what did you say ?   Oh, la, I thought she spoke !
I wish she was in heaven, and then her eyes
Would be two stars a twinkling in the skies.
There ! now she puts her hand upon her head—
I wish I was that hair—those curls instead,
That she might comb me when she went to bed.
   Jul. Oh, my ! I wish that nice young man would come !
   Rom. She speaks ! a sign she isn't deaf and dumb.
   Jul. O Romeo !—Romeo ! perhaps you're not to blame,
But it's a very shocking, ugly name ;
Go to your godfather, and refuse to wear it,
Or if you won't, be but my love, and swear it ;
And I'll leave home, and go live with you,
And be young Mistress Romeo Montague.
The name is not so bad—what's in a name ?
A Rose if Garlick call'd would smell the same.

The Friar's directions to Juliet are given in the course of a
song, of which the following is the opening verse :—

Here's a bottle of gin—do take it, dear,
Put it under your pillow, or somewhere near,
And when the old Nurse to her bed is gone,
First make yourself certain you're quite alone.
Then take this bottle—drink part of it off—
'Tis double distill'd, and may make you cough—
When presently through your veins will walk
A comical tremor—a wish to talk,
                  Oh, the bottle of gin !

When, in 1859, Andrew Halliday produced, at the Strand,
a " Romeo and Juliet Travestie, or the Cup of Cold Poison,"*

* This was the piece in which Miss C. Saunders played Romeo, and
Miss Marie Wilton Juliet.   Maria Simpson was the Mercutio, J. Clarke
the Nurse, Rogers the Apothecary, Bland the Friar, and Miss Bufton
the Paris.

he did better, I need hardly say, than his predecessor. His treatment of the balcony scene, for instance, was at least not vulgar :—

Romeo *appears on the top of the wall and comes down ladder.*

Rom. He jests at scars, who never wore a patch,
Or mounted garden wall and got a scratch
From row of broken bottles.

(Juliet appears on balcony.)

Jul.   Ha ! 'tis he !
Rom. Juliet !
Jul.   Romeo ! ah, yes ! 'tis he !
Rom. Oh, say that name again !
Jul.   Oh, me ! oh !
Romeo, wherefore art thou Romeo?
Rom. Well, 'pon my soul, my love, my sweet, my dear,
I haven't got the most remote idea ;
My father perhaps——
Jul.   Deny him.
Rom.   Then my mother.
She does not know I'm out.
Jul.   Oh, what a bother !
Rom. What is a bother, sweet ?
Jul.   That you,
My Romeo, should be a Montague,
And I a Capulet—and yet what's in a name?
Were you called Jones, I'd love you all the same ;
You'd be no worse : mark this, I do entreat—
The Serpentine by other name would smell as sweet.
Rom. Would I were some one else——
Jul.   But fate assigns
A bitter lot, and rules the hardest lines.
Rom. (*sneezes, and as if with cold in his head*) It's getting chilly,
         dear, but hear me swear—
By the boon, green cheese of heaven—look there,
Shining as brightly as a silver spoon.
Jul. (*sneezing, and with a cold*) Swear not by the boon—the
         inconstant boon,
Who changes oft, and twelve times in a year
Hooks it like a tenant in arrear.

> *Rom.* What shall I swear by, then, to gain a seat
> In your affections?
>   *Jul.*   Oh, do not swear, my sweet,
> At all. A good rule we now commence with :
> We take our seats—the oaths we do dispense with.

For the rest, the burlesque followed many lines of the original closely enough,[*] save that, at the end, Romeo, Juliet, Mercutio, Tybalt, and Paris, were all revived, much to the indignation of Shakespeare, a statue of whom appeared, with finger held up in a menacing manner.

The piece was well stocked with puns ; as, for example :—

> Who doubts Mercutio's courage him mistakes :
> He hates a *broil*, but he will fight for *stakes*.

And again :—

> By reason of this *bunion* on my toe,
> This *pilgrim's progress* has been very slow.

After "Romeo and Juliet," the first of Shakespeare's plays to be burlesqued was "Richard III.," of which Charles Selby, the comedian, and Stirling Coyne, the well-known man of letters, each perpetrated a travestie in 1844. Selby's piece [†] was founded on the Colley Cibber adaptation, and introduced Henry VI., who, at the end, was represented as coming to life again and quietly assuming the crown which Richmond was about to take. Richard also is resuscitated, after a fashion very popular in burlesques of Shakespeare. Of literary merit Selby's work had little.

---

[*] Juliet was sent to sleep, not by a potion, but by a perusal of the latest work of Mr. Tupper.

[†] Produced at the Strand, with Hammond as Richard, Wigan as Henry VI., Romer as Tressel, Miss L. Lyons as Lady Anne, and so on.

Take, for example, his arrangement of the scene in
which Richard woos the Lady Anne :—

Lady A. Well, I never ! You ugly, naughty man,
Why do you thus torment the wretched Anne ?
Richard. Torment ! sweet saint, recall that killing word,
And substitute adore.
Lady A.　　　　　Indeed ! I've heard
Old gossips say he's but a silly calf,
Who fondly thinks to catch old birds with chaff.
Look on that pattern of thy gentle love ! (*pointing off* R.)
Richard. I do, and weep, my pretty turtle-dove.
And yet methinks I can excuse myself.
Lady A. Wholesale butcher !
Richard.　　　　　Thou dost abuse thyself !
(*Rapidly, with great passion*) Thou art the cause of all my peccadilloes—
Thy beauty (like Battersean billows,
Which market barges smash to shivereens,
And cheat the town of *sparrow grass* and greens),
Thy fatal beauty, for whose dear sake,
Of all the world I'd Epping sausage make !
Or kill myself—(if thou shouldst wish me die)
One hour on that soft breast to lie.
Lady A. Nonsense ! I don't believe you ! get along !
　　　　　(*hitting him playfully with her fan.*)
Richard. I know, dear love, I've done thee grievous wrong !
But though by me thy husband's death was done,
'Twas but to help thee to a better one.
Lady A. His better does not wear a head.
Richard. He lives who loves thee better.
Lady A.　　　　　Whom ?
Richard.　　　　　Nay, guess.
Lady A. I can't.   I'm a dunce at riddle-me-ree.
Some lunatic, of course ?
Richard.　　　　Made so by thee ! (*kneels*)
Turn thy bright eyes on *this* devoted head—
Lady A. Would they were *baganets*, to stick thee dead ! (*crosses* R.)
Richard. I would they were—that I at once might hop the twig !
For now, with cruel scorn, they at me dig,

And *homœopathically* mill me.
If thou art determined, sweet, to kill me,
This " Trifle from Sheffield " in my buzzum stick,
And let the daylight through your loving Dick.

              (*kneels and gives her his sword.*)

Twenty-four years later, Mr. Burnand took up this subject. His work was called "The Rise and Fall of Richard III.," and was performed at the Royalty. His treatment of the wooing scene may well be contrasted with that of Selby. For instance :—

Richard. I see that you a passion for me foster——

Anne.   Passion for you ! High, mighty, double Glo'ster.

Rich.   Oh, call me double Glo'ster, if you please,
          As long as I, in your eyes, am the cheese.

Anne.   A cheese ! Why, then I cut you. (*going*)

Rich.   I've the daring
          To ask you to consider this cheese *paring*.

Anne.   You are hump-backed.

Rich.   Oh, hump-bug !

Anne.   And knock'd knee'd.

Rich.   A friend in-knee'd, ma'am, is a friend indeed.

In puns, and good puns too, this piece is particularly prolific. Thus, Richard's mother says of him that

     He as a child took early to the bottle,
     As all our family did, and my relations—
     I can look back on many *ginny*-rations.
     Yes, and my ancestors—they never fought
     With greater spirit than at A-*gin*-court.

Buckingham says to Richard—

     Don't be Protector, Richard—be Dick-tator.

Richmond says of him :—

     There Richard lays ;

whereupon Richard replies :—

         To order sir, I rise ;
     Who says " he *lays* " grammatically *lies*.

Of Richmond, the Duchess of York observes :—

> His hair is cut so short where once it flowed.
> *Richard.* 'Tis a French crop, like grass—'tis *à la mowed.*

Richmond, by the way, is supposed to be fresh from France, and talks broken English. The Duchess aforesaid asks him :—

> How are you, Richmond ? well ? or *Richmond 'ill ?*

Buckingham says to Anne :—

> I'll introduce, allow me, to your Grace,
> The Lord Mayor, the Recorder, and Jem *Mace.*
> *Anne.* Their robes are beautiful. Oh, nicey, nicey !
> Especially the *Mace*—he does look *spicey !*

But perhaps the best pun in the piece is that which is made apropos of the fact that Catesby and Tyrell have fallen over the coal-scuttle on the stairs and hurt themselves :—

> *Richard.* My friends are hurt, so you'll excuse them grinning.
> *Elizabeth.* Excuse ! oh, they're more shinned against than shinning !

Talfourd's " Macbeth, somewhat removed from the Text of Shakespeare," was first performed in 1847 at Henley-on-Thames during the regatta; next, at the Strand, in 1848; afterwards at the Qlympic, in 1853. At the last-named theatre it had the advantage of the aid of Robson in the title-part, of G. Cooke as Duncan, and of Mrs. A. Phillips as Lady Macbeth. It paraphrases the original fairly well until near the close, when, after Macduff has slain Macbeth, Duncan reappears (like Henry VI. in Selby's piece) and takes the crown from Malcolm. Similarly, Macbeth, his wife, and Banquo turn up again, and announce their willingness to die nightly.

In the first act Lady Macbeth comes in reading her husband's letter, as follows :—

> We met, 'twas on a heath, and on that day
> When victory had flushed us ; really they
> Both turned our blood to *curds* and stopped our *way* ;
> Sally, report has said, and I have got
> A gothic notion, they know what is what ;
> They called me, dear, all manner of rum things :
> While Cawdor's title in my noddle rings,
> Would you believe it ? but a flunkey brings
> The news of Cawdor's death ; I have to thank
> That queer old file for giving me his rank.
> One hailed me King—I pause to wipe my eye,
> For it's affecting.—Sally, dear, good-bye !
> Ever affectionately yours, till death
> Pops on his extinguisher,
>
> SAMUEL MACBETH.

Lady Macbeth comments on this :—

> Of all rum goes, this is about the rummest !
> Cawdor thou art, and shalt be—what thou'rt promised.
> Yet will thy scruples my intentions clog ;
> To go at once the unadulterate hog
> Is not thy nature.   Thou'rt the style of buck
> That has the *will* to sin, but not the *pluck*.

When Macbeth enters, she cries :—

> Welcome, great Glamis !—welcome, worthy Cawdor !
> Nay greater ! (*they embrace*).
>   *Macb.*   Ducky ! Duncan comes to-night,
> To stay and sup with us.
>   *Lady M.*   Yes, that's all right.
> (*Significantly*) When *goes* he hence ?
>   *Macb.*   To-morrow he'll endeavour.
>   *Lady M.* (*mysteriously*) Not if I knows it, Sammy—
> trust me, never !
>   *Macb.* What mean you?
>   *Lady M.*   Why, at such things you a muff are !

Macb. You wouldn't have me spifflicate the buffer?
I must think more of this.
    Lady M. Look (so thou wilt less
Suspicion rouse) particularly guiltless—
Leave all the rest to me.
    Macb. The *rest*? Don't fret at all;—
If I do this, no *rest* for me—you'll get it all.

Then they sing a duet, to the tune of " There's a good
time coming " :—

    Lady M. There's a good chance coming, Sam—
           A good chance coming !
           If the King comes here to-day,
           We're not such flats as throw away
           The good chance coming !
  Macb. But, my love, it's very wrong—
           Nothing could be wronger
           Than such a thing——
  Lady M. Well, hold your tongue,
    And wait a little longer !

[handwritten margin note: Robt. B. Brough b: 10/04/1828 d: 26/66/186?]
[handwritten margin note: William B. b: 28/04/1826 d: 13/03/1870]
[handwritten note: the Brough brothers:— Robt. Barnabas Brough + William Brough.]

The first burlesque of " The Tempest " made its appear-
ance at the Adelphi in 1848. It was from the pen of the
Brothers Brough, and was entitled " The Enchanted Isle,
or Raising the Wind on the most Approved Principles."
" O." Smith was Prospero, with Miss Taylor as his daughter
Miranda ; Miss ·Woolgar being the Ferdinand, with Paul
Bedford for her father—the Ariel Mme. Celeste, and the
Caliban Munyard. Some years were destined to elapse
before the subject again attracted the burlesque writer ; and
the writer then was Mr. Burnand, who gave to his work the
name of " Ariel," submitting it to the public in 1883 at
the Gaiety. Miss Ellen Farren took the title-part, with
Mr. Henry Monkhouse as Prospero, Mr. Frank Wyatt
as Sebastian, Mr. Dallas as Alonso, and Miss Connie

[handwritten note: Celine Celeste— Elliot? b. 16/08/1815? d. 12/02/1882]
[handwritten note: F. C. Burnand (Francis Cowley Burnand)]

Gilchrist as Miranda. This "perversion" was in three acts, and was one of the productions which led the way to the New Burlesque.

To Talfourd belongs the distinction of being the first to burlesque "The Merchant of Venice." He called his work "Shylock, or the Merchant of Venice Preserved: an entirely New Reading of Shakespeare, from an edition hitherto undiscovered by modern authorities, and which it is hoped may be received as the stray leaves of a Jerusalem Hearty-Joke." This came out at the Olympic in 1853, and again Talfourd had Robson as the exponent of his principal character. Again, too, he followed his original with some care, burlesquing rather in detail than on broad lines. Take, for example, his "reading" of a portion of the trial scene. Shylock has been foiled by Portia, and wishes to leave the court :—

Shy. Give me my principal, and I'll away.
Por. Best *carry out* your *principle* and stay.
Nay, Shylock, though you choose forgive the debt,
You'd find the law had hold upon you yet.
Shy. I say, young man, your practice rather sharp is.
Grat. Not when he practises on the *Jews-harp-ies.*
Ant. Shylock, although your conduct in this case
In its whole tenor has been thorough base,
On one condition I won't press the charge,
And you're at liberty to go at large.
Shy. At large? I feel particularly small,
(*Aside*) But thank my stars that I can go at all.
(*Shylock is going, but is prevented by the officers of the Court*)
Ant. There are two points, though, that I must insist on :
You'll shave your face and look more like a Christian,
And take your daughter to your arms again.
Shy. Well, since you've got the upper hand, it's plain
I must knock under—and I will, I swear,
Receive my heiress and cut off my *hair !*

(*Jessica and Lorenzo come forward.*)
Jess. You pardon us, pa?
Shy.   Yes, howe'er distressing
To my paternal feelings, take my blessing.
Fathers, I think, will own my case a hard 'un,
She's done for pa, and now she asks her *par-don.*

Gratiano, in this version, is represented as a flunkey, in which character he makes love to Ncrissa :—

Blush not that I'm a footman, I conjures ;
·Let not my *plushes* be the cause of yours.
You to the eyes—but, though more difficulter,
I to the knees plush as the *knee plush ultra.*

Everywhere the puns are as clever as they are bright. Portia says to Nerissa :—

                    Mind, a maiden should
Of kisses to a bearded man be chary.
Nerissa. Such a salute, ma'am, must be *salute-hairy.*

Launcelot, again, says to Jessica :—

But smile again, and all will sunshine be,
Sweet Israelite, you *is real light* to me !   . .
Mock not my misery—I know full well
I'm a poor *serf* and *he's* a heavy *swell.*

Once more, Shylock says :—

My only heiress, folks will say in mock,
Fled like a *timid hair* from a *Shy-lock* ! . . .
Unfeeling child, who's left her sire to sigh,
Without a *tie* or *prop* or *prop-er-ty.*

We come now to the production, at the Lyceum in 1856, of William Brough's perversion of "The Winter's Tale,"— " Perdita, or the Royal Milkmaid." * This was fitted with a prologue in which Time sang an effective song, descriptive

* See pp. 39, 40.

of the author's aims and intentions, and winding up with this ingenuous verse :—

> This period to match, in each single snatch
>   Of music to be sung, I've tried of
> The oldest tunes to get, including that as yet
>   Unknown melody the old cow died of.
>   And that all might be
>   In antiquity
>   Alike, I for my puns cry quarter,
>   For I've chosen, good folks,
>   The most ancient jokes
>   For this worthy old dramatist's slaughter.

When Autolycus appears upon the scene, with his pedlar's box, he is made to excuse his "conveying" propensities in a ditty suggested by the then popular song called "Bobbing Around" :—

> The shopkeeper who gives short weight
>   Is robbing all round, all round, all round ;
> The grocers who adulterate,
>   Like me go robbing all round.
> The milkman in his lowly walk
>   Goes robbing all round, all round, all round ;
> When, 'stead of milk, he walks his chalk,
>   And so goes robbing around.
> The publican dilutes our beer,
>   A robbing all round, all round, all round ;
> With water, and still worse, I fear,
>   So he goes robbing all round.
> In all we eat, or drink, or buy,
>   There's robbing all round, all round, all round,
> And tradesmen with each other vie,
>   Who'll best do robbing all round.
> Who'll first at me, then, throw a stone
>   For robbing around, around, around ?
> My trade's as honest as their own,
>   Since all go robbing around.

Mr. Burnand has written two burlesques on "Antony and Cleopatra"—one brought out under that title at the Haymarket in 1866; the other produced at the Gaiety in 1873, under the name of "Our Own Antony and Cleopatra." A third travestie of the tragedy, called "Mdlle. Cleopatra," and written by Mr. W. Sapte, junior, was seen at the Avenue in the present year.

VII.

BURLESQUE OF MODERN DRAMA.

WE now pass to a department of burlesque writing larger in extent and greater in variety than any other—that in which the finger of ridicule has been pointed at poetic and melodramatic plays (other than those of Shakespeare). This department is far-reaching in the matter of time. It goes back, for subject, so far as Lee's high-sounding "Alexander the Great" (better known, perhaps, as "The Rival Queens"), which, first produced in 1678, was travestied by Dibdin, in "Alexander the Great in Little," a "grand tragi-comic operatic burlesque spectacle," originally seen at the Strand in 1837, with Hammond as Alexander and Mrs. Stirling as Roxana. Seven years later there was performed at the Surrey a burlesque, by Montagu Corri, of Lillo's famous tragedy "George Barnwell" (1730), here called "Georgy Barnwell"—a title which H. J. Byron altered to "George De Barnwell" when in 1862 he travestied the old play at the Adelphi.

Home's "Douglas," which was given to the public in 1756, appears to have escaped stage satire until 1837, when it was taken in hand by William Leman Rede. The Adelphi was the scene of the production, and the performers included " O." Smith as Glenalvon, J. Reeve as Norval, and Mrs. Stirling as Lady Randolph. The piece does not supply very exhilarating reading. The ultra-familiar soliloquy, " My name is Norval," is here put into lyric form, and comes out as follows :—

My name is Norval, sir ; upon the Grampian Hills
My father feeds his flocks, beside the streams and rills.
He often said to me, "Don't roam about at nights."
But I had heard of sprees, of larks, and rows, and fights.
    Tol de rol lol tol lol, tol de rol lol lol lay.
    Tol de rol lol tol lol—list to what I say.

The moon rose up one night, as moons will often do,
And there came from left and right a ragged ruffian crew ;
They broke into our house, they swigged our beer and ale,
They stole our flocks and herds, and caught our pig by the tail.
    Tol, lol, etc.

The shepherds fled, the curs ! but I was not to be chizzled,
So with a chosen few after the fellows we mizzled ;
We fought and larrupped 'em all ! indeed, it isn't a flam,
I stole the togs of the chief, and, blow me, here I am !
    Tol lol, etc.

We have already seen that, in his " Quadrupeds of Quedlinburgh," Colman junior extracted some fun out of scenes in " The Stranger," " Pizarro," and " Timour the Tartar." The first of these plays was made the subject of more elaborate satire in 1868, when Mr. Robert Reece wrote for the New Queen's Theatre his burlesque called " The Stranger, Stranger than Ever ! " This, with Miss Santley as Peter, Mr. Lionel Brough as the Stranger, and Miss Henrietta Hodson as Mrs. Haller, had many points of attraction. In this *reductio ad absuraum* the lady's chief complaint is that her husband first neglected her and then deserted her, taking away the children. Moreover, " he

taught the infants all the comic songs," and so, "instead
of gloating over Peter Parley, the boy declared himself as
Champagne Charley." In despair the deserted one set to
work and took in washing :—

> You'll ask, " why washing ? "—give your fancy scope :'
> In that profession while there's life there's *soap* !
> Was I to live ?—of course came this suggestion !
> " *Tub* be or not *tub* be ? " that *was* the question.
> So with a will I turned me to my work,
> Carried a *blue bag* like a lawyer's clerk ;
> Yet still I grieved—the trade's of woe prolific,
> I couldn't sleep, for all this *soap-horrific* ;
> Hard was my lot, for I could plainly see
> My source of living must end *sud*-denly ;
> And in her downward course, say, what could stop her
> Whose sole subsistence was a single *copper* ?

As usual with Mr. Reece, the puns are excellent. Tobias
says of the stranger that

> Each evening you may see him sitting so,
> Under that *linden when the sun was low* ;
> On close inspection, too, you'll also see
> His noble *eye, sir, rolling rapidly.*

Then the Stranger says to Peter :—

> Mrs. Haller's gifts you showed,
> As hint that *I* should help you *Haller-mode.*

To the Countess he remarks :—

> Madam, this river-water's *eau-de-riverous* !

And of his children he says :—

> They're fighting through their alphabet. Oh, lor !
> I quit them in their *A-B-C-nian war* !

Of his wife :—

> When first I married thee (then somewhat shady),
> Oh, Adelaide ! I thought I *had a lady !*

But, in truth, there is no end to these *jeux-de-mots.*

"Pizarro," which nowadays has quite gone out of the
theatrical repertory, was dealt with from the comic point
of view by Leicester Buckingham, whose "Pizarro, or the
Leotard of Peru," was seen at the Strand in 1862, with
Johnny Clarke as the hero, and Miss Swanborough, Miss
Charlotte Saunders, Miss Bufton, Miss Fanny Josephs, Miss
Fanny Hughes, and Rogers, in other parts. Of the "literature" of this piece the following is a very fair example : it
is supposed to be spoken by Rolla :—

> Tho' to use vulgar phrases I've no wish,
> I may say, here's a pretty kettle of fish !
> But then the world's all fishy—poets fail
> To prove that life is not a tearful *wale !*
> Though fancy's prospect oft in-*witing* glows,
> Experience tends to *mull-it,* goodness knows ;
> Grave moralists aver that from our birth
> We are all *herring* mortals here on earth.
> Dancers stick to their *eels,* and live well by 'em ;
> And most folk can appreciate " *carpe* diem."
> Some statesmen—theirs is no uncommon case—
> Will give their *soul* in barter for a *place,*
> And call, to mend a diplomatic mess,
> The conger-eel's fond mate—a *conger-ess.*
> Nay, folks strive even in a college cloister
> Over a rival's head to get a *hoister.*

"The Wood-Demon," by "Monk" Lewis, played originally in 1811, suggested to Albert Smith and Charles Kenny
a travestie, of the same name, which they brought out at
the Lyceum in 1847. "Timour the Tartar," another of
Lewis's dramas, received equally satiric treatment at the

hands of John Oxenford and Shirley Brooks, whose work
made its appearance at the Olympic in 1860. In the
last-named year Messrs. Francis Talfourd and H. J. Byron
founded on Pocock's " Miller and his Men " (1813) a
" mealy-drama," similarly entitled, which was played at the
Strand.

Jerrold's " Black-ey'd Susan," first performed in 1822,
waited till 1866 for the travestie by Mr. Burnand, to which
I have already adverted. This " Latest Edition of Black-
eyed Susan, or the Little Bill that was Taken Up,"* was
made specially gay by a wealth of song and dance ; but
it had other merits. Here, for instance, is an amusing
soliloquy by Dame Hatley :—

> It's very hard, and nothing can be harder
> Than for three weeks to have an empty larder ;
> I'm in the leaf of life that's sere and yellar,
> Requiring little luxuries in the cellar.
> There are no *cellars* such as I requires,
> But there soon will be when there are some *buyers.*
> Destiny's finger to the " work "-us points,
> A stern voice whispers, " Time is out of joints."
> I used to live by washing ; now, no doubt,
> As I can't get it, I must live without.
> The turncock turned the water off—dear me !
> I showed no quarter—and no more did he.
> Thus, with the richer laundress I can't cope,
> Being at present badly off for soap.
> My son, the comfort of the aged widdy,
> Is still a sailor, not yet made a middy,
> But sailing far away ; it may be *my* son
> Is setting somewhere out by the horizon.
> He's cruising in the offing, far away,
> Would he were here, I very *offing* say.

---

* See p. 41.

Here also is the Wolsey-ish speech made by Captain Crosstree, after he has revealed himself as "alive and kicking," at the close :—

> Farewell, a long farewell to all imbibing !
> This is the state of man as I'm describing :
> To-day he takes a glass because he's dry,
> To-morrow, one to wet the other eye ;
> The third day takes one extra, just to shed
> A tear—he feels it gets into his head :
> The fourth day takes two extra ones, and feels
> 'Stead of his head it's got into his heels ;
> And in the morning, with perhaps two suits on,
> He finds himself—in bed, but with two boots on ;
> Then after that he's nowhere ; and that's how
> He falls as I did—which I won't do now.*

Five years after the production of Jerrold's play, the London stage was surfeited for a time with adaptations from the French, all bearing upon the evils of the gaming-table. These bore such titles as "The Gambler's Fate," "Thirty Years of a Gambler's Life," and so on, and were brought out at Drury Lane, the Surrey (by Elliston), and the Adelphi (by Terry and Yates). They did not last, however; and "The Elbow-Shakers, or Thirty Years of a Rattler's Life," in which Fox Cooper made fun of them, was scarcely needed to effect their overthrow. Reeve and Yates were the two Elbow-Shakers, but the piece had little intrinsic value.

In 1867, at the Haymarket, Mr. Gilbert Arthur a'Beckett brought out a travestie of Planché's "Brigand" (1829),

---

* Another burlesque on the same subject, called "Ups and Downs of Deal, and Black-eyed Susan," was seen at the Marylebone in 1867, with Miss Augusta Thomson as Captain Crosstree.

under the title of "The Brigand, or New Lines to an Old Ban-Ditty." In this, Massaroni, the hero, was represented by Compton as a poltroon, objecting very much to the dictation of Marie Grazia as portrayed by Ione Burke. Young Mr. Kendal also had a part in this production. Nor had we yet done with the old school of melodrama. Yet another specimen thereof was destined to come under the lash of the parodist—namely, the piece called "My Poll and my Partner Joe," written by J. T. Haines, first seen at the Surrey in 1838, and interpreted by T. P. Cooke as Harry Halyard, R. Honner as Joe Tiller, and Miss Honner as Poll (Mary Maybud). The "happy thought" of burlesquing this typical piece came to Mr. Burnand, who, in his travestie named after the original, made, at the St. James's in 1871, a success second only to that of "Black-ey'd Susan." It was in this burlesque that Mrs. John Wood (as Mary) had so notable a triumph with her song, "His Heart was true to Poll," which she still sings sometimes in public. Miss Emma Chambers was the Harry in this piece, and Mr. Lionel Brough the Black Brandon, with Harry Cox, Gaston Murray, and Miss Sallie Turner in other parts.

Now comes the turn of the poetic drama, as represented in and by the works of Lord Byron, Sergeant Talfourd, the first Lord Lytton, and Mr. W. S. Gilbert. The first of Lord Byron's plays to be burlesqued was "Manfred," which fell to the lot of Gilbert Abbott a'Beckett in 1834. In the "burlesque ballet opera," called "Man-Fred," which thus issued from A'Beckett's pen, Man-Fred figured as a master-sweep, very much perturbed and disturbed by the Act in reference to chimney-sweeping which had just been passed, and which, he plaintively declares, has killed the trade :—

> That horrible new act has marr'd his pleasure ;
> It really was a very *sweeping* measure.

His lady-love, Ann Starkie, is equally unfortunate in her business—that of apple-seller. As she remarks :—

> " The trade is at a stand," the people whine :
> If it be at a *stand*, 'tis not at mine.
> In vain down Fleet Street with my wares I go ;
> Though Fleet they call the street, its trade is slow.

In the course of the piece Ann appears disguised as Mme. Grisi, and some badinage is directed at the " stars " of the Italian Opera.

A'Beckett further undertook, along with Mark Lemon, a skit upon another of the Byronic dramas—" Sardanapalus " —which they reproduced as " Sardanapalus, or the ' Fast ' King of Assyria." The Adelphi was the theatre of operations; 1853 was the year; and while Miss Woolgar was Sardanapalus, Paul Bedford was Arbaces, Keeley was Salymenia (mother of the Queen), Miss Maskell was Beleses, and Miss Mary Keeley was Altada. Arbaces is here shown as impervious to the charm of melody :—

> Such music to my ears is a mere hum ;
> Of minims let me have the minimum.

Salymenia says to the King's favourite :—

> Your conduct, madam, 's not at all correct :
> If you're a Myrrha, why don't you reflect ?

Of such are the quips and the quiddities with which the piece abounds.

In 1858 came, from the workshop of H. J. Byron, the

first travestie of his "noble kinsman's" play, "Mazeppa."
This, produced at the Olympic, had Robson for its hero,
with other parts in the hands of Horace Wigan, Mr. Lewis
Ball, Miss Wyndham, Miss Bromley, and Mrs. W. S. Emden.
Of its punning dialogue, which throughout is in the genuine
H. J. Byronic manner, the following is a fair example.
Olinska is conversing with her father, the Castellan :—

    Oli. You hate romance,—are one of its deriders.
(*Very romantically*) Give me a summer-house with *lots* of spiders,
A poet-husband too, with rolling eyes,
In a fine phrenzy——
    Cas.   Poets I despise !
And in his phrenzy that you mention, daughter,
His *friends see* often nought but gin and water.
    Oli. In our sweet bower of bliss what could we fear ?
    Cas. Why, Quarter Day, which comes four times a year !
And although landlords show each quarter day,
They show *no quarter* when you do not pay,
Your poet-spouse grows thin, and daily racks his
Poor brains to pay the butcher or the taxes.
    Oli. A verse would pay the tax-man all we owed.
    Cas (*aside*). I think he'd be *averse*, though, to that mode.
To see with *my* eyes, if I could but make her !
    Oli. With a few *flowery* lines we'd pay the baker.
(*With enthusiasm*) Tradesmen with *gentle* feelings we'd pay so, sir ;
A comic song would satisfy the *grosser.*
A poet never yet was a great eater,
We'd pay the butcher with a little *meat-a.*

The subject of "Mazeppa" was afterwards treated by Mr.
Burnand in a burlesque brought out at the Gaiety in 1885.

    Of Sergeant Talfourd's dramatic works the only one,
apparently, that has been travestied is "Ion," which had to
submit to the ridicule of Fox Cooper in 1836. In that year
Cooper's perversion was played both at the Garrick Theatre
and at the Queen's, in the first case with Conquest as the

hero, in the latter with a lady in the *rôle*—an arrangement quite defensible, inasmuch as, in the original play, the name-part had been played (at the Haymarket) by Ellen Tree.

The pseudo-Elizabethanisms of Sheridan Knowles naturally attracted the attention of the comic playwrights. The opportunities were, indeed, only too tempting; and so I have to record the production of burlesques based upon five plays—" The Wife," " Virginius,". " Alfred the Great," "William Tell," and "The Hunchback." The first named has for its full title " The Wife: a Tale of Mantua." The "burlesque burletta," by Joseph Graves (Strand, 1837), is called " The Wife: a Tale of a Mantua Maker.' Mariana (first played by Ellen Tree) here becomes Mary Ann Phipps, the said mantua-maker; Floribel is Flora, a servant-of-all-work. Leonardo and Ferrardo Gonzaga figure as Marmaduke Jago, landlord of the Green Man, and Zachariah Jago, usurping that dignity; Count Florio is Floor'em (a police-sergeant), Julian St. Pierre is Jack Peters—and so forth. The travestie is fairly close, but the wit and humour are not of brilliant quality. Even less to be commended is " Virginius the Rum 'Un," perpetrated by William Rogers, the comedian, and performed at Sadler's Wells in the same year as Graves's effort. This is but a tedious assault upon " Virginius." The scene is laid in Islington, and Virginius is a butcher. Appius Claudius, here called Sappyis, is a sergeant of police. Dentatus is " Tentaties"; Icilius is " Isilyus." Claudius claims Virginia as his apprentice, and Virginius stabs her with a skewer; the instrument, however, sticks only in her stay-bone, and so no harm is done.

"Virginius" had very much more justice done to it when Leicester Buckingham made it the basis of a burlesque at the St. James's in 1859. Then Charles Young was the Virginius, Mrs. Frank Matthews the Virginia, and Miss Lydia Thompson a " Mysterious Stranger," introduced, apparently, only for the sake of a *pas seul*. In this piece the puns are very plentiful, if not always good. Thus, Virginia says :—

> Oh, deary me ! each day I'm growing thinner :
> Nurse says, because I never eat my dinner ;
> But that's not it ;—in my heart there's a pain
> Which makes me sigh, and sigh, and all in vain !
> I've lost the plump round waist I used to prize,
> And grow thin, spite of my long-*wasted* sighs.
> I love—oh ! such a nice young man !—but, oh !
> Does he love me ?—that's what I want to know.
> When we met at a party, I could see
> That he was just the party to suit me ;
> And to the words I spoke, on his arm leaning,
> Love lent a sigh to give a *si-lent* meaning.
> But he said nothing soft—that's what I cry for ;
> I sigh for one whose heart I can't dec*i-pher*.

Virginius, like so many other burlesque characters, delivers himself of a reminiscence of " To be or not to be," and at the close it is found that Virginius has not really killed his daughter, because she "pads."

"Alfred the Great," one of Knowles' historical plays, suggested portions of the burlesque called " Alfred the Great, or the Minstrel King," which Robert B. Brough wrote for the Olympic in 1859. In this, Robson was the King, Miss Herbert his aide-de-camp, and F. Vining his commander-in-chief, with other parts by Horace Wigan and Miss Hughes. Knowles's " William Tell " (1825), or the story embodied in it has been the basis of half a dozen travesties. First came Mr. Burnand's "William Tell," at Drury Lane, in 1856; next, Leicester Buckingham's, at the Strand, in 1857; next, Talfourd's "Tell! and the Strike of the Cantons, or the Pair, the Meddler, and the Apple!" at the Strand, in 1859-60; next, again, Byron's "William Tell with a Vengeance! or the Pet, the Parrot, and the Pippin," at the Strand, in 1867; a few days ater, A. J. O'Neill's "William Tell," at Sadler's Wells; and, lastly—so far—Mr. Reece's "William Tell told Over Again," at the Gaiety, in 1876. "The Hunchback" has been "guyed" less often than might have been expected, considering its popularity. Mr. Burnand brought out at the Olympic, in 1879, "The Hunchback Back Again," and this comic version of the hackneyed old play is not likely to be superseded.

The first Lord Lytton's verse-plays—bristling as they do with fustian and bombast—have naturally been frequently travestied. Note the number of occasions on which "The Lady of Lyons" has fallen a prey to the irreverent. Altogether there have been six notable burlesques of this drama. H. J. Byron wrote two, the first of which—"The Latest Edition of the Lady of Lyons"—was produced at the Strand in 1858. This, in the following year, was freshened up and re-presented to the public as "The Very Latest Edition" of the popular drama.

In 1878, at the Gaiety, came Mr. Herman Merivale's "vaudeville," "The Lady of Lyons Married and Settled," which is not only quite the best of the travesties on this topic, but one of the cleverest ever written. It sparkles with good things from beginning to end. Claude, it seems, has "taken to philosophy, and says we are all descended from monkeys."

It is not surprising, therefore, to find him singing a long song in praise of the Darwinian theory :—

Power to thine elbow, thou newest of sciences,
　All the old landmarks are ripe for decay ;
Wars are but shadows, and so are alliances,
　Darwin the Great is the man of the day.

All other 'ologies want an apology ;
　Bread's a mistake—Science offers a stone ;
Nothing is true but Anthropobiology—
　Darwin the Great understands it alone.

Mighty the great evolutionist teacher is,
　Licking Morphology clean into shape ;
Lord ! what an ape the professor or preacher is,
　Ever to doubt his descent from an ape.

Man's an Anthropoid—he cannot help that, you know—
　First evoluted from Pongos of old ;
He's but a branch of the *cat-arrhine* cat, you know—
　Monkey, I mean—that's an ape with a cold.

　　　.　　　.　　　.　　　.　　　.

Fast dying out are man's later Appearances,
　Cataclysmitic Geologies gone ;
Now of Creation completed the clearance is,
　Darwin alone you must anchor upon.

Primitive Life-Organisms were chemical,
　" Busting " spontaneous under the sea ;
Purely subaqeous, panaquademical,
　Was the original Crystal of Me.

I'm the Apostle of mighty Darwinity,
　Stands for Divinity—sound much the same—
Apo-theistico-Pan-Asininity
　Only can doubt whence the lot of us came.

Down on your knees, Superstition and Flunkeydom !
　Won't you accept such plain doctrines instead ?
What is so simple as primitive Monkeydom,
　Born in the sea with a cold in its head ?

This has some claim to rank with the ditties on the same subject by Lord Neaves and Mortimer Collins. But Claude has also gone in for something less innocent than Darwinianism. He is flirting with Babette, a pretty laundry-maid, the beloved of Gaspar. Of her, Gaspar sings as follows, in a clever parody of " Sally in our Alley " :—

> To catch a lover on the hip,
>   There's none like fair Babet-te !
> You'd love to kiss her rosy lip,
>   But, ah ! she'll never let 'ee !
> Yet shall she wash my Sunday suit,
>   Tho' she my suit refuses,
> For, oh ! she washes far the best
>   Of all the blanchissooses !
>
> For washing-day all round the year,
>   She ever sticks to one day ;
> She takes my linen Friday night,
>   And brings it back o' Monday !
> When I bestow the lordly franc,
>   'Tis sweet to hear her " Thankee "—
> She mends my hooks and darns my eyes,
>   And marks my pocky-hanky !
>
> She calls the wandering button home,
>   However hard I cuss it ;
> She's good at collar and at cuff,
>   And truly great at gusset !
> To catch a lover on the hip,
>   There's none like fair Babet-te !
> You'd love to kiss her rosy lip,
>   But, ah ! she'll never let 'ee !

In the course of the piece there is a good deal of direct parody of Lytton's style, both in prose and verse. For example, Claude says at one point to Babette :—

Come with me to my mother's lonely cot ! I have preserved it ever in memory of mine early youth ; and, believe me, that the prize of virtue never, beneath my father's honest roof, even villains dared to mar! Now, maiden, now, I think thou wilt believe me! Wilt come?

Babette. I wilt!

Again :—

In the sweet suburb of Richemont or Tedainton, on the banks of the broad Garonne, one of those expensive spots where, during the summer months, the river is at the bottom of the lawn—during the winter, the lawn at the bottom of the river—but where it is damp-pleasant all the year round ; there will we babble to the murmuring stream, and the babbling stream shall murmur back to us, and softly whisper——

Dowager Morier (coming down). Hold on !*

After Mr. Merivale's piece came one on the same subject by Mr. W. Younge (1879); another by Mr. Clifton (Lyne), played in the country in 1882 ; and yet another, by Mr. Reece (also played in the country) in 1884. This last was entitled " The Lady of Lyons Married and Claude Unsettled."

Ten years after the first burlesque of " The Lady of Lyons " appeared the first burlesque of Lord Lytton's " Rightful Heir." This was " The Frightful Hair " of Mr. Burnand, seen at the Haymarket in 1868-9. In 1868 also, publicity was given to " The Right-Fall Heir " of Mr. H. T. Arden.

In the autumn of 1873 Mr. Irving revived at the Lyceum Lord Lytton's " Richelieu," and the play was speedily followed at the Olympic by the " Richelieu Redressed " of Mr. Reece. This is remarkable, to begin with, as being written throughout in blank verse—an agreeable

---

* Mr. Merivale was fortunate in the cast of his production (played at the Gaiety in 1878). Mr. Edward Terry was the Claude, Miss Farren the Pauline, Mr. Royce the " Beauseong," Mrs. Leigh the Dowager Morier, and Miss Amalia the Babette, other parts being taken by Messrs. Elton, Maclean, Squire, and Fawcett.

departure from the time-honoured couplet. The general travestie is close, and there is a certain amount of direct parody, as where Richelieu is made to say that

> In the great Lexicon of Politics
> There's no such word as Truth !

In the "curse of Rome" scene, Richelieu draws around himself "the awful circle of the Daily Press!" Fun, too, is made of the well-known exit of Baradas at the words "All in despite of my lord Cardinal," and also of the various ways in which actors are wont to pronounce the simple word "Julie." The piece has a strong political flavour throughout, in compliment, no doubt, to the general election, which was then in prospect. Richelieu thus soliloquises :—

> A general election ! At the word
> Upspring a thousand hopes—ten thousand fears !
> From the great Limbo of past sessions rise
> The ghost of certain Legislative Acts
> To taunt me with my shifting policy :
> Amidst them, gaunt and frowning—Income-tax
> Broods o'er my heart—I cannot take it off!
> While lesser demons, labelled—Sugar, Tea,
> Malt, Hops, and kindred duties—hover round
> And gibber, " Where's your popularity ? "
> For this reward I have to bear the brunt
> Of deputations—tedious committees,
> The dull assaults of country members, and
> Whitebait as large as herrings. Ah, the fish
> At ministerial banquets should be *Plaice* !

Of Richelieu's genius for suspicion the Duke of Orleans and his party thus discourse :—

> *Duke.* Breathe not the words "'Tis wet." He'll twist that phrase
> Into reflections on th' existing *reign,*

W. L.—V.

Or with some public measure discontent
Because you chanced to say, " It isn't *fair* ! "
  Baradas. There's truth, sir, in your jest ; 'tis hard to say
What is a safe discussion nowadays !
  La Foix. Even the King falls under his distrust !
  Malesherbes. He treats him like a child in leading-strings !
  Duke. Ay ! at the royal breakfast Richelieu stands,
And cracks each egg—to see no treason's hatched.
  All (laughing). Well said !
  Duke.   His caution o'er the dinner broods,
And in each *pâté* sees a dangerous *spy.*
  Baradas. Escorts the King to bed, and, lest his charge
Should dream of *marriage*, secretly removes
The *Royal matches*, as suggestive !

It was characteristic of Mr. W. S. Gilbert that he should himself set the example of burlesquing his own work. I have already made reference to "The Happy Land," the travestie of his "Wicked World," which he and Mr. Gilbert Arthur a'Beckett prepared for the Court Theatre in 1873. It was in this piece that the personal appearance of three prominent living statesmen was closely imitated by certain of the performers, with the result of bringing down upon the culprits the veto of His High-and-Mightiness the Lord Chamberlain. In 1876 two of Mr. Gilbert's plays were burlesqued—"Broken Hearts" and "Dan'l Druce"; the former under the name of "Cracked Heads," the latter under that of "Dan'l Tra-Duced"; both being brought out at the same theatre—the Strand, and both being the work of the same author—Mr. Arthur Clements, who, however, had in "Cracked Heads" the assistance of Mr. Frederick Hay. "Dan'l Druce" was not a particularly good subject; but "Broken Heads," with its occasionally overstrained sentiment, was fairly open to polite ridicule. In the original, the Lady Vavir feigns love for a sun-dial, while the Lady Hilda expends much sentiment upon a streamlet. In "Cracked Heads" the Lady Vapid bestows her affections upon a clock, and the Lady Tilda hers upon a pump. Says the latter to the former :—

> Why do you love the clock, good sister ? tell.
> *Vapid.* The earth goes round ; the moon, with silvery smile ;
> The p'lice cerulean who the cooks beguile;
> The turncock, too, precursor of the spring ;
> The German band, and all that sort of thing.
> Most things go round, in fact ; and who shall mock ?
> The clock goes round : that's why I love the clock.

In this genial little piece, presented at the Strand in 1876, Mr. Edward Terry was the monster, here called Monsta ; Miss Lottie Venne and Miss Angelina Claude were the ladies Tilda and Vapid, and Mr. Harry Cox was the Prince Florian, here called Dorian. It will be remembered, by the way, that it has been the fate of one of Mr. Gilbert's comic operas to be parodied—surely a case of gilding refined gold ! The opera was " Ruddigore," which was chaffed, more or less effectively, in the little *pièce d'occasion* called " Ruddy George, or Robin Redbreast," brought out at Toole's Theatre in 1887.

The melodrama of the last half-century has received due attention at the hands of the stage satirists. Buckstone's " Green Bushes," for example, had its comic counterpart in H. J. Byron's "Grin Bushes," performed at the Strand in 1864. It was Byron, too, who burlesqued Boucicault's " Colleen Bawn," under the title of " Little Eily O'Connor " (Drury Lane, 1861). The story of Rip Van Winkle, made so popular in England by Mr. Jefferson, has been handled in the spirit of travestie both by Mr. Reece (at the Folly in

1876) and by Mr. H. Savile Clarke (in 1880). "The Lights o' London" suggested "The De-lights of London" (1882), which we owed to the co-operation of Messrs. Mackay, Lennard, and Gordon. After "The Silver King" came "Silver Guilt," a clever piece by Mr. Warham St. Leger, in which, at the Strand in 1883, Miss Laura Linden imitated Miss Eastlake to admiration. In like manner, after "Claudian" came the diverting "Paw Claw-dian" of Mr. Burnand, which, at Toole's in 1884, gave Miss Marie Linden the opportunity of emulating (as Almi-i-da) her sister's success. In this piece Mr. Toole, as Claudian, and E. D. Ward, as Coal-Holey Clement, were particularly amusing. "Chatterton," another of Mr. Wilson Barrett's triumphs, has lately reappeared, disguised as "Shatter'd Un"—the author in this instance being Mr. A. Chevalier. "In the Ranks" naturally led to the production of "Out of the Ranks" (by Mr. Reece, Strand, 1884) ; and "Called Back" was found especially provocative of ridicule, no fewer than three travesties being written—Mr. Herman Merivale's "Called There and Back" (Gaiety, 1884), Mr. Yardley's "The Scalded Back" (Novelty, 1884), and Mr. Chevalier's "Called Back again" (Plymouth, 1885).

In 1888 Mrs. Bernard Beere was playing at the Opéra Comique in "Ariane," a rather full-blooded drama by Mrs. Campbell Praed. This was at once burlesqued at the Strand by Mr. Burnand, whose "Airey Annie" (as rendered by Mr. Edouin, Miss Atherton, and Miss Ayrtoun) proved to be a very mirth-provoking product. The heroine, Airey Annie thus accounted for her sobriquet :—

> Untaught, untidy, hair all out of curl,
> A gutter child, a true Bohemian girl,

> Like Nan, in " Good for Nothing," so I played,
> And up and down the airey steps I strayed,
> Until the little boys about began
> To call me by the name of " Airey Anne."

Among miscellaneous satires upon the conventional stage products may be named Byron's " Rosebud of Stinging-Nettle Farm" (Crystal Palace, 1862), Mr. Reece's " Brown and the Brahmins" (Globe, 1869), and Mr. Matthison's " More than Ever" (Gaiety and Court, 1882)—the last-named being written in ridicule of the modern Surrey-side " blood-curdler."

So much for the travestie of English melodrama. When we come to deal with the burlesque of melodrama derived from the French, a large field opens out before us. Going back to 1850, we find that Hugo's " Nôtre Dame," as dramatised in England, has suggested to Albert Smith a comic piece called " Esmeralda," brought out at the Adelphi. The subject is next taken up by H. J. Byron, whose " Esmeralda or the 'Sensation' Goat " belongs to the Strand and 1861. Then Fanny Josephs was the Esmeralda, Marie Wilton the Gringoire, Eleanor Bufton the Phoebus, Clarke the Quasimodo, and Rogers the Claude Frollo. Gringoire was made to introduce himself in this punning fashion :—

> I am a comic, tragic, epic poet.
> I'll knock you off a satire or ode Venice on,
> Aye, or write any song like Alfred T*enny-song*.
> Something from my last new extravaganza—
> Come now (*to Clopin*), a trifling stanza shall I stand, sir?
> Let me in some way merit your esteem :
> *Ode to a creditor*—a first-rate theme.
>   *Clop.* Thankee, I'd rather not ; the fact is, you're——
>   *Gring.* But a poor author—that is, *rauther poor*.
> The baker, a most villainous character,
> Has stopped supplies. . . .

> The milk purveyor to my chalk cried "Whoa,"
> Because I did a trifling *milk-bill owe.*
> My tailor, who for years this youth hath made for,
> Closed his account, *account o' clothes* not paid for.
> The gasman, looking on me as a cheater,
> Finished my rhyme by cutting off my *metre.*

Esmeralda, who is a dancer, expresses her " delight in all things saltatory " :—

> Some people like dear wine, give me cheap *hops,*
> Where fountains spout and where the weasel pops ;
> My love for trifling *trips* I can't conceal :
> E'en when I read I always *skip* a deal ;
> I prefer *columbine* before all plants,
> And, at the play, give me a piece by *Dance.*

Phœbus, declaring his love for Esmeralda, makes use of a pun somewhat above the Byronic average :—

> Alonzo Cora loved with all his might,
> And Petrarch was forlorn for Laura quite :
> You're worth to me, dear maid, a score o' Coras ;
> Yes, to this bachelor, a *batch o' Lauras.*

In 1879, at the Gaiety, Byron returned to the topic, and produced the piece which he called " Pretty Esmeralda." At the same theatre, in 1887, one saw the same subject treated in the " Miss Esmeralda " of Messrs. F. Leslie and H. Mills—a piece in which Miss Marion Hood, as the heroine, played prettily to the Frollo of Mr. E. J. Lonnen, and in which the late George Stone laid the foundation of his too brief success.

Boucicault's version of " Les Frères Corses " was produced in London by Charles Kean in 1852, and was quickly followed by a travestie. This was furnished by Gilbert Abbott a'Becket and Mark Lemon at the Haymarket (April, 1852), under the title of " O Gemini ! or the Brothers of

Co(u)rse." Those who did not witness the production can nevertheless conceive how droll Buckstone must have been as the Brothers, and how well he was supported by Bland, also in a dual *rôle*—that of Meynard and Montgiron (or Montegridiron, as he was called)—and by Mrs. L. S. Buckingham as Chateau Renaud. The burlesque was not wholly of the punning sort; it relied chiefly upon its travestie of the incidents in the original play. Fabien was made to give (to the sound of " low music ") the following account of the extraordinary sympathy existing between himself and his brother :—

> Listen ! this hour, five hundred years ago—
> It may be more or less a second or so—
> In the Dei Franchi family there died,
> I think it was upon the female side,
> The very greatest of our great-great-grandmothers,
> Leaving ('tis often thus) two orphan brothers.
> They took an oath, and signed it, as I think,
> In blood—a horrid substitute for ink.
> They swore if either was in any mess,
> If either's landlord put in a distress,.
> Or of their goods came to effect a clearance,
> They'd to each other enter an appearance.
>   *Maynard.* But you have never seen a ghost—
>   *Fabien.*   That's true ;
> But I shall see one soon, by all that's blue :
> For 't is a fact not easily explained,
> The ghost has in the family remained,
> We've tried all means—still he has stalked about,
> And nobody could ever pay him out.
> We let apartments, sir ; but deuce a bit
> Will the ghost take our notices to quit.

Later, just before Louis' apparition, Fabien says :—

> I feel a pain about my ears and nose,
> As if the latter had repeated blows.

I'm sure my brother's in a fearful row—
I shouldn't wonder if they're at it now.
I'll write to him.   (*Writes*) "Dear brother, how's your eye?
Yours ever, Fabien.   Send me a reply."
I'm sure he's subjected to fierce attacks,
For as I seal my note I feel the *whacks* !

H. J. Byron, who travestied nearly everything, of course
did not let the "Corsican Brothers" escape him, and his
"Corsican 'Bothers'" duly figured at the Globe in 1869.
Messrs. Burnand and H. P. Stephens followed, at the Gaiety
in 1880, with "The Corsican Brothers & Co.," and in 1881
(at the Royalty) Mr. G. R. Sims made his *début* as a writer
of burlesque with "The Of Course-Akin-Brothers, Babes
in the Wood." In this he began the action with Fabien
and Louis as the Babes and Chateau Renaud as the Wicked
Uncle, introducing a certain Rosie Posie, who is maid to
Mme. dei Franchi and sweetheart of Alfred Meynard. At
the end of the first scene Father Time came on, and
summed up the situation in a song :—

Kind friends in front, you here behold a figure allegorical :
Excuse me if at times I pause and for my paregoric call.
I want to tell you all about this story Anglo-Corsican,
And do the best in spite of cough and voice that's rather hoarse I can.
Old Father Time I am, you guess ; 't is I who rule the universe,
And cause the changes which I sing in this the poet's punny verse !
So while the scene is changing, here I sing this song preparative,
To help you, as a chorus should, to understand the narrative.
    Ha, ha, ha ! Ho, ho, ho !
    As chorus to this tragedy, to act my painful doom it is.
    In spite of cough, sciatica, lumbago, and the rheumatiz.

The little boys who in the wood the robins saved from perishing
Are two young men for one young girl a hopeless passion cherishing.
In Corsica with his mamma young Fabien dei Franchi is ;
The other one in Paris lives, and growing rather cranky is.

Addison
~~C. A.~~ Sims.
of Seattle

Addison
~~G. R.~~ Sims.
of Seattle

Sweet Rosie Posie followed them. The ma of these phenomena
As lady-help accepted her for foiling the abomina-
Ble plans the wicked uncle laid the brothers to assassinate,
And Rosie still in Corsica contrives all hearts to fascinate.

To Paris went the uncle, too, to let coiffeurs their talent try,
And now he is an agèd buck and famous for his gallantry.
He's bought a wig, and paints his face—three times a day he'll
    carmine it,
He asks young wives to opera balls, and swears there's little harm
    in it.

In the second act Meynard brings a friend with him to
Corsica, and thus presents him to Mme. dei Franchi :—

A friend of mine who's come this trip with me,
The customs of the country for to see.
The customs, when he landed, landed him—
He's *cust 'em* rather, I can tell you, mim !
    Friend. 'Tain't pleasant when a chap on pleasure's bent
To find the call of duty cent. per cent.
    Mad. You're welcome, sir, although our customs seize you :
A triple welcome, and I hope the *trip 'll* please you.

Previous to the first entry of Louis' ghost, Fabien says :—

I feel so strange, I know poor Loo is seédy ;
I dreamt I saw his ghost all pale and bleedy.
I'll write him.   Where's the ink ?   Lor, how I shudder !
(*Looks about for ink*) I'm on the ink-quest now—poor absent brudder.
The ink !—the quill !   Ah ! this, I think, will do.
(*Sits and writes*) "Louis, old cock, how wags the world with you?"
(*Music—he shudders*) I feel as if a ghost were at my elbow handy.
This *goes to* prove I want a drop of brandy.

Of the other puns in the piece the following are perhaps
fair specimens.   At the *bal masqué*, Louis, meeting Emilie
de Lesparre, says :—

        Why are you here ?
    Emilie.   I came because I'm asked (*puts on mask*).

Louis. This is no place for you to cut a shine ;
'Tain't *womanly.*
    Emilie.   I know it's *masky-line.*

Again :—

Louis. My dagger awaits you—for your blood I faint !
Renaud. Your dagger awaits—you'*d aggerawate* a saint.

In the final tableau, Chateau Renaud is advised to take
some brandy; but he asks instead for "a go of gin—I want
the *gin-go* spirit."

The latest of the burlesques on this subject was supplied—
also for the Royalty—by Mr. Cecil Raleigh, whose " New
Corsican Brothers," played in 1889, had more than one
whimsical feature to recommend it. One of the brothers
(Mr. Arthur Roberts) was supposed to be an English linen-
draper, who, whenever anything was happening to the other
brother, had a wild desire to measure out tape—and so on.
The dialogue was in prose.

"Belphegor," the generic name bestowed upon the
numerous adaptations of " Paillasse," gave birth to at least
one travestie of importance—that by Leicester Buckingham,
which saw the light at the Strand in 1856, the year in
which Charles Dillon played in one of the adaptations (at the
Lyceum). "'The Duke's Motto," in which Fechter "starred"
at the same theatre, was the origin of H. J. Byron's " The
Motto: I am ' All There ' "—a piece seen at the Strand in
1863, with Miss Maria Simpson as the Duke Gonzaque,
George Honey as Lagardère, and Ada Swanborough and
Fanny Josephs as Blanche and Pepita. Among much
which is mere punning, though clever enough for that
commodity, I find this little bit of social satire :—

Receipt to make a party :—First of all,
Procure some rooms, and mind to have 'em small ;

Select a good warm night, so draughts may chill 'em ;
Ask twice as many as it takes to fill 'em ;
For though the half you ask may not attend,
The half that comes is sure to bring a friend ;
Select a strong pianist, and a gent
Who through the cornet gives his feelings vent ;
Give them some biscuits, and some nice Marsala ;
Make a refreshment-room of the front parlour ;
Garnish with waltzes, flirtings, polking, ballads,
Tongue, fowl, and sandwiches, limp lobster salads,
Smiles, shaking hands, smirks, simpers, and what not ;
Throw in the greengrocer, and serve up hot.

It is to H. J. Byron that we owe the burlesque of
"Robert Macaire," which, with Fanny Josephs and J. Clarke
as Macaire and Strop, brightened the boards of the Globe
Theatre in 1870. The drama of which Ruy Blas is the
central figure has been twice travestied among us—once
in 1873 by Mr. Reece ("Ruy Blas Righted," at the
Vaudeville), and more recently (in 1889) by Messrs. F.
Leslie and H. Clark ("Ruy Blas, or the Blasé Roué,"
at the Gaiety). "Diplomacy," adapted from "Dora,"
appealed to Mr. Burnand's sense of the ridiculous, and
the result was "Dora and Diplunacy" (Strand, 1878),
in which the weak spots of the original were divertingly
laid bare. In the same year, Mr. Burnand burlesqued, at
the Royalty, his own adaptation, "Proof, or a Celebrated
Case," under the title of "Over-Proof, or What was Found
in a Celebrated Case." To 1879 belong two clever travesties—"Another Drink," by Messrs. Savile Clarke and Clifton
(Lyne), suggested by "Drink," and brought out at the
Folly ; and "Under-Proof," Mr. Edward Rose's *reductio ad
absurdum* of "Proof." In the latter piece, besides many
well-constructed puns, there are many pleasant turns of

humour, as when Pierre satirises the conventional stage
pronunciation of his name :—

> In my native land, as you're aware,
> My Christian name's pronounced like this—Pi-erre,
> But here I'm made a nobleman of France,
> For everybody calls me *Peer* Lorance.

Of the Anglo-French melodrama of recent years, Mr.
Burnand has been the frequent and successful satirist.
He capped " Fedora " with " Stage-Dora " (Toole's, 1883),
" Theodora " with " The O'Dora " (same theatre, 1885), and
"La Tosca " with " Tra la la Tosca " (Royalty, 1890).   This
last contained some of the happiest of its author's efforts, in
the way both of ingenious punning and effective rhyming.
Here, for example, is a song put into the mouth of the
Baron Scarpia, the "villain " both of the play and of the
travestie :—

> I am the bad Baron Scarpia !
> You know it at once, and how sharp y'are.
> Than a harpy I am much harpier—
>   How harpy I must be !
> There never was blackguard or scamp
> To me could hold candle or lamp.
> I'm equal to twenty-five cargoes
> Of Richards, Macbeths, and Iagos !
> For nobody ever so far goes
>   As Scarpia—meaning me.

> I'm chief of the Italiani
> Peelerini Me-tropoli-tani !
> Around me they wheedle and carney—
>   They'd all curry favour, you see.
> And, buzzing about me like flies,
> Are myrmidons, creatures, and spies.

They're none of them mere lardy-dardy,
But cunning, unprincipled, hardy,
And come from Scotlandini Yardi,
    La Forza Constabular*ee*.

During the present year, the interest gradually excited by successive performances of plays by Henrik Ibsen has culminated in the production of the inevitable burlesques. More than one clever travestie of Ibsen has been printed—*e.g.*, those by Mr. J. P. Hurst and Mr. Wilton Jones; but the first to be performed was that entitled " Ibsen's Ghost, or Toole up to Date," which is from the witty pen of Mr. J. M. Barrie. This starts as a sort of sequel to " Hedda Gabler," which it mainly satirises; but there are allusions also to " Ghosts " and to " A Doll's House," with some general sarcasm at the expense of Ibsen's peculiarities. The dialogue is in prose, with a concluding vocal quartett; the writer's touch is as light as it is true; and the composition, as a whole, is thoroughly exhilarating. The three-act piece, " The Gifted Lady," in which Mr. Robert Buchanan sought to ridicule not only Ibsen but other " emancipating " agencies of the time, was, unfortunately, not so successful as Mr. Barrie's slighter and brighter work. It abounded in excellent epigram, but lacked geniality and humour. In " Ibsen's Ghost " Mr. Toole and Miss Eliza Johnstone renewed old successes, while Miss Irene Vanbrugh gave signs of aptitude for burlesque. In " The Gifted Lady " Miss Fanny Brough, Miss Cicely Richards, Mr. W. H. Vernon, and Mr. Harry Paulton showed all their usual skill, but, unfortunately, to no purpose.

VIII

WE have already seen that, in burlesquing mythology, faërie, and other matters, our comic playwrights have not been able to resist the temptation to introduce occasional travesties of things operatic. Opera, indeed, has always had a magnetic power over them. They have been unable to maintain their gravity in presence of the singularities which distinguish opera, even in its most modern guise, from the more natural and realistic drama. Operatic conditions demand, of necessity, certain stereo-typed regulations, especially of stage management, which detract from probability and excite derision. Especially is this so in the case of the older school of Opera, and notably in that of the Italian school, whose products were largely on the same simple and ingenuous model—a model on which the travestie writers were able to construct some genuinely entertaining imitations.

Beginning, then, with the. Italian school, we note that Donizetti has been particularly favoured by the parodists. His "Lucrezia Borgia," "Linda di Chamouni," "Elisir d' Amore," and "Fille du Régiment" have all had to submit to deliberate perversion. Of "Lucrezia" there have

been three notable burlesques—one by Leicester Buckingham, at the St. James's, in 1860 ; another by Sydney
French, at the Marylebone, in 1867 ; and the third by
H. J. Byron, at the Holborn, in 1868. Buckingham's was
entitled " Lucrezia Borgia ! at Home, and all Abroad," and
had Charles Young for the exponent of the title character.
Miss Wyndham was Johnny Raw ("known as Gennaro,
through the defective pronunciation of his Italian friends—
a British shopkeeper, who has left for awhile the counter-
tenor of his way, and is travelling on the Continent for his
pleasure "). Miss Cecilia Ranoe was Alfonso, and a small
part was played by Miss Nellie Moore. Lucrezia figures
in this piece as a dabbler in monetary speculations, the
failure of which gives opportunity for a speech parodying
some Shakespearean lines with more freshness than such
things usually possess :—

> Oh ! that dishonoured notes of hand would melt,
> Thaw, and dissolve themselves when overdue,
> And never leave the holder time to sue ;
> Or that in pickle no such sharp rod lay
> As the unpleasant writ called a *ca sa* !
> How weary, flat, unprofitable, stale,
> To kick one's heels inside a debtor's gaol !
> Fie on't ! 'Tis an unweeded garden clearly ;
> Blackguards and seedy swells possess it merely.
> That it should come to this ! At two months' date !—
> No, not two months ; six weeks is less than eight.
> So excellent a bill ! The blow will floor me !
> Is this a bailiff that I see before me,
> A capias in his hand ? Come, let me dodge thee ;
> Or in a sponging-house I know thou'lt lodge me.
> I've turned my back, and yet I see thee still !
> Canst thou then be two gentlemen at will ?
> Or art thou but a grim dissolving view—
> A phantom officer—in short, a *do* ?

I see thee yet—so palpable in form,
My prospects seem uncomfortably warm.
Thou marshall'st me to Whitecross Street, I see,
Clutching protested bills endorsed by me ;
Indictments, too, for fraud and false pretences !
Mine eyes are made the fools o' the other senses,
Or else I'm tight ! I see thee still, my man ;
And by thy side appears the prison van,
Which was not so before. There's no such thing !

In the course of the piece, Johnny Raw is poisoned by
Alfonso with publican's port, and afterwards Lucrezia seeks
to destroy Orsini and his companion with London milk.
Byron's burlesque on the subject was called " Lucrezia
Borgia, M.D."

" Linda di Chamouni " exercised the wit both of Mr.
Conway Edwardes and of Mr. Alfred Thompson. The
former writer's " Linda di Chamouni, or the Blighted
Flower," was played at Bath in 1869 ; the latter's work
was presented, later in the same year, at the Gaiety. In
Mr. Edwardes' book one is most struck by the multiplicity
and occasional felicity of the " word-plays." Here, for
instance, is what Pierotto says when he is asked to take
a cup of wine :—

Well, if you ask me *what* I'll take, I think
Tea I prefer 'bove every other drink.
For when I'm teazed, vex'd, worried beyond measure,
A *cup* of tea's to me a *source o'* pleasure.
Whene'er I play, the game is *tea*-to-tum ;
My fav'rite instrument's a " kettledrum."
I've faith, when suff'ring ills heir to humanity,
In senna tea that you may say's *insanitee.*
And also p'rhaps a little odd 'twill seem here,
That I prefer the scenery of *Bohea*-mia.
And if I were engaged in deadly strife,
I'd stab my en'my with a *Bohea* knife.

Two of Donizetti's operas—" L'Elisir d' Amore " and " La Fille du Régiment "—were travestied by Mr. W. S. Gilbert; the former under the title of "Doctor Dulcamara, or the Little Duck and the Great Quack," the latter under that of " La Vivandière, or True to the Corps." " Doctor Dulcamara " was played at the St. James's, with Frank Matthews in the title-part. " La Vivandière " (1868) was written for the Queen's Theatre, where it employed the talents of Miss Henrietta Hodson, Mr. Toole, Mr. Lionel Brough, Miss Everard (the original Little Buttercup), and Miss Fanny Addison.

Of Verdi's operas two have been singled out for special attention—" Il Trovatore " and " Ernani." The first of these suggested H. J. Byron's " Ill-Treated Trovatore," seen at the Adelphi in 1863, and another version by the same hand, played at the Olympic seventeen years after. Byron also wrote a travestie of " Ernani," which he called " Handsome Hernani " (Gaiety, 1879); but in this he had been anticipated by William Brough, whose work was seen at the Alexandra Theatre in 1865.

Three travesties have been founded on the " La Sonnambula " of Bellini. The first, which was played at the Victoria Theatre in 1835, was from the pen of Gilbert Abbott a'Beckett, and entitled " The Roof Scrambler " —a title explained in lines spoken by Rudolpho and Swelvino :—

> *Rud.* I tell you, there are beings in their dreams
> Who scramble 'pon the house-tops.
> *Swel.* So it seems.
> *Rud.* Roof-scramblers they are called ; for on the roofs
> They walk at night—Molly is one.

Molly is the name here given to Amina; Swelvino, of

W. L.—V.

course, is Elvino. He is a sexton, and has plighted his troth
to Lizzy; but before the piece opens, he has transferred
his affections to Molly Brown, a charity girl—"a Greasy
Roamer over the tops of houses." Swelvino and Molly are
about to be married, when there arrives at the village
Rodolpho, the new Inspector of Police, who introduces
himself as follows :—

> Ah, here I am again !—I know this scene,
> In which, when I was young, so oft I've been.
> I recognise each spot I see around,
> The stocks know me, and well I know the pound !
> The sight of these my eyes with tears is filling :
> I knew that pound when I had not a shilling !

Molly, walking in her sleep, enters Rodolpho's apartment,
and is found there by Swelvino, but is vindicated, like her
prototype in the opera, by being subsequently discovered in
a somnambulant condition. The story of " La Sonnambula "
is, in fact, followed closely, but caricatured throughout. W.
Rogers, who was the Swelvino, and Mitchell, who was the
Molly, appear to have been highly successful in exciting the
hilarity of their audiences. The latter portrayed the heroine
as " a waddling, thick-set, red-and-ruddy, blowzy-faced goblin,
with turn-up nose and carroty hair, wrapt in a pea-soup or
camomile-tea-coloured negligée, and carrying," in the sleep-
walking scene, " a farthing rushlight in one of Day &
Martin's empty blacking-bottles." Of Swelvino's appearance
we may judge from a remark made by Molly to her lover :—

> I, by looking in your face, can tell
> What are your feelings excellently well.
> Oh, yes ! the fulness of that ruby nose
> Your love for me doth passing well disclose ;
> Your agitated whisker shows full well
> What throbs of passion underneath it dwell !

The two other skits upon the opera were the work of H. J. Byron, who produced the first at the Prince of Wales's in 1865, under the title of " La! Sonnambula! or the Supper, the Sleeper, and the Merry Swiss Boy; being a passage in the life of a famous 'Woman in White': a passage leading to a tip-top story." Miss Marie Wilton was the Merry Swiss Boy (Alessio); Miss Fanny Josephs was Elvino; Mr. Dewar, Rodolpho; "Johnny" Clarke, Amina; Miss Bella Goodall, Lisa; Mr. Harry Cox undertaking the *rôle* of " a virtuous peasant (by the kind permission of the Legitimate Drama)." This was Miss Wilton's first production at the Prince of Wales's, and it was a great success. In 1878 Byron brought out at the Gaiety a piece which he called " Il Sonnambulo, or Lively Little Alessio." In this he introduced several variations on the operatic story; making the Count (Edward Terry) the somnambulist, instead of Amina—in burlesque of Mr. Henry Neville's sleep-walking scene in Wilkie Collins's " Moonstone." Miss Farren was the lively little Alessio, and Mr. Royce the "local tenor," Elvino.

Of Bellini's " Norma " the first burlesque produced was that which W. H. Oxberry, the comedian, contributed to the Haymarket in 1841. In this the title-part was played by Paul Bedford, with Wright as Adalgisa and Mrs. H. P. Grattan as Pollio. The piece had no literary pretensions, and it would be unfair to compare it, in that or any other respect, with " The Pretty Druidess, or the Mother, the Maid, and the Mistletoe Bough," which Mr. W. S. Gilbert wrote for the Charing Cross Theatre (now Toole's) just twenty-eight years later. This was one of the best of Mr. Gilbert's operatic travesties, the dialogue being characterised

by especial point and neatness.] Here, for example, is the
advice given by Norma (Miss Hughes) to the ladies pre-
siding over the stalls at a fancy fair. Hamlet's address
to the players is very happily suggested :—

> With pretty speech accost both old and young,
> And speak it trippingly upon the tongue ;
> But if you mouth it with a hoyden laugh,
> With clumsy ogling and uncomely chaff—
> As I have oft seen done at fancy fairs,
> I had as lief a huckster sold my wares.
> Avoid all so-called beautifying, dear.
> Oh ! it offends me to the soul to hear
> The things that men among themselves will say
> Of some *soi-disant* " beauty of the day,"
> Whose face, when with cosmetics she has cloyed it,
> Out-Rachels Rachel !—pray you, girls, avoid it.
> Neither be ye too tame—but, ere you go,
> Provide yourselves with sprigs of mistletoe ;
> Offer them coyly to the Roman herd—
> But don't you " suit the action to the word,"
> For in the very torrent of your passion
> Remember modesty is still in fashion.
> Oh, there be ladies whom I've seen hold stalls—
> Ladies of rank, my dear—to whom befalls
> Neither the accent nor the gait of ladies ;
> So clumsily made up with Bloom of Cadiz,
> Powder-rouge—lip-salve—that I've fancied then
> They were the work of Nature's journeymen.

The " Gazza Ladra " of Rossini lives on the burlesque
stage in the counterfeit presentment furnished by Byron's
"Maid and the Magpie, or the Fatal Spoon." This was one
of the writer's greatest triumphs in the field of travestie.
Produced at the Strand in 1854, with Miss Oliver as Ninette,
Miss Marie Wilton as Pippo, Bland as Fernando, and Clarke
as Isaac (the old-clothes man), it at once hit the public
taste, as it well deserved to do, for it is full of clever writing

and ingenious incidents. The best scene of all, perhaps, is that in which the broken-down Fernando reveals himself to Ninette—a happy satire upon a familiar melodramatic situation :—

Ninette (*entering*).   A stranger here !

Fernan. How beautiful she's grown ! I say, my dear !

(*she starts*) Start not—ha, ha !—do I alarm you ?

Ninette (*uneasily*).   Rather !

Fernan. (*hesitatingly*). Why, miss, you see—the fact is—I'm your father !

Ninette. Impossible ! I never had one !

Fernan.   Law !

Ninette. That is—I had none that I ever saw.

Fernan. Oh, why in battle did no friendly blow
Finish her luckless parent long ago ?
(*in choked accents*) Doth not the voice of nature seem quite clear—eh ?

Ninette. The voice of nature seems a little beery.

Fernan. (*seizing her arm—music piano*). Look at me well !

(*Ninette appears gradually to recognise him.*)

Ninette.   Upon a close inspection,
I seem to have a dreamy recollection
Of having seen those eyes of yours somewhere,
Also that most extensive head of hair ;
The accents of the voice, too, now I think,
Seem broken by emotion, not by drink ;
Yes, it's all coming back to me, of course.

Fernan. Remember, dear, I bought you once a horse,
A wooden toy—remember, you had lots—
It ran on wheels—all mane and tail and spots—
Also a dog, a little dog, I vow,
Which, when you squeezed it, used to go Bow-wow !
Likewise a spade, which, on your nurse's head
You broke, and got well spanked and sent to bed——

Ninette (*wildly*). A flood of memory rushes through my brain !

Fernan. (*excitedly*). Ninette, my daughter, look at me again.

Ninette (*seizing his nose*). Yes, yes, that nose decides me—yes—you are—

Fernan. At last—at last ! he—he ! she *knows* her pa !

In a mock love-scene with Ninette, Gianetto (Miss Ternan) draws the following comic picture :—

Fancy a bower with rose and jasmine graced,
Such as we see in small tea-gardens placed ;
Where friendly spiders and black-beetles drop
On to your bread and butter with a flop ;
Where mouldy seats stain sarsnet, satin, silk,
And suicidal flies fall in the milk ;
Where we can scorn the heartless world's attack,
Though daddy-longlegs may creep down your back ;
Smile at society's contemptuous sneer,
Though caterpillars tumble in your beer ;
Where chimneys never smoke, and soot don't fall,
Where income-tax collectors never call,
Where one's wife's mother never even once
Visits her darling daughter for six months ;
Where bills, balls, banks, and bonnets are not known—
Come, dwell with me, my beautiful—my own.

Turning to the burlesques of opera of the German school, we begin, naturally, with Mozart, whose " Don Giovanni " found humorous reflection in two pieces, by H. J. Byron and Mr. Reece. The former's " Little Don Giovanni " * belongs to 1865, when it was performed at the Prince of Wales's, with Miss Wilton (Mrs. Bancroft) as the hero, Clarke as Leporello, Miss Fanny Josephs as Masetto, Mr. Hare as Zerlina (probably his only appearance on the stage in petticoats), Miss Sophie Larkin as Elvira, and Miss Hughes as Donna Anna. Don Giovanni was the last burlesque part written by Byron for Miss Wilton, and, moreover, it was the last burlesque part she ever played. She records in her Memoirs that an amusing feature of the

* Byron's " Don Juan," brought out at the Alhambra in 1873, was about equally indebted for its plot to the libretto of Mozart's opera and to Lord Byron's poem.

piece was the spectacle presented in the last act by the Commandant's horse, which, in allusion to a recent freak in Leicester Square, had been covered with a variety of spots, and "looked like an exaggerated Lowther Arcade toy." Mr. Reece's burlesque was called "Don Giovanni in Venice," and came out at the Gaiety in 1873.

In 1842 Macready revived at Drury Lane Handel's delightful "Acis and Galatea," and the opera was promptly caricatured by W. H. Oxberry in a piece produced three days afterwards at the Adelphi. The travestie of "Acis and Galatea" which was seen at the Olympic in 1863 was from the pen of Mr. Burnand. Its full title was "Acis and Galatea, or the Nimble Nymph and the Terrible Troglodyte"; and the Nimble Nymph (described as "a Nymph of the Sea, who also visits the land—a nymphibious young lady") was played by Miss Hughes. The puns were prolific, and so were the parodies, the best of which are written in caricature of the absurd English translations in the operatic "books of the play." Here, for example, is a setting of the trio in "Trovatore"—"Il tuo sangue":—

Polyphemus. With you, oh, sanguine, I'd share your 'art, oh !
'Twould be a stinger, ho ! if no go.
(*As to her*) Dear ! (*as to himself*) Oh, folly ! be calm, oh ! I'm misty !
(*Holding his hands over his bursting heart—operatically singing*).
Eh, pooh, we've here a lump, oh ! (*alluding to his heart*).
No, eh, pooh, we've 'ere a
      Lump, oh no.
Ah ! de gal, oh, so de gal, oh, so coy, press 'art to (*enraptured*)
And it may then end in no go ! (*with a tinge of sadness*).
And it may then end in no go !
I'm a gent, oh, over-misty (*with his hand to his heart*),
Cease of her to be fond, ah, no !
      No ! fond ! ah ! no !
        Ah ! etc.

Phyllis. ⎧Come, ah ! come, will you o-ver-awe, eh? (*fiercely*).
Galatea. ⎩Come, ah ! come, will you o-ver-awe me? (*distractedly*).
Phyllis. ⎧You'll ar-ray, ah ! wi' Pol trudge, oh !* (*fiercely*).
Galatea. ⎩You'll ar-ray, ah ! wi' Pol trudge, oh ! (*distractedly*).
Phyllis. ⎧Veep ! ye'll ne'er go to rest o' shore, eh ! (*fiercely*).
Galatea. ⎩Veep ! we'll ne'er go to rest o' shore, eh? (*distractedly*).
Phyllis. Gay ! tomb ! ah ! one full ! no beau ! (*wildly and demoniacally*).
Galatea. Gay ! tomb ! ah ! one full ! no beau ! (*wildly and distractedly*).

Six years after the production of Mr. Burnand's piece, Mr. T. F. Plowman brought out at Oxford " a. piece of extravagance," to which he gave the name of " A Very New Edition of Acis and Galatea, or the Beau ! the Belle ! and the Blacksmith ! "

Of Meyerbeer's operas three have been burlesqued in England — " Dinorah," " L'Africaine " and " Robert le Diable." The first of these was parodied in " Dinorah under Difficulties," a burlesque by William Brough, which dates back as far as 1859 (at the Adelphi). " L'Africaine " was handled by Mr. Burnand six years later at the Strand. Three years more, and " Robert le Diable " was being travestied at the Gaiety by Mr. Gilbert, under the title of " Robert the Devil, or the Nun, the Dun, and the Sun of a Gun." † This last is on the old lines of " palmy-day " burlesque, and has not much in it that is characteristically Gilbertian. The lyrics are written chiefly to operatic airs, and there is no room, therefore, for rhythmical invention. In the dialogue, however, one comes across an occasional

---

* This, says Mr. Burnand in a note, is the poetic for " You'll get on your bonnet and accompany Polyphemus."

† In this Miss Farren, as Robert, was supported by Miss Constance Loseby as Raimbault, Miss Emily Fowler as Alice, Miss Annie Tremaine as Prince of Granada, and Joseph Eldred as Gobetto.

passage which strikes one as quite Gilbertian in its cynicism. Take, for example, these lines from the scene in which fun is made of the Tussaud " Chamber of Horrors " :—

> *Bertram.* These are all statues, raised from time to time
> To people who're remarkable for crime.
> *Robert.* But if their wicked deeds could so unnerve one,
> Why give them statues ?
> *Bert.*   'Cause they don't deserve one.
> That's our strict rule—a rule we never garble—
> Good deeds we write in sand, bad deeds in marble.

Some of the puns in the piece are worth recording. Thus, Alice says of a porter, to whom half a crown has been given :—

> He'll spend it all upon his favourite wets—
> He tipsy gets with all the *tips he gets.*

Again, Gobetto says of Robert :—

> He's smoking to a pretty tune, I'll bet, oh !
> *Prince.* That pretty tune must be " Il Cigaretto."

Gobetto says to Robert :—

> We saw you through the window, pouring fizz in !
> *Robert.* I liked the wines, but didn't like the *quizzin.*

Again :—

> *Alice.* Why, Robert, how you've changed in speech and tone !
> Your forehead, once so smooth, now bears a frown on it ;
> As for your mouth, 'tis evident you're down in it !
> *Robert.* Yes, though I'm young, it's plain to all who con it,
> Down *in* the mouth before I've down *upon* it !

Weber's " Der Freischutz " has been travestied both by Mr. Burnand and by H. J. Byron, both productions taking place in 1866, within two days of each other—the one at the Strand, and the other at the Prince of Wales's. Mr.

Reece is responsible for a burlesque of Flotow's "Martha," performed at the Gaiety in 1873, with Miss Constance Loseby, Miss Rachel Sanger, Mr. Lionel Brough, and Mr. Aynsley Cook in the leading parts.

Wagnerian "music-drama" has more than once been desecrated on the burlesque stage. First of all there came, at the Royalty in 1869, the "Flying Dutchman" of William Brough; then Messrs. Green and Swanborough brought out at the Strand, in 1876, "The Lying Dutch-man" (with M. Marius and Miss Lottie Venne); and the "Little Lohengrin" of Mr. Bowyer saw the light in 1884 at the Holborn Theatre.

So much for the German school. Of the French com-posers, Auber has had more pieces travestied in this country than has any one of his fellows. There is "Masaniello," for instance, and "Fra Diavolo," and "Les Diamans de la Couronne." "Masaniello, or the Fish 'oman of Naples," was the title given by Robert B. Brough to the "fish tale, in one act," which he wrote for the Olympic in 1857. He had, for the impersonator of his hero, Robson, whose presence in the cast suggested to Mrs. Wigan the addition to the mad scene of sundry indications of the actor's former successes at the Olympic. The result was very successful. Masaniello came on, crying—

> My lord, the Earl of Hammersmith is taken!
> Stop! That's in *Hamlet*! I'm Masaniello!
> To be or not to was—that's in *Othello*,
> Translated into Irish—for Ristori.
> Pop goes the Weasel—that's from *Trovatore*.

He then breaks off into a portion of the dagger dance from "Macbeth Travestie," following this up with a scrap from

Italian opera and part of the hornpipe in "The Yellow Dwarf." Then Borella says :—

> You are our chief! Do you not know me, sir?
> *Mas.* Excellent well! You are a fishmonger!
> And I'm your chieftain.
>   *Pietro.*   Are you not, my lad?
>   *Mas.* Ay, every inch a King-fisher—not bad! (*chuckles*).
> The monarch of the deep—my lord of scales;
> Here's a discovery—I'm Prince of Whales! . . .
> Think not to pierce this hide of Indian rubber (*weeps*).
> A whale! Oh yes! A whale of tears! All blubber!
>   *Suzanna.* Oh! this side-piercing sight!
>   *Mas.*   I'm very limp—
> And small—and flabby! Hang it! I'm a shrimp!

Then followed a song, in parody of "I'm Afloat" :—

> I'm a shrimp! I'm a shrimp, of diminutive size :
> Inspect my antennæ, and look at my eyes ;
> I'm a natural syphon, when dipped in a cup,
> For I drain the contents to the latest drop up.
> I care not for craw-fish, I heed not the prawn,
> From a flavour especial my fame has been drawn ;
> Nor e'en to the crab or the lobster I'll yield,
> When I'm properly cook'd and efficiently peel'd.
> Quick! quick! pile your coals—let your saucepan be deep!
> For the weather is warm, and I'm not sure to keep;
> Off, off with my head—split my shell into three—
> I'm a shrimp! I'm a shrimp—to be eaten with tea.

After this, Robson was wont to introduce a bit of "business" from "The Discreet Princess," ending with a ditty from the "Medea" burlesque. The travestie of the pantomime-action of the dumb girl Fenella was naturally another feature of Brough's work, which had the usual supply of puns, and, altogether, more than the usual amount of literary and dramatic merit. The little travestie, called

" Masse-en-Yell-Oh," written by Messrs. Harry Paulton and Mostyn Tedde for the Comedy in 1886, was an unpretending piece of work, not challenging comparison with its predecessor.

Auber's "Fra Diavolo" was another of the operatic originals on which H. J. Byron based his comic fancies. He wrote, to begin with, " Fra Diavolo, or the Beauty and the Brigands," first seen at the Strand in 1858; and then, twenty years after, " Young Fra Diavolo," which made its appearance at the Gaiety. "Les Diamans de la Couronne" fell to the lot of Mr. Reece, who, in 1875, prepared for the Holborn Theatre the piece entitled " The Half-crown Diamonds," a revised edition of which found its way to the stage of the Imperial Theatre just five years later.

Hérold's "Zampa" was burlesqued by Mr. T. F. Plowman at the Court in 1872, and by Mr. J. McArdle for the provincial stage in 1876. The "Mignon" of M. Thomas has also been transmogrified into the "Merry Mignon" of Mr. Wilton Jones (1882). The "Carmen" of Georges Bizet has had its mirthful side portrayed in no fewer than four comic pieces—the "Carmen, or Sold for a Song" of Mr. Reece (Folly, 1879); the "Cruel Carmen" of Mr. Wilton Jones (1880); the "Little Carmen" of Mr. Alfred Murray (Globe, 1884); and the "Carmen Up to Data" of Messrs. Sims and Pettitt (Gaiety, 1890). The Carmen of the first of these productions was Miss Lydia Thompson,—of the last, Miss Florence St. John, a charming vocalist, gifted with the true *vis comica*.

But the most popular, by a long way, of all French operas, for purposes of burlesque, has been the " Faust " of Gounod. Of the many travesties of this, or of the story embodied in it, the earliest was that of Halford, brought out at the Olympic in 1854. This was followed in 1857 by a piece called "Alonzo the Brave," written by Mr. Burnand for performance by University amateurs at Cambridge, and mingling the story of Alonzo, as told in the ballad, with that of Faust, in a fashion effective, if a little puzzling. In this piece of extravagance (in which, by the way, Mr. Burnand played Mephistopheles), Imogene is the heroine, taking the place of Marguerite in the affections of Faust. For a while, in the absence of Alonzo, she yields to the snares of the tempter; but, in the end, her first sweetheart appears to her as his own ghost, her inconstancy is forgiven, and Faust retires from the scene.

Seven years later Mr. Burnand wrote a burlesque called "Faust and Marguerite" for the St. James's. He had Ashley for his Faust, Charles Mathews and Mrs. Charles Mathews for his Mephistopheles and Marguerite, H. J. Montague for his Valentine, and "Johnny" Clarke for his Martha. In this instance he followed the story of the opera pretty closely till near the end, when Faust was sued for breach of promise of marriage, and escaped the clutches of Mephistopheles only by consenting to pair off with Martha! A visit to a music-hall formed part of the action, and gave occasion for some pointed lines. Said Faust :—

> I'm saddened by your modern comic singing;

and Mephistopheles went on to describe the scene :—

> There sat the draper's clerk, who wildly loves
> The tenth-rate *prima donna* in cleaned gloves;
> The would-be swell, who thinks it mighty grand
> To shake the comic singer by the hand;
> Who pays for his amusement through the nose,
> And stands not on the order of his "goes."

He thinks the dark girls dressed in blue first-raters,
And is familiar with the seedy waiters ;
He sips his sling or takes some sort of toddy,
And encores everything and everybody.

Marguerite says at one point—

That *circled orb,* you think, 's the moon ; it ain't :
We know 'tis but a *circle daub* of paint.

And she remarks elsewhere that

The minnow is the *minnow*-mum of fishes.

Faust says, in one place—

Our *prima donna,* sir, has gone, I guess,
To make herself *primmer* and to *don her* dress.

There is a diverting parody on " My Mother " :—

Who guided you o'er lake and fell,
Who told you all there was to tell,
Ne'er missed a place, but showed it well?
                                  Your Murray !

In 1869 Mr. Burnand was to the fore again with "Very
Little Faust and More Marguerite," which was played at
the Charing Cross Theatre (as the building was then
called). A few years later—in 1877—H. J. Byron entered
the field with " Little Doctor Faust," in which he had for
interpreters the Gaiety artists, headed by Miss Farren and
Mr. Edward Terry. Later still—in 1885—came a provincial writer with " Faust in Forty Minutes." In 1886 we
had at the Royalty a piece called " Mephisto," of which the
only characteristic feature was an imitation of Mr. Irving
by Mr. E. J. Henley, clever in its way, but not to be
compared for sustained truthfulness to the performance
given by Mr. H. E. Dixey in " Adonis " (at the Gaiety) a

week or two previously. In 1886, also, Mr. Burnand brought out at Toole's—with Mr. Toole as Mephistopheles (*à la* Irving)—"Faust and Loose"; and, two years after, we had at the Gaiety the "Faust up to Date" of Messrs. G. R. Sims and Henry Pettitt, of which more hereafter. A notable fact about "Faust and Loose" is the appearance on the stage, for the first time, of Marguerite's mother—a lady unaccountably neglected by all previous writers, serious or otherwise! In the burlesque she thus introduces herself :—

> My name it is—— Really,
> I can't state it clearly ;
> But I'll observe, merely,
>> That I'm not to blame.
> To save further bother,
> I'm Margaret's mother,
> And, as I've no other,
>> Why, that is my name.
>
> They can't do without me,
> The play's all about me,
> They flout me, they scout me ;
>> Oh ! I call it mean !
> Each version where Ma is,
> In London or Paris,
> Makes me Mrs. Harris,
>> Much talked of, not seen.
>
> I'm griping and grasping,
> I'm snoring, I'm gasping,
> With fear my voice rasping
>> Miss Marguerite fills.
> They speak thus behind me—
> You'll speak as you find me—
> But all have maligned me,
>> From Goethe to Wills !

English serious opera has not often fallen a prey to the

untender mercies of the parodist.   Balfe and Vincent
Wallace alone have been victimised in that way—Balfe
through his " Bohemian Girl " and " Rose of Castile ";
Wallace through his " Maritana."   The " Bohemian Girl "
has taken four different shapes on the burlesque boards.
In' 1851, as transmogrified by the Brothers Brough, she
figured at the Haymarket as " Arline."   In 1864, under the
auspices of Messrs. Best and Bellingham, she appeared
at Sadler's Wells under the same designation.   At the
command of Mr. W. S. Gilbert she posed at the Royalty
in 1868 as " The Merry Zingara."   In 1877, as portrayed
by H. J. Byron at the Opéra Comique and Gaiety, she
appeared as " The Bohemian Gy-url."   For his Arline Mr.
Gilbert had Miss " Patty " Oliver; for his Gipsy Queen,
Miss Charlotte Saunders; for his Count Arnheim, Fred
Dewar; and for his Devilshoof, Danvers.   Byron's piece
was interpreted by the Gaiety Company.   "The Rose of
Castile," as treated by Mr. Conway Edwardes, was seen in
1872 at the Brighton Theatre as " The Rows of Castile."
" Maritana," of course, was the origin and basis of Mr.
Burnand's " Mary Turner " (Holborn Theatre, 1867), as
well as of Byron's " Little Don Cæsar de Bazan " (Gaiety,
1876), in which Mr. Terry was such an entertaining King
Charles.

BURLESQUE OF FICTION AND SONG.

THE writers of stage travestie have gone less to fiction for subject-matter than might have been expected. Half a dozen romances previous to Scott, half a dozen of Scott's own stories, about the same number of modern novels, and still fewer foreign masterpieces—these represent the sources of all the most important of the burlesques which have been based upon invented prose narrative.

The earliest of the tales which have been thus dealt with is "Robinson Crusoe." Of this time-honoured story, the first whimsical treatment was that which took the shape of a piece called "Crusoe the Second, or the Shipwrecked Milliners," presented at the Lyceum in 1847. This was written by Stocqueler, and had for interpreters Mr. and Mrs. Keeley, with Alfred Wigan (as Crusoe). It was followed, in 1860, at the Princess's, by the "Robinson Crusoe" of H. J. Byron. Seven years later, no fewer than six writers joined in the production of a perversion of Defoe's tale, brought out at the Haymarket in 1867, and bearing the names of H. J. Byron, W. S. Gilbert, T. Hood, jun., H. S. Leigh, W. J. Prowse, and Arthur Sketchley. In this (which was given at a *matinée* for the benefit of the family of Paul Gray, the artist) the parts were all sustained by well-known

W. L.—V.

13

men of art and letters. After this there came, in 1876, at the Folly, the " Robinson Crusoe " of Mr. H. B. Farnie,* which, in its turn, was followed, just ten years later, by yet another arrangement of the story, in which Mr. Farnie had the co-operation of Mr. Reece.

To the Adelphi, in 1846, belongs an "extra extravagant extravaganza," founded by Gilbert Abbott a'Beckett and Mark Lemon on the "Peter Wilkins" of Robert Paltock (first printed in 1750). This burlesque had for its full title —"Peter Wilkins, or the Loadstone Rock and the Flying Indians," and had for its chief interpreters—Miss Woolgar as the hero, Paul Bedford as Jack Adams, and Miss E. Chaplin as Youriwkee. Dr. Johnson's "Rasselas" attracted the attention of William Brough, and was made, in 1862, the foundation of a burlesque produced at the Haymarket.

In 1765 Horace Walpole published his mediæval imagining, "The Castle of Otranto," by which so many of us have in our youth been thrilled. In 1848 Gilbert Abbott a'Beckett set himself to make fun of its singularities, and the result was a very brightly written piece, enacted at the Haymarket.† In this, Manfred's son Conrad is found imprisoned under the gigantic helmet of Alphonso, and the distracted father at once begins to give way to comic word-splitting :—

> If he's beneath that hat,
> His bier, by this time, must be precious flat !
> I'll not believe it ! no, my life upon it !
> No one would dare my Conrad thus to bonnet.

* With Miss Lydia Thompson as Robinson, Mr. Lionel Brough as Jim Cocks, and Mr. Willie Edouin as Man Friday.
† With Keeley as Manfred, Bland as the Marquis Vincenza, Miss P. Horton as Theodore, Miss Reynolds as Isabella, and Mrs. W. Clifford as Hippolita.

> But stay !—has anybody got a lever,
> To give a lift to this gigantic beaver?
> (*The helmet is raised at the back ; Manfred looks under it.*)
> Alas ! he speaks the truth—my son lies low,
> Poor little chap, under this great *chapeau.*
> My Conrad gone !—This is a sad disaster,
> The die is cast by this unlucky castor !
> Can no one tell me how or whence it came?
> Is there no ticket with the hatter's name?
> If I knew grief before, this hat has capped it,—
> My boy, crush'd 'neath this hated nap, has napped it !

In the opening scene, Hippolita, Conrad's mother, ventures to suggest to Manfred that the boy is not of marriageable age, sixteen summers not having yet passed o'er his head :—

> *Man.* Time flies, you know ; thro' life one quickly flings
> One's sixteen summersets, after sixteen springs.
> *Hip.* 'Tis my maternal tenderness that speaks :
> As yet no whiskery down adorns his cheeks.
> *Man.* I'll hear no more ! talk not of down to me—
> The boy's as downy as a boy need be.

In the year following the publication of " The Castle of Otranto," the " Vicar of Wakefield " was given to the world. It appears to have escaped travestie until 1885, when— thinking more, no doubt, of Mr. Wills's " Olivia " than of Goldsmith's *chef d'œuvre*—Messrs. Stephens and Yardley brought out at the Gaiety " The Vicar of Wideawakefield," in which Mr. Arthur Roberts and Miss Laura Linden sought, not unsuccessfully, to reproduce and heighten some of the artistic peculiarities of Mr. Irving and Miss Ellen Terry. Mrs. Shelley's " Frankenstein," published in 1818, received its first dramatic *reductio ad absurdum* in 1849, when the Brothers Brough made it the subject of a burlesque ;—its second in 1887, when Messrs. " Richard Henry " turned out at the Gaiety a travestie, of which I shall have something to say in my next chapter. In the Broughs' version Wright was Frankenstein and Paul Bedford the Monster, and much fun was made out of the finishing touches which Frankenstein gave to his work. " O." Smith, Miss Woolgar, and Miss Chaplin were also in the cast.

Sir Walter Scott's novels have obtained a fair amount of notice from the comic dramatists. " Ivanhoe," for example, has exercised the humorous powers of three—of Robert Brough (at the Haymarket in 1850), of H. J. Byron (at the Strand in 1862), and of T. F. Plowman (at the Court in 1871). Byron (who called his work " Ivanhoe in accordance with the Spirit of the Times "*) had the aid of Miss Charlotte Saunders as his Wilfred, of Charles Rice as his Brian de Bois-Guilbert, of " Johnny " Clarke as his Isaac of York, of Miss Eleanor Bufton as his Black Knight, of Miss Swanborough as Rowena, of Jenny Rogers as his Rebecca, and of Miss Polly Marshall, Miss Fanny Hughes, and Poynter in other parts. In the provinces he was his own Isaac of York.

" Isaac of York," by the way, was the title given by Mr. Plowman to his effort, which had a good deal of ingenuity and " go." Here, for example, is an extract from the scene at the banquet at which Cedric entertains his guests. Ivanhoe is soliloquising aside, and his utterances

---

* This burlesque has been used, during the present year, as the foundation for a travestie played by the Cambridge Amateur Dramatic Company, under the title of " Ivanhoe à la Carte " (in allusion to Mr. D'Oyly Carte's production of Sir Arthur Sullivan's " Ivanhoe "). To this adaptation, it is said, new lyrics were contributed by Messrs. J. K. Stephen and R. C. Lehmann.

are interrupted by the demands of the *personæ* sitting at
table :—

> *Ivanhoe (soliloquising aside).* 'Tis strange once more my native
> boards to tread,
> Beneath the roof where I was born and——
> *Rowena.*   *Bread !*
> *Ivan.* If she should recognise me, she'd be flustered.
> My utmost self-possession must be——
> *Rebecca.* ·   *Mustard !*
> *Ivan.* She's lovelier than ever.   Happy fate,
> Her beauteous face once more to contem——
> *Isaac.*   *Plate !*
> *Ivan.* That scamp, Sir B., I'll challenge—that's quite clear,
> And (if I can) despatch him to his——
> *Cedric.*   *Beer !*
> *Ivan.* I'll meet him boldly with my——
> *Isaac.*   *Knife and fork !*
> *Ivan.* And fight till one of us is dead as——
> *Sir Brian.*   *Pork !*
> *Ivan.* When Richard comes he'll stop such idle praters,
> These plottings Normans and base agi——
> *Isaac.*   *Taters !*
> *Ivan.* He'll make 'em in their knavish doings halt ;
> His action will be battery and as——
> *Reb.*   *Salt !*
> *Ivan.* Out of his land he'll soon make each a stepper,
> When he returns, by Jove, he'll give 'em——
> *Isaac.*   *Pepper !*

In another scene Isaac gives vent to a piece of mock-
heroic execration directed against Brian de Bois-Guilbert :—

> Avenge me, then, ye fates, I do implore.
> May he, like me, be martyr to lumbage*r*,
> Tic-doloreux, sciatica, and ag*er*,
> Sore-throats, neuralgia, hooping-cough, and sneezings,
> Rheumatics, asthma, colds, and bronchial wheezings.
> And while the north-east wind doth round him blow,
> Ye clouds, hail, mizzle, drizzle, sleet, and snow ;

Rain rakes and pitchforks, kittens, cats and dogs,
While down his throat pour vapours, mists, and fogs.
May broken chilblains ever stud his toes,
May icicles hang pendent from his nose,
May winter's cold his shaving-water freeze,
May he be stopped whene'er he's going to sneeze.
And when appalled you loudly call for helps,
May palsies seize you——
      Sir B.   Oh, shade of Mr. Phelps ! *

Next to " Ivanhoe " in popularity for travestie we may place " Rob Roy." Mr. Sydney French took it in hand at the Marylebone in 1867, and Mr. William Lowe gave it a very Scotch rendering, in 1880, under the title of " Mr. Robert Roye, Hielan Helen his Wife, and Dougal the Dodger." But the " standard " burlesque on the subject is, of course, Mr. Burnand's " Robbing Roy " (Gaiety, 1879), in which Mr. Terry was such a diverting " Roy," with Miss Farren as Francis, Miss Vaughan as Diana, and Mr. Royce as an admirable Dougal. Of the " Bride of Lammermoor " there have been two burlesque versions—Oxberry's, at the Strand in 1848 ; and H. J. Byron's, at the Prince of Wales's in 1865. " Kenilworth " has been similarly honoured. There was the piece brought out at the Strand in 1858 by Andrew Halliday and a collaborator, and there was that which Messrs. Reece and Farnie contributed to the Avenue Theatre in 1885. " Guy Mannering " has engaged the attention of Mr. Burnand : we can all remember his " Here's another Guy Mannering," brought

* Mr. Plowman had Mr. Righton for his Isaac, Miss Kate Bishop for his Ivanhoe, Miss Nelly Bromley for his Rowena, Miss Oliver for his Rebecca, Mr. Alfred Bishop for his Brian de Bois-Guilbert, and Mlle. Cornélie d'Anka for his Richard Cœur-de-Lion.

out at the Vaudeville in 1874. For the solitary travestie of "The Talisman," the late J. F. M'Ardle is responsible. It was first played at Liverpool in the year last named.

Lord Lytton's novels and romances have been ridiculed on the stage very much less frequently than have his dramas. "The Very Last Days of Pompeii," by Mr. Reece, and "The Last of the Barons," by Mr. Du Terreaux, are, so far as I know, the only stage works in which his prose fiction has been perverted. The former was seen at the Vaudeville in 1872, and the latter at the Strand in the same year. In "The Last of the Barons," Atkins was the King-maker, Mr. Edward Terry portraying Edward IV. as a great dandy, and endowing him with an amusing lisp.

When we turn to the stories of more recent times, we think at once of the "No Thoroughfare" of Charles Dickens and Wilkie Collins, and of the "Foul Play" of Charles Reade and Dion Boucicault, as having suffered at the hands of the irreverent scribes. The former romance suggested to Hazlewood junior his "No Thorough-fair beyond Highbury, or the Maid, the Mother, and the Malicious Mountaineer." This was in 1868; and in the following year the elder George Grossmith emulated Hazlewood's example at the Victoria Theatre. "Foul Play" was parodied by Mr. Burnand, not only in the pages of *Punch*, but in "Fowl Play, or a Story of Chikkin Hazard," produced at the New Queen's in 1868.* Of the bright writing in this "book," no better specimen could well be

---

* In this piece Mr. Toole was the Robert Penfold, Mr. Lionel Brough the Joseph Wylie, Mr. Gaston Murray the General Rolling-stone, Mr. Wyndham the Arthur Waddles, and Miss Ellen Farren (then in her novitiate) the Nancy Rouse.

furnished than the song which Wylie sings in description‚
of the scuttling of the *Proserpine.* This I give in full :—

I'm a werry wicked cove, with my one, two, three
    Characters in the history as follars
Of a sickly gal and me, and a missionary*ee*,
      In a choker white and nobby pair o' collars.
      The *Proserpine* an' guns
        Weighed such a lot of tuns,
    And I was the mate and the butler,
        And as I wanted funs
        You gave two thousand puns
    To me to go below, and so to scuttle her.
Both. $\left\{\begin{array}{l}\text{He's}\\\text{I m}\end{array}\right\}$ a werry wicked cove, with $\left\{\begin{array}{l}\text{his}\\\text{my}\end{array}\right\}$ one, two, three
Cha*rac*ters in the history as follars ;
Of the sickly girl and $\left\{\begin{array}{l}\text{he}\\\text{me}\end{array}\right\}$ and the missionary*ee*,
    In a choker white and nobby pair of collars.

There was copper there and gold, both o' yours not mine,
    'Twas a werry awful risk, but I ran 'un ;
And the Copper, labelled Gold, went aboard the *Proserpine*
    And the Gold, labelled Copper, on the *Shannon.*
      Oh, it went down like a line,
      On board the *Proserpine*,
And it was not my little game to stop'er,
    And the gold comes safe in the *Shannon* ship,
While you gets the walue for the copper.

The *Proserpine* went down in a one, two, three,
    Which she did to the werry bottom ;
They called out for the boats, and the ropes, and floats,
    But couldn't get 'em cos I'd *got* 'em.
      So they got a boat and sail,
      As wouldn't stand a gale,
And the lady and the gent jumps *in* her,
      And the missionary*ee*
      Took a pound of tea,
But they hadn't got no grub for their dinner.

Both. $\begin{cases} \text{I'm} \\ \text{You're} \end{cases}$ a very wicked cove, with my one, two, three,
   Which is a quotation from Cocker ;
   But I mourns for that Gal and the Missionary*ee*
   Which is both gone down to Davy Jones's Locker.

Among other recent fictions which have obtained the distinction of stage travestie may be named " Lady Audley's Secret," " Little Lord Fauntleroy," and " The Strange Case of Dr. Jekyll and Mr. Hyde." In the first of these instances H. J. Byron was the operator—the scene, the St. James's Theatre in 1863. Mrs. Burnett's pretty conception was tortured into " The Other Little Lord Fondleboy " (1888), and Mr. Stevenson's weird invention into " The Real Case of Hide and Seekyll" (Royalty, 1888), for which the younger George Grossmith must bear the blame.

The literature of dramatic parody does not owe much to foreign fiction. Farnie gave us " Little Gil Blas " at the Princess's in 1870, and in the same year Mr. Arthur Wood produced at the Olympic a comic paraphrase of " Paul and Virginia." It was in 1870, too, that Messrs. Eldred and Paulton turned out, at Liverpool, " The Gay Musketeers," which was followed at the Strand in 1871 by " The Three Musket-Dears " of Messrs. J. and H. Paulton. Of the " Monte Cristo Junior " of Messrs. " Richard Henry " I shall have something to say anon.

Dividing Song for the moment into Poem and Ballad, we note that the poems of Lord Byron have been the inspiring cause of at least four notable burlesques. His lordship's " Don Juan " suggested the " Beautiful Haidee " of H. J Byron (1863) and the " Don Juan Junior " of the " Brothers Prendergast " (1880) ; while his " Corsair " is the basis of William Brough's " Conrad and Medora " (Lyceum,

1856), and his " Bride of Abydos" prompted the piece with
the same title which H. J. Byron wrote for the Strand
Theatre. In "Conrad and Medora" Miss Marie Wilton
was "the Little Fairy at the Bottom of the Sea," the title-
parts being given to Miss Woolgar and Mrs. Charles Dillon,
and that of Birbanto to Mr. Toole. The Bride of Abydos
—Zuleika—had Miss Oliver for her representative.

With Byron it seems natural to associate his friend Tom
Moore, whose " Lalla Rookh " has had exceptional favour
with the parodists. Four of these have been fascinated by
her charms—Mr. J. T. Denny in 1885, Mr. Horace Lennard
in the previous year, Vincent Amcotts in 1866, and last,
but not least, William Brough (at the Lyceum) in 1857. It
was to be expected that, when travestying Moore, Brough
should parody "The Minstrel Boy," and so we have from
him the following lines, sung by Miss Woolgar as
Feramorz :—

> The minstrel boy through the town is known,
>   In each quiet street you'll find him,
> With his master's organ—it is ne'er his own,
>   And his monkey led behind him.
> " Straw laid down ! " cries the minstrel boy,
>   " Some sick man here needs quiet ;
> ' Bobbin' around' will this house annoy,
>   At any rate, I'll try it ! "

> The minstrel grinds, and his victims pay ;—
>   To his claims he's forced compliance !
> To the poet's study then he takes his way—
>   To the men of art and science.
> And cries, " My friends, in vain you'd toil
>   At books, at pen, or easel ;
> One roving vagabond your work shall spoil,"—
>   He plays " Pop goes the Weasel."

Elsewhere, Namouna, the Peri, gave utterance to the following reflections on the levelling power of love * :—

> Love makes all equal—scorns of rank the rules ;
> Makes kings and beggars equal—equal fools.
> Love brings (distinctions overboard all pitchin')
> The low-born peeler to the grandee's kitchen ;
> Makes the proud heiress of paternal acres
> Smile kindly on the young man from the baker's.
> Kings will forget their state at love's dictation,
> Cabmen their rank, and railway-guards their station.
> Love makes the housemaid careless—masters wroth,
> And makes too many cooks to spoil their broth.

In this piece Mrs. Charles Dillon was the Lalla Rookh, and Mr. Toole represented " a fabulous personage, not found in the poem," called Khorsanbad.

One, at least, of our burlesque writers—Mr. Gilbert Arthur a'Beckett—has had the courage to tackle a poem of Coleridge ; to wit, his " Christabel," from which, however, Mr. A'Beckett derived only certain suggestions for his work.   In his " Christabel, or the Bard Bewitched," represented at the Court in 1872, the Bard, Bracy, was played by Mr. Righton, who made a special feature of a travestie of Mr. Irving in " The Bells."   He pretended that he had murdered a muffin-man, and that, consuming all he could of the muffins left in the man's basket, he had deposited the remainder in the area.   Miss Nelly Bromley was the Christabel.

Scott's " Lady of the Lake " gave Mr. Reece the idea for a burlesque performed at the Royalty in 1866.   In the

---

* Reminding one of H. J. Byron's couplet :—

> Love levels all—it elevates the clown,
> And often brings the fattest people down.

same year Andrew Halliday brought out at the Adelphi a comic piece, happily entitled " The Mountain Dhu, or the Knight, the Lady, and the Lake." Mr. Toole was the impersonator of the Mountain Dhu, Paul Bedford the Douglas, Miss Hughes the Malcolm Graeme, Miss Woolgar (Mrs. Mellon) the Fitzjames, and Miss Furtado the Lady of the Lake. " The Lady of the Lane " was the title given by H. J. Byron to the travestie from his pen which saw the light at the Strand in 1872. In this case Mr. Edward Terry was the Roderick and Miss Kate Bishop the Ellen, Mrs. Raymond making a great hit as the demented Blanche.

Our present Laureate provoked in 1870 the satiric powers of Mr. W. S. Gilbert, whose " Princess," played at the Olympic, was described by the author as " a whimsical allegory," as well as " a respectful perversion of Mr. Tennyson's poem." * In this production Mr. Gilbert wrote his lyrics to the melodies of popular airs, after the manner of the time.] The major portion of the travestie is familiar to present-day audiences as having formed, in the main, the text of " Princess Ida," for which Sir Arthur Sullivan composed such charming music. Nevertheless, I cannot refrain from quoting, as a happy specimen of Mr. Gilbert's later manner in burlesque,† the speech addressed

---

* Mr. David Fisher was the King Hildebrand, and Miss Maria Simpson (Mrs. W. H. Liston), his son Prince Hilarion ; Miss Augusta Thomson being the Cyril, Miss Mattie Reinhardt the Princess Ida, Miss Fanny Addison the Lady Psyche, Mrs. Poynter the Lady Blanche, and Miss Patti Josephs the Melissa.

† In a sense, all Mr. Gilbert's comic operas are burlesques, for they are full of travestie, especially of the conventionalities of grand opera and melodrama. At the same time, they cannot be called burlesques in the everyday, theatrical sense of the term.

by the Princess to her disciples—a speech marked by agreeable *naïveté* and happy mock-heroics :—

In mathematics Woman leads the way !
The narrow-minded pedant still believes
That two and two make four !   Why, we can prove—
We women, household drudges as we are—
That two and two make five—or three—or seven—
Or five-and-twenty, as the case demands ! . . .
Diplomacy ?   The wily diplomate
Is absolutely helpless in our hands :
He wheedles monarchs—Woman wheedles him !
Logic ?.   Why, tyrant man himself admits
It's waste of time to argue with a woman !
Then we excel in social qualities—
Though man professes that he holds our sex
In utter scorn, I'll undertake to say
If you could read the secrets of his heart,
He'd rather be alone with one of you
Than with five hundred of his fellow-men !
In all things we excel.   Believing this,
Five hundred maidens here have sworn to place
Their foot upon his neck.   If we succeed,
We'll treat him better than he treated us ;
But if we fail—oh, then let hope fail too !
Let no one care one penny how she looks !
Let red be worn with yellow—blue with green,
Crimson with scarlet—violet with blue !
Let all your things misfit, and you yourselves
At inconvenient moments come undone !
Let hair-pins lose their virtue ; let the hook
Disdain the fascination of the eye,—
The bashful button modestly evade
The soft embraces of the buttonhole !
Let old associations all dissolve,
Let Swan secede from Edgar—Grant from Gask,
Sewell from Cross—Lewis from Allenby—
In other words, let Chaos come again !

Into the region of the Ballad the comic playwrights have

made comparatively few incursions. "The Babes in the Wood," "Lord Bateman," "Billy Taylor," "Villikins and his Dinah," and "Lord Lovel,"—these are the stories which have been most in favour with burlesque purveyors. R. J. Byron took up the first-named subject in 1859, when the company at the Adelphi (where the piece was produced) included Miss Woolgar (Sir Rowland Macassar), Mr. Toole and Miss Kate Kelly (the Babes), Paul Bedford (the First Ruffian), and Mrs. Billington (the Lady Macassar). Then, in 1877, there came a provincial version by Messrs. G. L. Gordon and G. W. Anson; and, next, in 1884, at Toole's Theatre, the "Babes" of Mr. Harry Paulton, in which Mr. Edouin and Miss Atherton were the central figures. The first travestie of "Lord Bateman" was made by Charles Selby at the Strand in 1839; then there was the production by R. B. Brough in 1854 at the Adelphi; and, still later, there was the piece by H. J. Byron, at the Globe (1869). Passing over the "Billy Taylor" of Buckstone (1829), we arrive at "The Military Billy Taylor" of Mr. Burnand, which came out forty years later. It is to Mr. Burnand, also, that we owe "Villikins and his Dinah," played by amateurs at Cambridge, as well as "Lord Lovel and the Lady Nancy Bell," which he wrote for the same place and performers.

X.

THE NEW BURLESQUE.

WITH the year 1885 there dawned a new epoch for stage travestie in England. The old Gaiety company had broken up, Miss Farren alone remaining; and with the accession of fresh blood there came fresh methods. The manager who had succeeded Mr. Hollingshead recognised the tendencies of the times; and with "Little Jack Sheppard"—a travestie by Messrs. Stephens and Yardley of the well-known story, familiar both in fiction and in drama—a novel departure was made.

[In the "palmy" days, burlesque had not, as a rule, formed the whole of an evening's entertainment. The one-act travestie had grown on occasion into two and even three acts; but, until recent years, the one act (in several scenes) had usually been deemed sufficient, the remainder of the programme being devoted to comedy or drama. The musical part of the performance had generally been made up of adaptations or reproductions of popular airs of the day—either comic songs or operatic melodies: very rarely had the music been special and original. The scenery had never been particularly remarkable; nor, save during the various *régimes* of Vestris, had there been any special splen-

dour in the dresses. For the most part, the old school of
burlesque did not rely upon a brilliant *mise-en-scène.* In the
prologue to his "Alcestis," produced just forty-one years
ago, we find Talfourd expressly drawing attention to the
simplicity of the stage show. Speaking of the productions
at the houses of serious drama, he said :—

> Plays of the greatest and the least pretence
> Are mounted so regardless of expense
> That fifty nights is scarce a run accounted—
> Run ! They should gallop, being so well *mounted*

But with "Alcestis" it was to be different :—

> What you enjoy must be all "on the quiet."
> No horse will pull *our* play up if it drag,
> No banners when our wit is on the flag ;
> No great effects or new-imported dance
> The drooping eye will waken and entrance ; . . .
> But an old story from a classic clime,
> Done for the period into modern rhyme.

A very different policy was to characterise the New
Burlesque. The pieces, having now become the staple of
the night's amusement, were to be placed upon the boards
with all possible splendour. Money was to be spent
lavishly on scenery, properties and costumes. Dancing was
to be a prominent feature—not the good old-fashioned
"breakdowns" and the like, but choregraphic interludes
of real grace and ingenuity. The music was to be
written specially for the productions, and pains were
to be taken to secure artists who could really sing.
Something had already been done in each of these directions. So long ago as 1865 Mr. Burnand's "Windsor
Forest" had been fitted with wholly new music ; and at

the Gaiety, under Mr. Hollingshead, burlesque had grown in elaborateness year by year. Not, however, till the production of "Little Jack Sheppard," in 1885, had the elaboration been so marked and complete in all departments.

Meanwhile, how were the librettists to be affected? Clearly, they would have to give more opportunities than usual for musical and saltatory illustration; and accordingly we find the book of "Little Jack Sheppard" full of lyrics —solos, duets, quartetts and choruses, all of them set to new airs by competent composers. At the same time, the authors took care not to omit the element of punning dialogue. In this respect the old traditions were to be maintained. Byron, for instance, might very well have written the lines which follow, in which the interlocutors strive to outdo one another in the recklessness of their *jeux de mots :*—

> *Thames Darrell.* Wild and Uncle Roland trapped me,
> They caught this poor *kid napping*, and *kidnapped* me ;
> Put me on board a ship in half a crack.
> *Winifred.* A ship ! Oh, what a *blow* !
> *Thames.* It was—*a smack* !
> When out at sea the crew set me, Thames Darrell,
> Afloat upon the waves within a barrel.
> *Win.* In hopes the *barrel* would turn out your *bier.*
> *Thames.* But I'm *stout*-hearted and I didn't fear.
> I nearly died of thirst.
> *Win.* Poor boy ! Alas !
> *Thames.* Until I caught a fish——
> *Win.* What sort ?
> *Thames.* A *bass.*
> Then came the worst, which nearly proved my ruin—
> A storm, a thing I can't *a-bear, a brewin'.*
> *Win.* It makes me pale.

W. L.—V.

> *Thames.*　　　　　　It made me *pale* and *ail.*
> When nearly coopered I descried a sail ;
> They did not hear me, though I loudly whooped ;
> Within the barrel I was *inned and cooped.*
> *All's up,* I thought, when round they quickly brought her ;
> That ship to me of safety was the *porter.*

"Little Jack Sheppard"—which had for its chief exponents Miss Farren, Mr. Fred Leslie (a brilliant recruit from the comic opera stage), Mr. David James (who had returned for a time to his old love), Mr. Odell, Miss Harriet Coveney, and Miss Marion Hood (who had graduated in Gilbert-Sullivan opera)—was followed at the Gaiety by "Monte Cristo Junior," in which Messrs. "Richard Henry" presented a bright and vivacious travestie of Dumas' famous fiction, greatly aided by the *chic* of Miss Farren as the hero, and the inexhaustible humorous resource of Mr. Leslie as Noirtier. Here, for example, is a bit of the scene between these two characters in the Château d'If :—

> (*Noirtier, disguised as Faria, pokes his head through the hole in the prison wall. He wears a long grey beard, and is clad in rags.*)
>
> *Dantès* (*startled*). This is the rummiest go I e'er heard tell on !
> *Noirtier.* Pray.pardon my intrusion, brother felon—
> I'm Seventy-Seven.
> *Dantès.*　　　　　You look it—and the rest !
> *Noirtier* (*with senile chuckle*). Ah ! youth will always have its little jest.
> My *number's* Seventy-seven : my age is more !
> In point of fact, I've lately turned five score :
> Time travels on with step that's swift, though stealthy.
> *Dantès* (*aside*). A hundred years of age ! This prison's healthy,
> To judge by this old joker. (*aloud*) What's your name, sir ?
> To which I'd add—and what's your little game, sir ?
> *Noirtier.* My name is Faria—I'm a ruined Abbé—
> All through my country's conduct, which was shabby.

They've kept me here since I was three years old,
Because I wouldn't tell of untold gold—
Of countless coin and gems and heaps of treasure
Which I'd discovered in my baby leisure—
(*chuckles*) But we will foil their schemes, and that ere long.

 Dantès (*aside, touching forehead significantly*). The reverend
  gentleman has gone quite wrong.

 Noirtier (*clutching Dantès wildly*). But, ah, they starve me !
  Hence thy strange misgiving—

For what's a parson, boy, without his living ?
Hast e'er a bone to give an old man squalid ?

 Dantès. Not me ! They never give us nothing solid ;

They seem to think an appetite's unlawful :
In fact, their bill of fare is fairly awful.

 Noirtier. But now to business ! You must know, fair youth,
Though I in prison lie, I love the truth.
Therefore—— But stay (*glancing suspiciously around*)—are we
  alone ?

 Dantès. Of course we are, old guy fox ! (*business*).

 Noirtier. Then now I will confess my little game.

(*Removes wig, beard, rags, etc., and appears in convict dress, with*
 [77] *conspicuously marked on breast.*)

And so, behold !

 Dantès.   What ! Noirtier?

 Noirtier.   The same !

Here, again, is the duet sung by the same characters in
the course of the same scene :—

I.

 Dantès. Here in this gloomy old Château d'If
We don't get beer, and we don't get beef.

 Noirtier. They never give us mutton or veal or pork,
On which to exercise knife and fork.

 Dantès. No nice spring chicken, or boiled or roast—
No ham-and-eggs, and no snipe-on-toast !

 Noirtier. So no wonder we're rapidly growing lean
On the grub served up from the prison cuisine.

  (*With treadmill business.*)

Both. Poor prisoners we ! Poor prisoners we !
With skilly for breakfast and dinner and tea,
And such dismal diet does not agree
　　Noirtier. With Seventy-seven !
　　Dantès.　　　　　　　　　And Ninety-three !
　　　　　　　　　　　　(*Grotesque pas de deux.*

II.

Dantès. Our wardrobe has long since run to seed,
For *ci-devant* swells we are sights indeed !
　　Noirtier. I shiver and shake, and the creeps I've got—
I'd give the world for a " whiskey hot ! "
　　Dantès. And as in my lonely cell I lie,
I think of *her* and the by-and-by.
　　Noirtier. Don't buy or sell, or you'll come to grief,
And never get out of the Chateau d'If !
　　Both. Poor prisoners we ! etc.　　　(*Dance as before.*)

After " Monte Cristo Junior " there came, at the same
theatre and from the pens of the same writers, a travestie of
" Frankenstein," produced in 1887, with Miss Farren as
the hero, and Mr. Leslie as the Monster that he fashions.
Here much ingenuity was shown in the management of the
pseudo-supernatural business connected with the Monster.
Previous to the vivifying of the figure, Frankenstein thus
soliloquised :—

Frankenstein. At last I am alone—now let me scan
My wondrous figure fashioned like a man.
All is now ready—every joint complete,
And now to oil the works—and then—*toute suite* !
O Science ! likewise Magic ! lend a hand
To aid the awful project I have planned.
　　(*Sings*) I've invented a figure
　　　　　　Of wonderful vigour,
　　　　　　　A gentleman-help, so to speak ;
　　　　　A chap automatic
　　　　　Who'll ne'er be erratic,
　　　　　　Who'll live upon nothing a week

It will fetch and will carry,
And won't want to marry,
  Or try on the wage-raising plan ;
It will do all my bidding
Without any kidding—
  My Patent Mechanical Man.
Now to my cell I'll post with due cell-erity,
And do a deed that shall astound post-erity.
But thrills of horror now run through my veins.
What if I fail in spite of all my pains ?
A nameless dread doth in my bosom lurk.
My scheme is good—but what if it won't work ?

The Monster's first utterances were as follows :—:

Monster. Where am I ? also what—or which—or who ?
What is this feeling that is running through
My springs—or, rather, joints ?—I seem to be
A comprehensive (*feeling joints*) joint-stock companee ;
My veins—that's if they are veins—seem to glow——
I've muscles —yea—in quarts—I move them—so !
(*Creaks horribly all over : fiddle business in orchestra.*)
Horror ! I've broken something, I'm afraid !
What's this material of which I'm made ?
It seems to be a sort of clay—combined
With bits of flesh and wax—I'm well designed —
To see, to move, to speak I can contrive—
I wonder if I really am alive !
(*Sings*) If my efforts are vain and I can't speak plain,
    Don't laugh my attempts to scorn !
For, as will be seen, I am but a machine
    Who doesn't yet know if he's born.
I can move my feet in a style rather neat,
    And to waggle my jaws I contrive ;
I can open my mouth from north to south,
    I—I—wonder if I'm a-live, a-live !
    I wonder if I'm a-live !

In 1888 Mr. G. R. Sims and Mr. Henry Pettitt joined
forces in burlesque, and the result was seen in a piece happily

entitled " Faust up to Date." In this version Marguerite (Miss Florence St. John) figures first as a barmaid at an Exhibition. She is a young lady of some astuteness, though she insists upon her general ingenuousness :—

I'm a simple little maid;
Of the swells I am afraid,
I tell them when they're forward they must mind what they're about.
I never go to balls,
Or to plays or music-halls,
And my venerated mother always knows when I am out.
When I leave my work at night,
I never think it right
To talk to any gentleman I haven't seen before.
But I take a 'bus or tram,
Like the modest girl I am,
For I know that my big brother will be waiting at the door.

Martha introduces herself thus :—

I'm Martha, and my husband's never seen ;
Though fifty, my complexion's seventeen.
In all the versions I've one *rôle* to play,
To mind Miss Marguerite while her *frère's* away.
You ask me why she don't live with her mother,
And I reply by asking you another—
Where is my husband ?   I oft wonder if
The public know he left me in a tiff,
And not a single word from him I've heerd
Since Marguerite's mother also disappeared.
Not that I draw conclusions—oh dear, no !
The gents who wrote the opera made them go.
And Goethe lets a gentleman in red
Inform me briefly my old man is dead.
These details show my character's *not* shady—
I am a widow and a perfect lady.

When Valentine returns home and hears the scandal

about his sister, he breaks out into the following terrific
curse :—

> When to the drawing-room you have to go,
> With arms all bare and neck extremely low,
> For four long hours in biting wind and snow,
> May you the joys of England's springtime know!
> Whene'er you ride, or drive a prancing pair,
> May the steam roller meet you everywhere!
> When thro' the Park you wend your homeward way,
> Oh, may it be a Home Rule gala day!
> When for a concert you have paid your gold,
> May Mr. Sims Reeves have a dreadful cold!
> May you live where, through lath-and-plaster walls,
> Come loud and clear the next-door baby's squalls!
> Your husband's mother, when you are a wife,
> Bring all her cats, and stay with you for life!

At the end, when Mephistopheles (Mr. E. J. Lonnen)
comes to claim Faust, it turns out that Faust and Marguerite
have been duly married, but have been obliged to conceal
the fact because Marguerite was a ward in Chancery.
Moreover, Old Faust reappears, and insists that, as it was
he who signed the bond, it is he and not young Faust who
ought to suffer for it.

"Faust up to Date" includes some clever songs and
some excruciating puns, of which these are perhaps the
most excruciating :—

> *Marg.* These sapphires are the finest I have seen.
> *Faust.* Ah! what I've sapphired for your sake, my queen!
> *Marg.* An opal ring, they say, bad luck will be ;
> This one I opal not do that for me.

Again :—

> *Mephis.* Along the Riviera, dudes her praises sing.
> *Val.* Oh, did you Riviera such a thing?

"Atalanta," the travestie by Mr. G. P. Hawtrey brought out at the Strand in 1888, was fitted with prose dialogue, much of which was very smart and amusing. The songs were numerous and well-turned, and certain details of the travestie were ingenious. Hippomenes, the hero, wins the race he runs with Atalanta, by placing in her path a brand-new "costume," of modern cut and material, which she finds it impossible not to stop for. For the rest, while possessing a decidedly "classical" flavour, "Atalanta" was, in essence, a racing burlesque, abounding in the phraseology of the turf, and introducing in the last scene counterfeit presentments of a number of well-known sportsmen.

An agreeable cynicism ran through both the talk and the lyrics, from one of which—a duet between King Schœneus and his High Chamberlain, Lysimachus—I extract the following satire on turf *morale* :—

Lys. There's a time to win and a time to lose.
Sch.　　　　Of course, of course, of course.
Lys. You can make 'em safe whenever you choose—
Sch.　　　　By force, by force, by force.
Lys. Then doesn't it seem a sin and a shame
　　　To stop such a pleasant and easy game?
　　　If a horse doesn't win, why, who is to blame?
Sch.　　　　The horse, the horse, the horse.

Lys. If it's cleverly managed, I always think—
Sch.　　　　Proceed, proceed, proceed—
Lys. At a neat little swindle it's proper to wink.
Sch.　　　　Indeed, indeed, indeed!
　　　I don't understand what it's all about;
　　　But a man must be punished, I have no doubt,
　　　If he's such a fool as to get found out.
Lys.　　　　Agreed, agreed, agreed.

Lys. It's all because jockeys have played such tricks—
Sch.   They go too far, too far.
Lys. That the stewards are down like a thousand of bricks—
Sch.   They are, they are, they are.
    For a season or two, you'll observe with pain,
    They'll hunt out abuses with might and main ;
    Then the good old times will come back again.
        Hurrah, hurrah, hurrah !

Elsewhere, there is a diverting bit of parody suggested by the extreme cautiousness and bad grammar of some newspaper racing prophecies. Hippomenes and Atalanta are the sole competitors in the race, and the local " tipster " thus discusses their prospects :—

I have from time to time gone through the chances of the several competitors, so that to repeat what I have written is to go over very well-worn ground. Although the race is reduced to a match, it has lost none of its interest in the eyes of the public. It is a difficult race to meddle with, but the plunge must be made ; I shall, therefore, give my vote to Atalanta, which, if beaten, it may be by Hippomenes.

Of " Joan of Arc," the " operatic burlesque " written by Messrs. J. L. Shine and " Adrian Ross " to music by Mr. Osmond Carr (Opéra Comique, 1891), the distinguishing feature—apart from the fact that the music is all original and all the work of one composer—is the neatness of the lyric writing, with which special pains appear to have been taken. Of Joan herself her father is made to sing as follows :—

    Oh, there's nobody adepter
      Than our Joan, Joan, Joan !
    She is born to hold a sceptre
      On a throne, throne, throne ;
    She's the head of all her classes,
    And in fervour she surpasses
    All the Hallelujah lasses,
      As they own, own, own !

Don't call her preaching dull, for
  It is not, not, not!
She can do Salvation sulphur
  Hot and hot, hot, hot!
She can play the drum and cymbal,
With her fingers she is nimble,
And the pea beneath the thimble
  She can spot, spot, spot.

She can tell you by your faces
  What you'll do, do, do;
She can give you tips for races
  Good and new, new, new!
She can cut a martial swagger,
She's a dab at sword and dagger,
And will fight without a stagger
  Till all's blue, blue, blue!

Of all the songs in the piece, however, perhaps the most vivacious is that in which De Richemont (Mr. Arthur Roberts) describes how he " went to find Emin " :—

Oh, I went to find Emin Pasha, and started away for fun,
With a box of weeds and a bag of beads, some tracts and a Maxim gun ;
My friends all said I should come back dead, but I didn't care a pin,
So I ran up a bill and I made my will, and I went to find Emin !
I went to find Emin, I did, I looked for him far and wide,
I found him right, I found him tight, and a lot of folks beside ;
Away through Darkest Africa, though it cost me lots of tin,
For without a doubt I'd find him out, when I went to find Emin !

Then I turned my face to a savage place, that is called Boulogne-sur-
    Mer,
Where the natives go on *petits chevaux* and the gay *chemin de fer* ;
And the girls of the tribe I won't describe, for I'm rather a modest man.
They are poor, I suppose, for they're short of clothes, when they take
    what they call *les bains* !
And they said to me, " *Oh, sapristi !* " and the men remarked, " *Sacré !* "
And *vive la guerre aux pommes de terre*, and *vingt minutes d'arrêt* !

Voulez-vous du bœuf? j'ai huit! j'ai neuf! till they deafened me with
    their din,
So I *parlez*'d *bon soir* and said *au revoir*, for I had to find Emin!

   .   .   .   .

And at last I found Emin, poor chap, in the midst of the nigger bands
Who daily prowl, with horrible howl, along the Margate sands;
I heard the tones of the rattling bones, and I hurried down to the beach—
Full well I know that they will not go till you give them sixpence each!
Said they, "Uncle Ned, oh! he berry dead, and de banjo out ob tune!
Oh! doodah, day! hear Massa play de song of de Whistling Coon!
If you ain't a snob, you'll give us a bob for blacking our blooming skin"—
But I took that band to the edge of the sand, and there I dropped 'Emin!

I have not thought it necessary, in the preceding pages,
to offer any apology for stage burlesque. One must regret
that it sometimes lacks refinement in word and action,
and that in the matter of costume it is not invariably
decorous; but that we shall always have it with us, in some
form or other, may be accepted as incontrovertible. So long
as there is anything extravagant in literature or manners—
in the way either of simplicity or of any other quality—so
long will travestie find both food and scope. That is the
raison d'être of theatrical burlesque—that it shall satirise
the exaggerated and the extreme. It does not wage war
against the judicious and the moderate. As H. J. Byron
once wrote of his own craft:—

> Though some may scout it, . . .
> Burlesque is like the winnowing machine:
> It simply blows away the husks, you know—
> The goodly corn is not moved by the blow.
> What arrant rubbish of the clap-trap school
> Has vanished—thanks to pungent ridicule!
> What stock stage-customs, nigh to bursting goaded,
> With so much "blowing up" have been exploded!
> Had our light writers done no more than this,
> Their doggrel efforts scarce had been amiss.

In this defence of his calling, Byron had been anticipated by Planché, who, in one of his occasional pieces, introduced the following passage, in which Mr. and Mrs. Wigan and the representatives of Tragedy and Burlesque all figured. When Burlesque entered, Tragedy cried out—

Avaunt, and quit my sight ! let the earth hide thee.
Unreal mockery, hence ! I can't abide thee!
   Burlesque. Because I fling your follies in your face,
And call back all the false starts of your race,
Show up your shows, affect your affectation,
And by such homœopathic aggravation,
Would cleanse your bosom of that perilous stuff
Which weighs upon our art—bombast and puff.
   Mr. Wigan. Have you so good a purpose, then, in hand?
   Burlesque. Else wherefore breathe I in dramatic land?
   Mrs. Wigan. I thought your aim was but to make us laugh
   Burlesque. Those who think so but understand me half.
Did not my thrice-renownèd Thomas Thumb,
That mighty mite, make mouthing Fustian dumb?
Is Tilburina's madness void of matter?
Did great Bombastes strike no nonsense flatter?
When in his words he's not one to the wise,
When his fool's bolt *spares* folly as it flies,
When in his chaff there's not a grain to seize on,
When in his rhyme there's not a grain of reason,
His slang but slang, no point beyond the pun,
Burlesque may walk, for he will cease to run.

FINIS.

Printed by Hazell, Watson, & Viney, Ld., London and Aylesbury.

GREAT SUCCESS.

◆

THE BOOK OF THE HOLIDAY SEASON.

-THIRD EDITION (WITHIN A FORTNIGHT OF PUBLICATION).

◆

THE BACHELORS' CLUB.

By I. ZANGWILL,

Crown 8vo.   348 pp.   3s. 6d.

With ILLUSTRATIONS by GEORGE HUTCHINSON.

BRIEF EXTRACTS FROM FIRST PRESS NOTICES.

ST. JAMES'S GAZETTE: "Some exceedingly clever fooling, and a happy audacity of whimsical invention."

DAILY GRAPHIC: "A genuine humourist. We own to having laughed heartily, and appreciated the cleverness and the cynicism."

STAR: "Mr. Zangwill has an original way of being funny. He is full of clever and witty, paradoxical and epigrammatical, surprises. His book is a splendid tonic for gloomy spirits."

EVENING NEWS: "Not one in a score of the amusing books which come from the press is nearly so amusing as this."

SUNDAY TIMES: "Read, laugh over, and profit by the history of 'The Bachelors' Club,' capitally told by a fresh young writer."

GLOBE: "A clever and interesting book. Agreeable satire. Store of epigram."

REFEREE: "A new comic writer. There is a touch of the devilry of Heme in Mr. Zangwill's wit."

SCOTSMAN: "Any one who has listened to what the wild waves say as they beat the shores of Bohemia will read the book with enjoyment and appreciate its careless merriment."

FREEMAN'S JOURNAL: "Very clever and amusing; highly interesting, humorous and instructive."

PICTORIAL WORLD: "One of the smartest books of the season. Brimful of funny ideas, comically expressed."

MAN OF THE WORLD: "Witty to excess. To gentlemen who dine out, the book will furnish a stock of 'good things' upon every conceivable subject of conversation."

GRANTA: "A book of genuine humour. Full of amusing things. The style is fresh and original."

NEWCASTLE DAILY CHRONICLE: "Really clever and amusing; brimful of genuine humour and fun."

YORKSHIRE HERALD: "A quaint, fresh, delightful piece of humour. Hood or Douglas Jerrold might have written the book."

NORTHERN DAILY NEWS: "The reader must be very dyspeptic who cannot laugh consumedly at his funny conceits."

SPORTING TIMES: "No end of fun. Not a dull line in the book."

JUDY: "It's Zangwillian, which is saying a very great deal indeed in its favour."

ARIEL: "The cleverest book ever written" (Author's own review).

LONDON: HENRY & CO., 6, BOUVERIE STREET, E.C.

The Whitefriars Library of Wit and Humour.

Edited by W. H. DAVENPORT ADAMS.

A New Series of Monthly Volumes designed to supply the Public with Entertaining Literature by the Best Writers.

Crown 8vo, cloth, with Portrait, 2s. 6d. each.

Vol. I.—ESSAYS IN LITTLE.

By ANDREW LANG. Sixth Thousand.

Also a Large-Paper Edition (limited to 150, all sold upon subscription).
Crown 4to. 10s. 6d. net.

OPINIONS OF THE PRESS.

" If it is well to judge by firstfruits (and, generally speaking, the judgment is right), the new 'Whitefriars Library' should compass the very laudable designs of its projectors. The first monthly volume of the new series may fairly be said to be aflush with the finest promise. Mr. Andrew Lang's 'ESSAYS IN LITTLE' is one of the most entertaining and bracing of books. Full of bright and engaging discourse, these charming and recreative essays are the best of good reading. Hard must be 'the cynic's lips' from which Mr. Lang's sportive pen does not 'dislodge the sneer,' harder that ' brow of care' whose wrinkles refuse to be smoothed by Mr. Lang's gentle sarcasms and agreeable raillery. . . . 'ESSAYS IN LITTLE' ought to win every vote, and please every class of reader."—*Saturday Review.*

" The volume is delightful, and exhibits Mr. Lang's light and dexterous touch, his broad literary sympathies, and his sound critical instinct to great advantage."—*Times.*

" 'The Whitefriars Library' has begun well. Its first issue is a volume by Mr. Andrew Lang, entitled 'ESSAYS IN LITTLE.' Mr. Lang is here at his best —alike in his most serious and his lightest moods. We find him turning without effort, and with equal success, from 'Homer and the Study of Greek,' to 'The Last Fashionable Novel'—on one page attacking grimly the modern newspaper tendency to tittle-tattle (in a 'Letter to a Young Journalist'), on another devising a bright parody in prose or verse. Mr. Lang is in his most rollicking vein when treating of the once popular Haynes Bayly, the author of 'I'd be a Butterfly' and things of that sort. With Bayly's twaddling verse Mr. Lang is in satiric ecstasies; he revels in its unconscious inanity, and burlesques it repeatedly with infinite gusto. . . . His tone is always urbane, his manner always bright and engaging. No one nowadays has a style at once so light and so well bred. . . . It is always pleasant, and frequently delightful."—*Globe.*

Vol. II.—SAWN OFF: A Tale of a Family Tree.

By G. MANVILLE FENN.   *[Fourth Thousand.*

Vol. III.—"A LITTLE IRISH GIRL."

By the Author of "Molly Bawn."   *[Ready.*

Vol. IV.—THREE WEEKS AT MOPETOWN.

By PERCY FITZGERALD.   *[Ready.*

Vol. V. A BOOK OF BURLESQUE.

By WILLIAM DAVENPORT ADAMS.   *[Ready.*

Vol. VI.—"IN A CANADIAN CANOE."

By BARRY O. E. PAIN, B.A.   *[July.*

The services of Messrs. OSCAR WILDE, G. A. SALA, JUSTIN M'CARTHY, M.P., G. A. HENTY, F. C. BURNAND, W. CLARK RUSSELL, RUDOLPH C. LEHMANN, R. E. FRANCILLON, HARRY FURNISS, ARTHUR À BECKETT, J. BERNARD PARTRIDGE, and others, have been secured.

LONDON: HENRY & CO., 6, BOUVERIE STREET, E.C.;
And at all Booksellers' and the Railway Stalls.

By W. H. DAVENPORT ADAMS.

A BOOK ABOUT LONDON:
Its Memorable Places, its Men and Women, and its History. Crown 8vo. 6s.

PART I.—STORIES OF HISTORICAL SCENES AND EVENTS.
PART II.—STORIES OF FAMOUS LOCALITIES AND BUILDINGS.
PART III.—STORIES OF CRIME AND MISADVENTURE.

In this volume an attempt has been made to present in a series of striking episodical narratives the principal events in London history, and some of the more striking aspects of London life. Full particulars are given of plots and conspiracies, forgeries and murders, executions and hair-breadth escapes; and many favourite old stories, not easily accessible now, are brought forward in a new dress, with all the light of recent research thrown upon them.

A COMPANION VOLUME. BY THE SAME AUTHOR.

A BOOK ABOUT LONDON.
The Streets of London:

An Alphabetical Index to the principal Streets, Squares, Parks, and Thoroughfares, with their Associations—Historical, Traditional, Social, and Literary. Crown 8vo. 3s. 6d.

This work is the result of very extensive labour, and offers, it is believed, a completer view than has before been attempted of the diverse associations which lend so profound an interest to the Streets of London. It contains more than a thousand succinct references to remarkable persons, incidents, and scenes, with illustrative anecdotes and full explanations gathered from a vast number of authentic sources.

By LADY FLORENCE DIXIE.

NEW WORK FOR THE YOUNG.

ANIWEE;
Or, The Warrior Queen.

A Tale of the Araucanian Indians and the Mythical Trauco People. By the Author of " The Young Castaways," etc. In large crown 8vo, with Frontispiece. 5s.

"A story of pure adventure, full of incident, and related with much smoothness and animation. As a story simply this work appeals to, and will be heartily accepted by, the boys and girls to whom it may be presented."—*Globe*.

" Another pleasant book for the young from Lady Florence Dixie. The boys and girls—and we hope they are many—who have drunk in delight from her ' Young Castaways ' will find their reward in this new story of ' Aniwee.'"—*Echo*.

"The story is romantic and interesting enough to delight boys and girls alike, and the adventures with the Trauco people are as novel as they are thrilling."—*Daily Graphic*.

LONDON: HENRY & CO., 6, BOUVERIE STREET, E.C.,
AND AT ALL LIBRARIES AND BOOKSELLERS'.

Lightning Source UK Ltd.
Milton Keynes UK
UKHW02f1833270218
318590UK00005B/318/P